D1248608

# IRANIAN CIVILIZATION AND CULTURE

# Iranian Civilization and Culture

*Before Islam and its Impact on*
*Islamic Civilization and Arab Literature*

MOHAMMAD MOHAMMADI-MALAYERI

*Translated by*
SHAHROKH MOHAMMADI-MALAYERI

MANOHAR
2012

First Published by Tehran University in 1944
2nd edition 1977
Published in India in 2012

ISBN 978-81-7304-950-7

*Published by*
Ajay Kumar Jain *for*
Manohar Publishers & Distributors
4753/23 Ansari Road, Daryaganj,
New Delhi 110 002

*Printed at*
Salasar Imaging Systems
Delhi 110 035

# Contents

# Preface

Mohammad Mohammadi-Malayeri was born in Malayer in western Iran in 1909. He studied Arabic under the tutelage of his father, Hedayatollah, who was the Marja' Taghlid and Hakem Shar' (religious leader and shari'a judge) of that region. When Tehran University was established, he enrolled and selected Arabic Literature as a major, completing his studies with distinction. He was then sent by the Ministry of Education and Culture to the American University of Beirut (AUB) to continue his studies in Arabic literature. He taught Persian language and literature, while he simultaneously completed his Doctorate. During that period he benefited from the opportunities present in the academic environment and continued his research on the historic ties between the Arabic and Persian languages, a subject of great interest to him. He prepared two theses in Arabic for his degree on the subject of the impact of Iranian culture on different aspects of Arabic literature. But these could not be published in Beirut at the time and were later revised and translated into Persian and published in Tehran in 1944 under the title *Pre-Islamic Iranian Culture and its Impact on Islamic Civilization and Arabic Literature*. This book was later revised and republished by Tehran University in 1977. It is this revised edition which is now being published in English.

The motive for this subject of research which constituted the core for all of Prof. Mohammadi's writings throughout his life, in both Persian and Arabic, was his observation that prominent Arab writers on this subject in Egypt and Lebanon, the two main centres for Arabic literature at the time, did not pay much attention to the impact that Persian language and culture (as well as Persian speakers) had on the development and enrichment of Arabic language and literature after Islam. This was due to two reasons: one was that writers on this subject were themselves unaware of such impact; and the other was that within the literary community of the time, Arabic was more prominent than Persian, and the dependence of the Persian language on the Arabic language was considered a matter of fact, but the dependence of the Arabic language during the period of its development and expansion on the Persian language was difficult to comprehend and accept. Prof. Mohammadi believed that the history of the Arabic language and literature would remain incomplete and vague without proper attention to the links between the two languages and cultures. This would also make it easier to comprehend the rapid pace of development of Arabic as a medium for literary expression in the first centuries of Islam, since its causes cannot be found within the Arabic language alone, but must be sought in external factors, namely the Persian language and Iranian culture. And, as Prof. Mohammadi's studies in this area continued, it became clearer to him that the impact of the Persian language and culture went beyond the Arabic language and literature to the Islamic civilization as a whole.

Prof. Mohammadi's second assignment to Beirut in 1957 was to establish the Department of Persian Language and Literature at the newly-founded Lebanese University. As he began his work, he discovered that the Persian language and its historical links, and impact on the growth and development of Arabic language and literature was virtually unknown in academia. This was a vital issue that had to be addressed. He therefore established a bilingual Persian and Arabic periodical in the Department of Persian Language and Literature of the Lebanese University titled *Al Derasat al Adabyah* (Literary Studies), which was published during nine years of his ten years' tenure as Head of that Department. The periodical covered various aspects of the inter-linkages between the two languages and literatures, and its articles were written by both Persian-speaking and Arabic-speaking scholars, became one of the significant literary periodicals on the subject of comparative Persian and Arabic literature. The periodical continues to be published to this date. During that period, in Beirut, Prof. Mohammadi also published three books in Arabic. One book was titled *Al Rawafed al Faresyah fil Adab al Arabi— Kotob al Taj wal Ayeen* (Persian Roots in Arab Literature—The

Books of Taj and Ayeen) in which the Sassanid *Tajnamehs* and *Ayeen Namehs* that had been translated into Arabic are covered. Another book was titled *Al Tarjamah wal Naghl a'nel Faresiyah fil Ghoroon al Islamiyahl Oulah* (Translation and Transcription from Persian in the First Centuries of Islam) covering other translated works. And the third book was titled *Al Adab al Faresi fi Aham Adwarehi wa Ashhar A'lamehi* (Persian Literature—Its most important periods and Most Renowned Elements).

In 1968, Prof. Mohammadi was appointed Dean of the faculty of Elahyat at Tehran University, where he established a periodical titled *Maghalat va Barresiha*, which was generally a continuation of his efforts to bring together the Persian and Arabic languages and literatures.

Prof. Mohammadi retired from Tehran University in 1979 and dedicated his academic efforts towards organizing the results of more than forty years of research into his most comprehensive literary work titled *Iranian History and Culture in the Period of Transition from the Sassanid to the Islamic Periods*, published in Tehran in five volumes. This series received Iran's Book of the Year award in 2003.

Prof. Mohammadi passed away in Tehran in 2002.

As this book was written long before Prof. Mohammadi completed his research on this subject, it would be useful to extract from the introduction to his latest work, information that can provide the reader with a conceptual framework to the subject, and a better understanding of the contents of this book. He explains in Chapter one of Volume one of *Iranian History and Culture* that, in his school days, while he studied the two subjects of the history of Iran, as well as the history of Iranian literature, one question preoccupied him most: why did the history of Iranian literature begin after Islam with the recording of Persian poetry in the third and fourth centuries of the Hijra, while the history of Iran went back more than a millennium before Islam? He indicates that what led him to the path of seeking to find an answer to this question was Edward Brown's book on the literary history of Iran. Brown had divided Iran's literary history into three distinct phases: the Achaemenian period from 550 to 330 BC, the Sassanid period from AD 226 to 652, and the Islamic period from AD 900 to the present. Thus, there were two breaks in the long history of Iranian literature: a period of 550 years between Alexander's conquests and the beginning of the Sassanid Empire, and a period of approximately 250 years between the collapse of the Sassanid Empire and the beginning of recording of Persian poetry in the Islamic period. Prof. Mohammadi indicates that the break between the end of the Achaemenian period and the beginning of the Sassanid period is understandable as the Ashkanid Empire, that had inherited the legacy of Iranian civilization and culture from the Achaemenians, and the Sassanids who had inherited that legacy from them, had both perished. What was questionable was the break following the collapse of the Sassanids, because the Islamic period that inherited the cultural legacy of Iran from the Sassanids had not perished and still continues; and while there is little hope that reliable information can be found regarding the first break, it is possible that by studying the roots of Islamic civilization and culture, some of the missing links in the second break can be found, and so, that period can be termed as a period of transition rather than a break.

Prof. Mohammadi explains that, in discussing Iranian history before and after Islam, it is the norm to talk about two distinct periods separated by a 'wall', on one side lies the destroyed and perished period, and on the other side the newly-emerged period. This is an incorrect perception. Iranian civilization did not perish because of the fall of the Sassanid Empire. When the Arabs took over the capital of the Sassanids at Tisphoon (or Mada'en, near Baghdad today) and became masters of the whole of Iraq, they found a complex administrative and financial system in place. Since they did not have the capacity to take over that system or modify it, they realized it was in their interest to maintain it, and even to modify some of their earlier practices in order to better adapt to it. One of those practices was to distribute conquered land among the fighters. As they anticipated great difficulties to apply such a practice in Iraq, the Caliph Omar decided to keep the *dehghans* (landowners) in charge of their land, and to maintain the *kharaj* institutions (accounting system) that had been established by Khosrow Anooshiravan intact.

This was the case with the *divan* system (administration) of the Sassanids as a whole, which was adopted by the Caliphate. Here also, it was necessary to maintain the services of the *dabirs* (administrators) of the *divan* to ensure that it functioned effectively. As the Islamic state grew and expanded, it was the *divan* system that made it possible to govern the vast territories and the diversity of the peoples covered by the Caliphate. It must also be mentioned that the administrative divisions of the Sassanid period, and particularly in Iraq, survived intact for several centuries into the Islamic period.

The fact that the *dehghans* and *dabirs*, who represented two pillars of Sassanid civilization and culture, survived the transition from the pre-Islamic to the Islamic period meant that the economic and administrative systems of the Sassanids out lived the collapse of their political system. It was through them that pre-Islamic Iranian culture spread within the Islamic society and played an important role in the expansion and development of Islamic culture and civilization.

The Iranian calendar, which was a solar calendar, was also adopted by the Caliphate. This was because the Arab calendar was lunar, and thus not convenient for setting the *kharaj* of agricultural lands, whose revenues were based on crops that depended on a solar cycle. With the calendar, many of the Iranian cultural practices that depended on it found their way into the Islamic world, such as the Nowrooz feast that marked the beginning of the *kharaj* year.

The question is why has this process not been more apparent and visible? The most important reason that Prof. Mohammadi presents for this is *ta'reeb*, or Arabization. He writes: *Ta'reeb* means presenting a non-Arabic word or noun in an Arabic format such that its origins are in time erased and forgotten. One such case is the Arabization of names of individuals, by ignoring their ethnic names and giving them Arabic names and even devising Arab ancestry for them. This was a practice that Arab tribes had in the Jahili period. When tribes defeated other tribes, they would take their wealth as booty, capture their members into slavery, and then establish for them family allegiances within their own tribe, which would also apply to their descendants after them, and would continue to apply to them even when they were able to gain their freedom. Such people they would call *mawali*. This practice was limited among Arab tribes, but became widely practised in the Arab conquests of Iran, so much so that it left a serious impact by suppressing the history of Iran and of Iranians in that period. This is because, in references in Arabic books to these *mawali*, whose numbers were ever increasing during the first centuries of Islam, they were considered people of no identity or ancestry, and were known only as a result of their links to this or that Arab individual or tribe. The obscuring effect of this practice on the history of Iran in that period can be better understood when we consider the fact that most of the impact that Iranians had in the expansion of Islamic civilization and culture was through these same people called *mawali*, whose Iranian identity is not clearly recorded.

Another dimension of Arabization concerns that of history. Prof. Mohammadi explains that what is meant by the Arabization of history is not the fact that all history books on that period were written in Arabic, when the writers of those books were mostly Iranians. This means that, reading those histories gives the general impression that in those days and within the vast territories of Islam, no other peoples or cultures existed besides those migrating Arab tribes, no other events were taking place except what was related to those tribes and their activities, and no other language was used by people except Arabic. This is partly because the contents of Arab history books were often based on tales recounted orally by individuals known as *rawi* (narrator), and therefore reflected only what those individuals had witnessed, or heard from others. And since these tales usually went back to an Arab *rawi*, the contents of these tales rarely went beyond what was taking place among the migrant Arabs, which those *rawis* witnessed or became aware of, and rarely covered any of the other important events that were taking place outside the limited circles of those Arab migrants. The only way that an occasional reference is made to other events is when these are related to an Arab, and so were marginally mentioned. Prof. Mohammadi refers to an important event that occurred in Iraq almost seven decades after the Arab conquests of that area. The event was the transformation of the *divan* from Persian to Arabic, with all the complexities involved in such a transformation, such as the modification of systems and the recruitment and training of *dabirs*. This was a very significant development in the history of Iran and Islam, and if it had been described in the history books with its details and complexities, it could have clarified many of the hidden aspects of the history of that period. But the only reference to this event is a short tale, namely that Hajjaj transformed the *divan* of Iraq from Persian to Arabic.

Yet another dimension of Arabization that Prof. Mohammadi has referred to is that of avoidance of reference to Iranian sources even when they were available. Tabari, for example, is known in the Islamic world as the father of history. In the section of his book which he dedicated to Iranian history before Islam, he covered material that existed in Iranian sources that were still available in his days either in original Persian or in Arabic translation. He could have used those sources and even made reference to them, but he chose to write in the prevailing format by recounting tales from Arab individuals and *rawis*. In his entire book there is no reference to even one Iranian book or piece, even in its Arabic translation. Where he referred to Persian scholars, he refrained from naming even one of them. This kind of approach to Iranian literary works resulted in their being gradually forgotten and any occasional reference to them was only within mainstream Arabic literature.

Another reason for the vagueness of Iranian history of the first centuries of Islam is that Iranian history became intertwined with Arab and Islamic history simultaneously. Iranians and Arabs are two nations that coexisted and interacted for centuries before Islam. When Islam brought these two nations under the same cover, it introduced an element into the joint history of Iranians and Arabs that had its own parameters and went beyond national identity. Viewing Arab conquests and expansion, as well as the Islamization of Iran from the same perspective, and as a single event, added confusion to the history of that period, the effects of which can be felt even today. Although the spread of Islam in Iran was hastened as a result of the Arab conquest of Iran, nevertheless each event is distinct and has its own causes and effects. Also the time frames for the two events are not that close to support considering the two events as one.

A last point to raise concerns the Persian language. In the book there are repeated references to the Pahlavi language that was in use in Iran in the Sassanid period, implying that it was a distinct language that fell out of use in the Islamic era. Prof. Mohammadi provided the following comment on this subject in his introduction to the later Persian edition of this book:

Following scholars whose works have been the sources for this book, wherever there was a reference to the Iranian language before Islam, it is identified as the Pahlavi language. This to me was evident and beyond doubt. But, as my studies continued, questions emerged that indicated otherwise, such that, if I was writing this book today, I would substitute Pahlavi with Persian in most instances. The reasons for this change of position I have covered in a section of the book *Iranian History and Culture* dedicated to the Persian language.

Prof. Mohammadi's objective was to help clarify the hidden aspects of the interdependence of Iranian and Arabic literature and culture. It is hoped that this book can be a step towards achieving that objective.

*August 2011*                            SHAHROKH MOHAMMADI-MALAYERI

# Introduction

The Sassanid period is of great significance in the history of Iran and the orient because during that period, Iranians were able to establish a powerful state and rule over vast areas of the orient for 400 years; and more importantly, because the cultural, organizational and administrative achievements of that period survived for centuries after the fall of the Sassanids and became the model for those states that succeeded them in this region. In order to better comprehend the significance of that period in the history of Iran, it is sufficient to state that it was due to the historical and cultural heritage of that period that Iranians were able to maintain their prominent position in Islamic culture and civilization, even when they did not hold sway in the political arena.

Several centuries before Ardeshir Babakan, the founder of the Sassanid dynasty ascended the throne of Iran, this region had been conquered by Alexander the Macedonian and governed by the Greeks. The primary objective of Alexander and his successors was the destruction of the bases of Iranian culture and national unity, as a result of which Hellenization flourished in Iran and the culture acquired a Greek character. Although Greek domination did not last long, as Iranian clans began to infiltrate the structure of Greek government and rapidly destroyed it within the span of one century, it took a long time for Iranian civilization and culture to shed its Hellenic influences, and for Iranians to establish a powerful state by asserting their intellectual freedom and reviving their national culture. In other words, to transform that period of subordination and humiliation into one of revival and vitality, called for a fundamental national transformation, both in form and in spirit. This transformation occurred in the Ashkanid period. The

Ashkanids provided the medium in which Iranian national identity developed which it reached its zenith with the establishment of the Sassanid empire.

Professor Arthur Christensen has described this aspect of the Sassanid empire in his valuable book *Iran Under the Sassanids*, by pointing out that Roman historians had failed to grasp the significance of the transformation that occurred in Iran following the establishment of the new dynasty. Dion and Herodien only briefly referred to the victory of Ardeshir over Ardavan. The Romans received the new empire as mightier than its predecessor, and therefore a bigger threat to the eastern frontiers of their empire, but they failed to grasp the fact that this new empire was in essence and foundation different from its predecessor. Moreover, they did not realize that the emergence of the Sassanid empire was the ultimate phase of a long process of transformation that was in progress during the Ashkanid period under a façade of Greek civilization. During that period some elements of Greek influence were rejected by Iranian society and others were absorbed by it and were transformed. When Ardeshir was establishing his control over the state, Iranian society was gradually emerging as an integrated national entity and the manifestations of this integration were increasingly apparent in various aspects of social and cultural life. Therefore, the change from one dynasty to another was not merely a political change, but also a manifestation of the emergence of a new spirit within the Iranian empire.[1]

The Sassanids consolidated their empire by strengthening the national culture and reviving Iranian religion, which became their strongest base of support. The foundations of the empire were laid by Ardeshir Babakan who rendered invaluable service to the people of Iran by retrieving the scattered pieces of *Avesta*,[2] and expanding the religion of Zoroaster. This wise policy of Ardeshir, followed by his successors, had a miraculous impact on reviving the national unity of Iran, and making Iranians strong; a policy that attracted the attention of the contemporaries of the Sassanids. With this initiative,

[1]  Arthur Christensen, *L'Iran Sous les Sassanids*, p. 92.
[2]  *Avesta—Zoroaster's Holy Book.*

Ardeshir integrated the dispersed communities of Iran along a united path, under one religion and one flag.

Islamic historians have narrated numerous accounts, confirmed by historical evidence, about the policy of the Sassanid shahs to support and promote enlightenment. Khosrow Anooshiravan's reign could be considered a period of cultural renaissance, a period of particular significance in the history of Iran, mainly because of its exclusive national character and Iranian flavour. During this period, Iranians not only focused on their own scientific and cultural heritage, but also evinced a keen interest in the contemporary sciences of India and Greece, and strove to obtain Indian and Greek books and translate them into Persian. Anooshiravan's aim was to transform Tisphoon, the capital of Iran and by then the most significant political centre of the orient, into an important centre for knowledge and culture, a position that two centuries later was occupied by the city of Baghdad built in the Abbasid period at the same location. Anooshiravan did not live long enough to complete what he had initiated. The flame that he had kindled did not die after him and Iranian scholars pursued their efforts to promote scholarship and achieve significant results after the Sassanid period, however, they strove in the name of Islam and the intellectual fruits of their labour were in the Arabic language.

The Sassanid empire had a dramatic end, which coincided with the dawn of a new era in the history of the orient. Far from the western frontiers of Iran, a religious movement called Islam emerged in the Arabian Peninsula that triggered a transformation in that part of the world. The Sassanid empire, passing through a period of weakness and impotence, was unable to withstand the Arab and Islamic conquests, and after a futile struggle, the banner of Iranian independence was eventually toppled. Fate had turned a page in the history of this ancient and valiant people, which proved to be a hard lesson for the Iranian nation. A chapter in the history of the orient had ended and another chapter was about to begin. From being the seat of the biggest empire in the orient, Iran now became a part of another empire known as the Arab or Islamic empire.

It was expected that with the collapse of Iranian sovereignty and the weakening of the foundations of Iranian national civilization and culture, Iranians would no loger play a prominent role in the politics of the orient. But, it soon became evident that Iranians had not lost their excellence, and were able to secure for themselves a stature that was worthy of them.

The end of the initial period of Islamic conquests was followed by the dawn of an era of peace and stability. Vast territories that had been conquered had to be administered by the Islamic government. However, if conquest had been possible only through holy war, retaining and administering the conquered territories required a sound mind and wisdom, mature thinking and experienced men. The Arabs, who regarded themselves as the first holy warriors of Islam, were desert nomads and were not familiar with the intricacies of politics and government, they lacked the knowledge and culture required for the administration of such a vast state. Among the Islamic peoples, none were as fit for this task as the Iranians, who had ruled over a major part of these territories for centuries and had the requisite knowledge and experience. This was the best opportunity for Iranians to put their talents and capabilities to use and strive for the advancement of the Islamic community, of which they formed the majority. Taking advantage of this opportunity, Iranian scholars participated in the administration of the caliphate and the affairs of the state, they promoted knowledge and culture and laid the foundations of the flourishing cultural movement of Islam.

The new society that emerged, despite differences in race and intellect, remained a united one during the first centuries of Islam. This unity was based on unanimity of thought and faith. All the different peoples of the Islamic society followed the same beliefs, and pursued the same objectives and goals. Since the Koran was the solid link among them, the language of the Koran became the universal language used by different Islamic peoples to communicate among themselves. Thus, they expressed themselves and disseminated the fruits of thought and intellect to the other members of that vast society in that language. The outcome was that the Arabic language, which before the advent of Islam was a simple nomadic language in terms of vocabulary and structure, developed within a short time and at an unprecedented pace and soon became the only scientific and literary language of the Islamic east. The Arabic language maintained this position for several centuries, and is one of the greatest languages of the orient to this day.

The transformation of the Arabic language and its use for diverse branches of sciences and literature was not the result of the efforts of one nation alone; rather, it was the product of the intellect of different nations who chose to produce their scientific and religious works in the Arabic language, and contributed to its development according to their capacities and capabilities. For this reason scholars have designated the totality of the scientific and literary achievements in the Arabic language as Islamic civilization and culture.

As attested by history and confirmed by Arabic literary sources, one of the major groups that strove to strengthen the Arabic language and to enrich it with the sciences and the arts were the Iranians. This is substantiated by the number of eminent personalities in the philosophical, mystical, narrative and historic areas of Arabic literature, as well as religious jurisprudence and methodology, and the area they belonged to. Moreover, it must be borne in mind that the scientific and literary movement of Islam was launched in a place that had been for centuries the capital and centre of Iranian rule, and it began in a period which prominent historians have described as the period of Iranian influence and the golden era of Islam. This was an era in which the Arabs lost the authority and decisive influence that they had enjoyed in the Islamic world under the Amavids, and they were no longer the sole political masters of the Islamic community. It was in this period that the eastern Islamic state based in Baghdad, reached the peak of its achievements in all fields and its fame spread throughout the known world.

Conflicts that erupted from time to time among the various Islamic nations, particularly between Iranians and Arabs, did not affect the Islamic environment encompassing all Islamic nations. Nor did they affect the growth and expansion of the Arabic language, which all Moslems accepted as the language of Islam. This is confirmed by the fact that nationalistic Iranians, whom the Arabs called *Sho'oubiyah*[3] were the most ardent promoters of Islamic culture, and

---

[3] *Sho'oubiyah*: A movement within the Islamic community of nations that refused to recognize any privilege for the Arabs over other Islamic nations.

the forefathers of science and literature in the Arabic language. From the beginning, Moslem Iranians distinguished between Arabic Islam (which Arab racial fanatics promoted and which portrayed the Arabs as first among equals in the Islamic world under the pretext that Islam emerged in Arabic among Arabs) and universal Islam (with its universal message of brotherhood and equality), and did not confuse the one with the other; while on the one hand they strongly resisted Arab fanaticism, on the other hand, they strove for the expansion of Islam and the Arabic language. Not only were the Iranians the first people to promote Islamic knowledge outside the Arab peninsula, but also Iranian culture was the first non-Arab culture that interacted with Arabic literature and laid the foundation for its growth and development.

Those who have studied Arabic literature and examined the factors which led to its rapid expansion and progress during the Abbasid period are unanimous in attributing this transformation to the interaction of Arab literature and culture with the culture and literature of other nations, primarily Iranian and Greek. Needless to say that Greek philosophy and thought had a tremendous influence on Arab thinking and Islamic philosophy; but, as is discussed in this book, the decisive element that had a considerable impact on the transformation and growth of Arabic literature and culture was Iranian and not Greek culture.

The fact that Iranians were able to gradually secure their autonomy within a century or two after the advent of Islam, and their ability to maintain Persian as a living language as distinct from Arabic, was not an accident of history or fate; but it was due to a series of implicit and explicit factors, and the result of the efforts of Iranians in this period of languish.[4] They were able to receive this despite the fact that Arabic had become more stronger and fulfilled the roles of both the language of religion and of politics. Considering the fact that among all the nations neighbouring Arabia that endorsed Islam and

[4] Period of languish: The period between the fall of the Sassanid empire and the re-emergence of autonomous Persian dynasties, during which Iranian literary and cultural works were produced in the Arabic language rather than Persian.

accepted the Arabic language as the language of Islam, Iranians were the only people who succeeded in preserving their own language and culture, the significance of their efforts in this regard during the first ·two centuries of Islam becomes clear. It must be noted here that the scientific and literary efforts of Iranians did not wither with the fall of the Sassanid state, but continued to bear fruit, the only difference was that in the first periods of Islam they produced their literary works in Arabic. However, with the passage of time, when they were able to establish independent states, their literary and artistic works were again in Persian, while Arabic remained the language of religion.

On the question of the impact of Iran on Islam and its causes, Inostranzev has opined that Islam in its internal and external history owes much of its heritage to Iran. According to him, the influence of Iran on the history of Islamic peoples is both clear and continuous; whenever favourable conditions prevailed, Iranian elements would surface, and whenever conditions were not conducive they would go under cover, but would maintain their substantive presence. The reason for this is hidden and unveiling it has tremendous significance for human heritage and calls for the study of numerous interrelated issues and questions. In general, however, it should be pointed out that Iran's impact was due to the fact that its historical and cultural heritage survived through the Islamic period and continued to develop.[5] Jackson, a professor of Iranian and Indian languages at Columbia University, has summarized this issue by drawing an analogy between the conquest of Iran by the Moslems and the conquest of England by the Normans, and between the two battles of Qadesiyah and Nahavand and the battle of Hastings.[6] He has added that although the Iranians lost their political independence, they maintained their autonomy of spirit and thought because they were more cultured and had a more advanced civilization compared to their conquerors; the flame of freedom continued silently to burn in their hearts and was rekindled whenever an opportunity arose.

In his review of the revival of the art of painting in Iran in the thirteenth century AD, and with reference to the ceramic and

---

[5] Inostranzev, *Iranian Influence on the Moslem Literature*, p. 56.
[6] Jackson, *Early Persian Poetry*, p. 14.

porcelain paintings of that period found in Rey, Arnold has pointed out that the paintings of that period reflect the same characteristics and intricacies as are seen in the Sassanid empire which collapsed in the sixth century AD. The ancient style and character that had originally developed in a Zoroastrian environment had strangely enough survived for six centuries and had surfaced again in an Islamic environment. This was despite the fact that the main element of Zoroastrian style painting, i.e. the drawing of human figures, was not compatible with Islam. Arnold has argued that this is a clear indication of the deep and vibrant nationalistic feelings of the Iranians, which they harboured even when they were subjugated.[7]

With advancement in the tools and methods of research, the impact of Iranian civilization and culture on Arabic and Islamic literature and culture is an area that has increasingly attracted the attention and interest of scholars. According to some reasons, this is one of the most significant topics that should be of concern to those who study Islam, because research in this area will alter many of the prevailing premises regarding the sources and foundations of Islamic civilization and culture. It must, however, be borne in mind that such scientific and historical scholarship and debate in oriental cultures is new and incomplete. Until the middle of the nineteenth century when research in Arabic literature was a new field for European orientalists, few of them addressed this issue. As their research progressed and their awareness of the different fields of Arabic and Islamic sciences as well as the history and culture of pre-Islamic Iran grew, it became increasingly apparent to them that Islamic sciences and Arabic literature are clearly integrated with Iranian thinking and intellect and an understanding of the historical developments in Arab culture is not possible without studying Iranian civilization and culture and its historical evolution.

Among those whose efforts have led to a greater understanding of this topic and who have paved the way for its further growth and expansion, mention must be made of scholars like Goldziher, von Kremmer, Noeldke, Brockelmann, Arnold, Baron Rosen, Zutemberg, Huart and Edward Browne. Inostranzev has discussed

---

[7] V. Arnold, *The Islamic Book*, p. 56.

this issue in many of his writings and has highlighted its significance in the history of Islam. Christensen has shed light on many hidden aspects through his unrivalled research on Iran in the Sassanid period.

Prominent researchers have compared the Iranian people in the east to Greeks and Romans in the west. In other words, just as Greek and Roman cultures had a significant impact on the civilization of Western nations, and are viewed as the foundation of Western cultures, so has Iranian culture and Iranian thought had a great impact on the peoples of the east. As a result, Iranians have played a significant role in the advancement of human civilization and culture. It would be relevant to cite here Browne's views.

In his affirmation of Iranian independence during this country's period of languish, he has pointed out that the destruction of a finite being, whether an individual or a nation, represents a loss for the living world, and therefore, is considered as pure evil and a great sin. The reason why ancient Greeks and Romans have attracted the attention of other peoples of the world and have become the subjects of their affection and interest is that they have left behind a great industrious and literary heritage through which they have indebted human civilization and culture to their strife. It is for this reason that the modern nations of Italy and Greece have aroused the interest of the peoples of the world and have reaped great political benefits in process. Browne has expressed the belief that Iran is at par with those two nations, because the Iranian people have made numerous literary and scientific contributions to human civilization and culture. Therefore, the absence of Iran from the community of free states of the world is not only a loss to the people of Iran, but also to her mankind.

# ONE

# Iranian Literary Heritage and Its Fate in the Arab Campaign

**Attitude of Invaders towards the Heritage of Conquered Nations** The first century of Islam was not very conducive for Iran's literary productivity. The *bedwin* holy warriors who had become the masters of the Islamic world were still not familiar with the manifestations of learning and enlightenment, and they did not comprehend the essence of the value that the Koran had attached to knowledge and learning. As a result, they felt no interest in books and manuscripts, particularly when they considered them as belonging to the infidels. Thus, even if they did not consider the destruction of such literature as a duty, they did not consider their preservation to be desired either. Therefore, at the dawn of Islam and during the period of conflict, disorder, looting, and the changing of religions and scripts, a portion of the literary and scientific heritage of Iran was destroyed; and the portion that was preserved, was later used as a primary source by scholars, and was translated into Arabic and interacted with and became part of the Islamic culture.

In a number of historical sources there are general references to the destruction of Iran's books during the Arab conquest, and others contain narratives about the burning of these books by the invaders. There are varying views on the attitude of the Arabs towards the libraries and cultural vestiges of nations whose territories were captured during the Islamic conquests. Some believe that when the Arabs captured the territories that later became part of the Islamic empire, they destroyed all books and scientific works which they came across, giving the justification that the Koran superseded everything that came before it. Thus, they either burnt the books of Iran and Egypt or drown them in water. In the later centuries, however, as the Arabs became more enlightened and discovered the value of the treasures that they had destroyed, they considered such claims against the first holy warriors of Islam unbefitting, and they removed all traces and evidence of such behaviour that existed in historic sources, and as a result, many such references were lost. Others have considered such accusations as unfounded, and they have described the few references that do exist on the subject as the product of animosity and hostile bigotry. It is obvious that ascertaining the truth in such a situation, if not impossible, is at least very difficult. In any case this should not prevent one from discussing here what has been said or referred to in general on the matter in historic sources.

Georgy Zaidan, the Egyptian author, whose writings include two well-known series of books, the *History of Islamic Civilization* and the *History of Arab Literature*, has written extensively in his *History of Islamic Civilization*, about the library of Alexandria and its burning during the Arab conquest. According to him, he had initially considered the attribution of the burning of the library of Alexandria to the Arabs as untrue, and had stated this view in a book entitled *The History of Modern Egypt* that had written early in his scholarly career. However, in his subsequent studies on the history of Islam, he chanced upon other evidence, and abandoned his earlier belief. According to him, the reasons that led him to alter his position were:

1. The inclination of Moslems at the dawn of Islam to destroy any book other than the Koran, based on what they quoted from the Holy Prophet and his companions.
2. A tale that Abul Faraj Malti has narrated about the conquest of Egypt in the book *A Short History of States*, which in brief is that when Amru bin A'as conquered Alexandria, he wrote to Omar and asked for instructions about what to do with the books there; Omar wrote in response and instructed him to destroy them because with the Koran at hand, he saw no further need for other books.
3. A number of narratives about the books of Iran and their destruction by the Arabs, that have been recorded (which will be referred to later).
4. Evidence that during those periods burning the opponents' books was one of the means of revenge in conquests, which is also confirmed by numerous historical events.

5. Evidence that when the followers of one religion became dominant over the followers of another religion, they destroyed their temples and their holy books.

6. Tales revealing that many of the eminent pious men during the dawn of Islam, such as Ahmad bin abu Hawari and Abu Amru bin Ala', destroyed their own books because of their piety, which indicates that the early Moslems were not so enamoured of books.

After giving his reasons, Georgy Zaidan concluded that, at the time of the initial expansion of Islam, whatever ancient scientific and literary books that the Arabs came across, they burnt in support of Islam, and when their state established itself and they turned to acquiring knowledge, they produced several times over what they had destroyed.[1]

**Iran's Heritage Partially Destroyed and Partially Preserved** This summarizes what Georgy Zaidan has elaborated on the library of Alexandria. Regarding the Iranian cultural heritage and its fate during that period there are other accounts that are worthy of mention. Georgy Zaidan has quoted in his discussion two tales on this issue, one from Ibni Khaldoon and the other from Haj Khalifah, the author of *Kashf ul Zonoon*. In his writing, Ibni Khaldoon has raised the question: 'where did the science and knowledge of Iran go which Omar decreed its destruction at the time of conquest?'[2]

Haj Khalifah has described the event in greater detail. According to him, As the Moslems conquered Iran and captured the books of the Iranians, Sa'ad bin Abi Waqqas wrote a letter to Omar and asked for an opinion on them, and Omar wrote him in response, to drown the books in water, because, he explained, if they are intended to guide us, God has guided us with a better book, and if they are intended to mislead us, God has rendered us in no need of them. Thus, the Moslems threw those books into the water (or fire) and with them the sciences of Iran also perished.[3]

---

[1] Georgy Zaidan, *The History of Islamic Civilization*, vol. III, pp. 42-7.
[2] Ibni Khaldoon, The Introduction, vol. I, p. 32.
[3] *Kashf ul Zonoon*, vol. I, p. 446.

Haj Khalifah has referred elsewhere in the same book to the behaviour of the Arab holy warriors and has said that whatever books the Moslems found in their conquests they burnt.[4]

As mentioned earlier, details of such events are not available in any of the classical Islamic sources, and despite the vital significance that these events have for the study of the evolution of Islamic civilization and culture, the only information that is available is confined to incomplete and ad hoc references scattered in different historical sources of Islam. For example, the *Nehayat ul Erab* mentions that when the Moslems captured Tisphoon, the capital of the Sassanid state, and set fire to the curtain of the Eyvan Kasra, 100,000 gold *dinars* were extracted from it.[5] Of course, there is no mention of books and libraries here, but reading this tale, one cannot but wonder that, under such circumstances, what became of the books and writings which were preserved in the treasuries and archives?

More information can be obtained from what Abu Reyhan Birooni has written about Kharazm and the fate of its scientific heritage. Birooni himself was from Kharazm, and as is apparent from his writings, he was an inquisitive and knowledgeable man who has rarely written anything unauthenticated. As such his writing can be viewed with confidence. He writes that when Qutaybah bin Muslim Bahili captured Kharazm and killed its writers and the *Hirbadan* (clerics in charge of the fire temples) and burnt their books and letters, the people of Kharazm fell into ignorance, and whatever that they knew of the codes and the sciences, was transmitted by word of mouth from generation to generation, and they could recount only from memory.[6] Referring to Qutaybah's second visit to Kharazm, Birooni writes that, as Qutaybah had eliminated in this land all those who were well versed in the Kharazmi script and were knowledgeable of the heritage of this land, and had brought destruction and disunity in this area the heritage of this land was lost after Islam, and there was no hope of regenerating it.[7]

[4] Ibid., p. 25.
[5] *Nehayat ul Erab*, vol. I, p. 366.
[6] *Al-Akhbar al Baghyah*, p. 48.
[7] Ibid., pp. 35-6.

Although Birooni has written on the cultural heritage of Kharazm in eastern Iran from his writings one can deduce to some extent the fate of the literary heritage in other regions of Iran. It must be borne in mind that the first campaign of Qutaybah to the eastern parts of Iran, that is Bokhara, Soghd and Farghaneh east of Khorasan, took place in the 87th year of Hijra, nearby seventy years after the Arab conquest of the western cities and the capital of Iran. Although during this period the Arabs had become more familiar with the manifestations of civilization and culture following their exposure to Islamic teachings, and the civilization of nations which were more cultured, such was their attitude towards the heritage of Kharazm and its scholars and books. It has therefore been assumed that seventy years earlier, their attitude towards what they found in the west of Iran, or in the treasuries of Tisphoon, could not have been better.

It must be borne in mind that burning the books of opponents was practised by most community around the world during different historic periods and is evident even today. The Arabs were no exception to this practice, and various such accounts are available about other periods as well. For example, an event related to Iranian books that occurred in the early years of the fourth century of the Hijra was the burning of the books of the Manavis. It has been recorded that in the year 311 they burnt the painting of Mani and fourteen sacks of his followers' books at the Bab ul Ammah of Baghdad. As a number of researchers have assumed that these books, like most or all Manavi books, contained drawings and decorations and perhaps even gold and silver inlays, their loss is an irreparable blow to the field of art and painting in Iran.[8]

Regardless of the treatment of Iran's cultural heritage by the Arabs, it should not be considered the only reason for the destruction of many of Iran's scientific and literary works. Among other reasons which have had a considerable impact on this was that many Iranians after embracing the Moslem faith no longer cared for the literary heritage of their forefathers, and were not interested in their preservation. Some Iranians even viewed this heritage as alien and did not hesitate to destroy it under the pretext that it was the

[8] V. Arnold, *The Islamic Book*, p. 2.

heritage of the Zoroastrians. According to Dolatshah Samarqandi, when someone brought the book of the story of Vamegh and Azra, a Pahlavi book, to Abdullah bin Taher, he decreed that it be drowned in water and that any such books found in the territories within his jurisdiction should be destroyed.[9]

**Reasons for Partial Preservation of Iran's Heritage**

So far the discussion has focused on those factors that were not conducive to the preservation of the scientific and literary heritage of Iran, and they in fact contributed to the destruction of a part of that heritage. It is, however, equally necessary to discuss other factors that have had great impact on the preservation of some of Iran's books and cultural masterpieces, and have contributed, during those periods of turmoil and uncertainty, to the survival of a part of this heritage in the later periods. One of these factors is the Persian language.

**The Persian Language in the Period of Languish**

It was mentioned in the introduction that after the spread of Islam, Arabic which was considered the language of Islam, gradually spread among the Islamic nations, and soon it became the official and religious language of Moslems. It should be added here that in Iran the Arabic language never crossed this threshold and never became the language of the masses. Of course, many Iranians who interacted with the Arabs learnt Arabic and used it to satisfy their needs, but the common language in the towns and villages of Iran remained Persian and its various dialects.

The main reason why the Arabic language gradually lost its initial grandeur in Iran, and was overshadowed in the realms of politics and literature by Persian, was that Arabic was unable to penetrate the core of Iranian family life. It would be erroneous to assume that as the Sassanid state collapsed within a short period, Iranian literature also withered away in the same way and no trace was left of it. The political power of a state can be destroyed by a military defeat, but language, literature and customs, and the heritage that constitutes the

---

[9]   *Tazkareh Dowlatshah Samarqandi*, Brill Edn, p. 30.

character of a nation, do not fade away in a short time, particularly if that nation has a deep-rooted culture.

From the narratives of Islamic historians, one can clearly grasp the scope and the significance of the Persian language even during this period of languish. It has been recorded that when the envoys of Abdul Malik came to the camp of Ibn-i-Ashtar, they did not hear even a single word of Arabic in the entire camp. The armies of Ibn-i-Ashtar and Mukhtar were all recruited from among Iranians, and although they lived among the Arabs and interacted with them, they continued to communicate in their own language and did not speak Arabic. Ibrahim Imam, the propagator of the Abbasid call, wrote in his letter of guidance and advice to Abu Moslem: 'If you can manage not to leave a single Arab speaker in Khorasan, then do so'. By Arab speaker Ibrahim was referring to members of Arab tribes that had migrated from Arabia and had settled in this region, which indicates that Arabic was confined only to Arab migrants.

Even in the *diwans* of the provinces of Iran, Persian continued to be used as the official language for a fairly long time. In Baghdad too, Persian continued to be widely used even after the city had become the capital of the Arabic and Islamic Caliphate. Explaining why most of the titles that were used by the government of Egypt were Persian, Ghalaghshandi writes that, although Egypt did not border Iran, the seat of the caliphate was in Baghdad and often its officials and leaders spoke in Persian, and these titles spread to Egypt from there.[10]

### Zoroastrians in the First and Second Centuries of Hijra

One must also consider the Zoroastrians and their institutions in Iran in the first centuries of Islam as another important factor in the preservation of part of the Iranian literary heritage. One of the realities about Iran and Islam is that the spread of this new religion in Iran and the change in the national religion of the Iranians from Zoroastrian to Islam did not occur within the same short span of time that the Sassanid empire was transformed into an Islamic Caliphate. The progress of Islam in Iran was gradual and there is no evidence that this process was the

---

[10] *Sobhi-al-A'asha*, vol. IV, p. 453.

result of coercion or pressure exerted by the conquerors on the local population; rather, there are numeous indications to the contrary.

It is true that until Iranians began to understand Islam, they actually remained hostile to it and strongly resisted it; but once they grasped the essence of Islam, not only did they cease their hostility towards it, but they also joined the lines of the holy warriors themselves, and spared no effort in spreading and promoting it. The progress of Islam in Iran gained momentum as people's comprehension of it grew, such that during the days of the Amavid Caliphate, some of its functionaries expressed discontent with Iranians embracing Islam, and their shifting in flocks from the Ahl i Zimmah (those who paid the *jezyah* (taxes levied on non-Moslems) and were under the protection of the Moslems) to the masses of Moslems; this was because their conversion reduced the enormous annual revenue of the state from the *jezyah*.

At the same pace that Islam was finding its way into the hearts of Iranians, the Zoroastrian religion was losing ground, and its followers were diminishing in number. Since this was a slow process, during the first centuries of Islam Zoroastrians continued to enjoy the respect and relative freedom that they had in society; and thus, their numbers remained relatively high and their impact on the social and cultural life of the country was considerable. Islamic historians have named several Iranian clans which remained Zoroastrian until the second or third or even the fourth centuries of Hijra, before they converted to Islam. Saman Nia Samanian of the nobility of Balkh converted to Islam around the second century, Kareem, the son of Shahriar, the first reigning member of the clan of Ghaboos, converted at the beginning of the third century, and Abu Hassan Mehyar Deylami, the renowned poet whose *divan* is well known in Arabic literature, converted to Islam in the year 394 of Hijra, or towards the end of the fourth century of Hijra.

The people of Tabarestan and the northern regions of Iran were unaware about the new religion for 300 years after Hijra and remained hostile to the Caliphate. Most of the people of Kerman were Zoroastrian during the entire Amavid period.[11] During the

---

[11]   *Masalek-ul-Mamalek*, pp. 126, 194; *Ya'qoobi*, pp. 274, 279-80.

time of Estakhri, the Zoroastrians of Iran constituted a substantive number;[12] according to Maghdesi, they had a considerable impact on the social life of this region, and although they were considered by the state at par with other religious minorities and the Ahl i Zimmah, they enjoyed a higher standing among the people. For example, the Zoroastrians of Shiraz did not have to wear the mark that the Ahl i Zimmah had to wear for easy identification, and their customs and codes were common in the entire region; and on the occasions of their feasts all the bazars of the city were decorated,[13] and during the festivities of *Nowrooz* and Mehregan in particular the people of the city joined them in their celebrations.

Until the time of Estakhri, and perhaps even later, the Iranian calendar and months remained in use in the province of Fars, and even the *divan* of this region continued to be written in the same manner and with the same calendar as it had been during the Sassanid period.[14] Ibni Hawghal writes:

Nowhere are there as many Zoroastrians as in *Fars*, because this region was the seat of their state and their religion and the center of their books and their fire temples, and the heritage that they have inherited from generation to generation and which they still own.[15]

What has been discussed here reveals the extent to which Zoroastrians enjoyed freedom in the first centuries of Islam. These conditions did not last for ever and in the later centuries, as the fanaticism of Moslems increased, Zoroastrians felt more confined and restricted in their religious rituals and social living conditions, and their lives became increasingly harsh until hordes of them left the lands of their ancestors and migrated to India.

There is no reference in Zoroastrian literature to this exodus except for one vague account that is known as the Story of Senejan, which according to Inostranzev, was written around the sixteenth century AD. In brief, this story recounts that after the victory of the Moslems over the Iranians and their conquest of Iran, the followers

[12] *Masalek-ul-Mamalek*, p. 139.
[13] *Ahsan ul Taqaseem*, p. 429.
[14] Ibid., p. 44.
[15] *Sourat al Ardh*, vol. II, p. 292.

of Zoroaster remained in Iran for nearly a century and settled in the mountainous regions of this land, but they eventually began to migrate. Initially, they migrated to the island of Hormoz from where they went to Gujrat, where they held discussions with the chief of the region of Senejan, in following which settled in that region permanently and were joined by other groups of migrants through Khorasan. According to Inostranzev, this migration occurred gradually and in small groups because had it been in one move or at one time, there would have been detailed references to it in Arabic literary sources.[16]

The fact that during the period of languish Zoroastrians lived in Iran in great numbers and enjoyed relative freedom of action had a very positive outcome for the preservation of a part of Iran's scientific and cultural heritage. Because of the affection that Zoroastrians had for the heritage of their forefathers and the great events of their history, they strived hard to preserve this heritage and even succeeded in saving a part of it, particularly their religious writings, and passed it on to future generations. The impact of Zoroastrians on the preservation of this heritage can be better understood if one considers that in the first and second centuries of Islam, Zoroastrian life continued in Iran with all its manifestations, and the fire in many of the *Ateshkadehs* continued to burn and they remained active centres where Zoroastrian Moobadan continued their religious and educational activities among their followers.

**The Moobadan**   According to the available narratives, during the first Islamic periods Zoroastrian Moobadan were treated with dignity and respect whether by the Caliphs and their envoys or by the people, and if even they were insulted by a Moslem fanatic, the guilty would be punished by the Moslem rulers.[17] There are papers in Persian and Pahlavi giving details of debates between Zoroastrian thinkers and Moslems in the presence of the Caliph. One such debate was between a Zoroastrian teacher and a Moslem

---

[16] Inostranzev, pp. 13-14. Also refer to Taghi Zadeh, *Gah Shomari* in *Ancient Iran*, pp. 159, 304.

[17] Arnold, *Preaching of Islam*, p. 179.

jurist on Ahuramazda and Ahriman, and another paper is attributed to Moslem scholars. There is a paper in Pahlavi entitled *Gojasteh Abalish* (or *Abalish* the Damned)[18] which describes a debate between a Zoroastrian Moobad named Azar Faranbagh, the son of Farrokhzad, and Abalish, a non-believer Zoroastrian. What is significant in this debate is the fact that it took place in the presence of Ma'moon, the Caliph and Grand Judge of Islam, with the participation of the leaders of the Jewish and Christian communities. This stands witness to the personal concern of the Caliphs for such matters, and also the relative freedom that Zoroastrians and the Moobadan enjoyed. Jahiz has provided a detailed account of his discussion with a Moobad which also supports this fact.[19]

The service that the Moobadan and Zoroastrian scholars have rendered to Iranian culture is more in the fact that they preserved what they possessed of the literary heritage of Iran in the *Ateshkadehs* and other safe places, through copying, studying and debating them. Perhaps they even restored parts of what had been lost or damaged during the period of turmoil and instability. While studying Iranian history, customs and religious sects, Islamic historians and scholars often used this group of Moobadan and Hirmandan as their sources. These same groups were among the most important sources of Mas'oodi, Hamzeh Esfahani, Abu Reyhan Birooni and other historians who have evinced an interest in the history of Iran. The *Khodai Nameh*, the greatest book of the history of Iran, was safeguarded for several centuries by the Moobadan until it was eventually immortalized by Ferdowsi. Similarly, the *Ayeen Nameh*, which was also one of the great works of the Sassanid era, was preserved by this group until it was translated into Arabic and found its way into Arabic literature. The Moobad of the city of Shapoor, was one of the scholars who translated the *Khodai Nameh* into Arabic.

---

[18] This paper was translated into Persian by Sadegh Hedayat, and published in Tehran in HS 1318. For more information on this paper, refer to its introduction.

[19] *Al-Hayawan*, vol. V, p. 25.

**Mesmoghan and the Holy Seat of Rey**

Apart from the Moobadan, who continued to live in Islamic society and dedicated their lives to teaching and debating the Zoroastrian heritage, there were others who continued to live in autonomy in remote areas or in strong fortresses, and who did not heed to the authority and rule of the Caliphs for a long period after the fall of the Sassanid empire. Islamic books mention the name of a location in Rey that was under the rule of the Grand Moobad and which maintained its independence from the Islamic caliphate until the second half of the second century of Hijra.

According to Pourdavood, Rey was among the cities that were considered holy in ancient times, and was a holy seat for Iranian clerics. The Grand Moobad who had the title of Zarathustrotema[20] lived in Rey and, like the Pope in Italy, had a seat of monarchical authority, and the province of Rey was the domain of his material and spiritual reign. Arabic authors have referred to the Grand Moobad as *Mesmoghan*. This means the greatest of the Moghs. *Mes* in Pahlavi means the same as the word *Meh* in Persian,[21] and is the equivalent of great in English.

At the time when Rey and its surrounding areas came under the rule of the Caliphs, Mesmoghan lived in a strong fortress located in the mountains of Damavand, and his rule extended over that region. It can be deduced from what Ibn-i-Faghih has written, that this fortress, which he has called Ayreen, was a famous green and beautiful castle built on an elevated and solid mountain. Writing about the construction of this castle, which he has attributed to Arma'il; he says that Arma'il came to a village named Mandan, and on its eastern mountain built a castle in which he laid out extravagant gardens and constructed houses with running fountains; and among those houses was one that was exceptionally decorated with teak and ebony wood, and there was no house in the orient more elevated and more beautiful than it. This building remained untouched until Mahdi (the Abbasid Caliph) gave the son of Mesmoghan immunity

---

[20]   Means 'as Zarathustra'.

[21]   The Introduction of Bargatha, pp. 25-6.

and lured him down from Ayreen and had him beheaded. When Haroon Rashid, the successor of Mahdi, came to Rey and heard of this place, he went there and ordered that it be dismantled and taken to Baghdad.[22]

There are different accounts of the conquest of this centre that remained, until the middle of the second century, outside the authority of the Moslems. According to Tabari, the conquest of Estonavand and the capture of Mesmoghan and his brother took place in the year 141 of Hijra. Marquart, a German professor, has written that in the year 131 of Hijra, Abu Muslim asked Mesmoghan to heed and when he resisted, Abu Muslim dispatched Musa bin Ka'ab to fight him. Musa, however, failed to subjugate him and Mesmoghan remained in control of his seat till the time of Mansoor when he was eventually defeated and captured along with his brother Parviz and his two daughters in the fortress of Estonavand.[23] In his account of the events that occurred during the reign of Khaled Barmaki in Tabarestan, Ibn-i-Faghih has also referred to Mesmoghan and the story of his being sent to Baghdad: 'Mesmoghan came out of the fortress with his women to Khaled and sat on the ground in his presence. Khaled felt pity and sat him on a carpet, then he sent him with his daughters to Mansoor.'[24]

It is not possible to determine from these narratives the exact date when this area lost its autonomy and came under the control of the Caliphs. It appears that Estonavand was conquerted twice; the first time during of the Caliphate of Mansoor and during the Welayah of Khaled Barmaki over Tabarestan and the northern parts of Iran, and again during the Caliphate of Mahdi. The explanation for this may be that after the surrender or entrapment of Mesmoghan during the Caliphate of Mansoor, his son took his place and managed his estate, but with expressed allegiance to the Caliph. As time passed, his insubordination to, and autonomy from the Caliph, became apparent and Mahdi was compelled to dispatch an army to subdue him. Although he had been given immunity, Mahdi broke his vow

---

[22] Ibn-i-Faghih, *Al-Buldan*, p. 257.
[23] Marguart, *Iranshahr*, p. 127.
[24] *Al Buldan*, p. 314.

and killed him. Ibn-i-Faghih has given the title of *Mesmoghan* to the first story and *Son of Mesmoghan* to the second one.

No further information in available about this mountainous region and its small spiritual seat that maintained its autonomy from the Caliphate for nearly 150 years. Moreover, there is no information about the cultural treasures that it may have contained, and therefore it is not possible assess the impact that it may have had on the preservation of Iran's heritage and the role that it may have played in the cultural history of Iran, in a manner that it deserves. However, it is likely that this Zoroastrian centre, during 150 years of its independence under the authority of the Grand Moobad and away from the influence of the Caliphs and the Arabs, was one of the important centres for the preservation of Iranian cultural works and a refuge for the Moobadan.

**Hosn al Jass According to Estakhri and Ibni Hawghal**

Another of these centres was a fortress which has been described by Estakhri and Ibni Hawghal. This fortress has been referred to in Arabic books as 'Ghal'at ul Jass' or 'Hosn al Jass', and the basis of the account of these two Islamic historians, where researchers have pointed out the significance of this location in the cultural history of Iran and have drawn the attention of scholars to it.[25] This fortress

---

[25] In the English translation of Inostranzev's paper, this location is referred to as 'Shiz' (pp. 19-22), while Estakhri and Ibni Hawghal, Inostranzev's sources, have called this fortress *Hosn al Jass* or *Qal'at ul Jass*. As this location may be mistaken for another Iranian Zoroastrian centre, the following clarification may be added: Shir was located in Azarbaijan in which the largest of Iran's *Ateshkadehs*, that is, the *Ateshkadeh* of Azargashasb was located, together with the imperial palace of Ganzak, that housed the most precious treasures of Khosrow Parviz, including the *Taghdis* throne. (Refer to *Al-Boldan*, p. 268; and *Al-Tanbih wal Eshraf*, Egypt, p. 83; *Masalek-ul-Mamalek* of Ibni Khordadbeh, p. 121; and *Mo'jam ul Boldan*, vol. V, p. 326; for further information on the throne of Taghdis, see Christensen, pp. 460-2). The fortress described here was in Fars, and in this region there was no area known as Shiz. Apparently, the word Shiz in Inostranzev's paper

was located in the region of Arrajan between the provinces of Fars and Khouzestan.

Commenting on the strong fortresses of this region, Estakhri writes about this fortress, 'Ghal'at ul Jass is located in the Arrajan region, and there sit Iranian Zoroastrians and storytellers and engage in the study and debate of their historical heritage; and that is a truly sturdy fortress.'[26] Elsewhere he has described the area of Shapoor, which was located in the same region:

> In the area of Shapoor there is a mountain on which the figures of each of the renowned Shahs and Marzbans of Iran and the prominent chiefs of *Ateshkadehs*, and great Moobadan have been carved, and the paintings of these persons and their biographies are kept in chests; and in charge of maintaining them is a group who sit in the region of Arrajan in a place known as Hosn al Jass.[27]

Ibni Hawghal has given a similar account of the area of Shapoor and the figures carved there.[28]

It is known from the *Mo'jam-ul-Buldan* of Yaghoot that, since the Sassanid period, this area had been a place of scholarship and debate and one of the centres of Iranian culture where the recording of the sciences took place. According to Yaghoot, at the time of Iranian rule, the *Gashteh Daftaran* lived in this area. He has identified the Gashteh Daftaran as manuscript writers who used a script that he has called 'Kitabat ul Jastagh'. They wrote in this script books on medicine and astrology.[29] Although during the time of Yaghoot this

---

is the same as the word Jass, which has been transformed through transcription to the Russian and English scripts.

[26] *Masalek-ul-Mamalek*, p. 11. For further information, refer to Inostranzev, p. 19 and references on that page.

[27] *Masalek-ul-Mamalek*, p. 150.

[28] Refer to the book *Description of the Iranian Territory of Iraq from the Book Al Masalek wal Mamalek of Ibn-i-Hawghal*, p. 28.

[29] *Mo'jam-ul-Boldan*, vol, IV, p. 350. Among the seven Persian scripts that Ibn i Nadeem has quoted from Ibni Mughaffa', he has referred to two scripts—Kastaj or Kashtaj, and half Kastaj. He mentions that Kastaj had twenty-eight letters and was used for the imperial *farmans*, official letters as also the script on stamps, cloth, carpets and coins. The half Kastaj

area had lost its scientific significance, on the basis of what has been discussed earlier, it can be seen that at least up to the fourth century of Hijra, copies of Iranian books could be found which, according to Inostranzev, were probably in the Pahlavi language and contained material on the history of Iran and were illustrated in the same style as the figures carved in shapoor mountain in Shapoor.[30]

Undoubtedly, research on this location and what has been found there has great significance not only for the study of Iranian books that were translated from Pahlavi into Arabic in the first centuries of Islam, but also for the original sources of the *Shahnameh* of Ferdowsi. One of the translators of Pahlavi books into Arabic was a man who has been described by Ibni Nadeem as the Moobad of the city of Shapoor. Inostranzev has asserted that this Moobad probably obtained the books that he translated from this place. The information that is available about this location dates to a period that approximates to Ferdowsi's period. It is likely that in composing his *Shahnameh*, Ferdowsi may have depended upon the same sources. The available narratives on this region reveal that Sassanid books of history contained illustrated writings, a claim that is supported by other historical evidence as well.

---

which also had twenty-eight letters was used for books of medicine and philosophy (*Al-Fehrest*, p. 13). It can be concluded from the writings of Ibni Faghih that all or some of the tablets carved on rocks were written in the Kashtaj script. In the description of a huge rock in Hamedan and the script that he found on it, he says that the script was known as Kashtaj (*Al-Buldan*, p. 243). Kashtaj is the Arabic form of Gashteh, and apparently the *Kashtah Daftaran* referred to in *Mojam-ul-Boldan* is the Arabic form of *Gashteh Dabiran*. Regarding the small discrepancy that exists between Ibni Nadeem and Yaghoot about the usage of this script, nothing definite can be said. However, the writing of Ibni Nadeem who has quoted in greater detail from Ibni Mughaffa' about the usage of the various Persian scripts, is more reliable.

[30] The region of Arrajan maintained its Iranian character throughout its history, unlike a number of other regions of Iran that were influenced by the Arabic environment. When Al Motannabbi, the renowned Arab poet, passed through Arrajan, he found his language to be alien in that region, and he composed a verse to express his disappointment.

**The *Ateshkadehs***    Another element of Zoroastrian heritage that survived long after the spread of Islam is the Ateshkadehs. In this period of languish, a large number of *Ateshkadehs* were intact and active in most cities and provinces of Iran. These *Ateshkadehs* and their affiliated institutions were among the important centres of Zoroastrian Moobadan and scholars. In the fourth century of Hijra, the *Ateshkadehs* of Fars were so numerous that Estakhri was unable to recall their names from memory; according to him, there was hardly any province or city or district which did not have at least a number of *Ateshkadehs*. The flame of the *Ateshkadeh* of Mehr Nersian, which Mehr Nersi, the Grand Vazir of Bahram Gour, had constructed in the Dashtbarin of Fars, continued to burn ever during the time of Tabari, the renowned historian of the third century.[31] The *Ateshkadeh* of Azargoshasb in Farahan was active till the end of the third century of Hijra, and was put out in 282 of Hijra. Ibn-i-Faghih giving an account of putting out the flame of this *Ateshkadeh* has written,

When in the year 282, Broun the Turk was appointed by the Caliph as the Wali of Qom, he came to this location and besieged it, and unleashed his chariots and catapults upon it until he captured it; then he destroyed its tower and put off its flame, and took its element to Qom; and since then this *Ateshkadeh* ceased to exist.[32]

Ibn-i-Rastah has referred to one *Ateshkadeh* that remained active even in his time,[33] and has mentioned another *Ateshkadeh* in the village of Akhorin near Holvan in Kordestan, which was flourishing in his days and people from afar made a pilgrimage to it.[34] Yaghoot has written in the seventh century about the big and famous *Ateshkadeh* of Azargoshasb in Gazan, which the Arabs called Shiz and which was located in Azarbayjan, and has described the silver crescent that topped it. Although Ziad bin abi Sofyan had ordered that the flame of the *Ateshkadeh* of Karian in Fars be put out following his appointment in this region in the first century of

---

[31]   *Tarikh Tabari*, p. 870.
[32]   *Al-Buldan*, p. 247.
[33]   *Al A'lagh al Nafisah*, p. 153.
[34]   Ibid., p. 165.

Hijra, the Zoroastrians had revived it and it was active during the time of Yaghoot; people from distant lands made a pilgrimage to it and carried its flame everywhere.[35]

**Iranian Vaspouharan**   It would be relevant to briefly discuss
**and Dehghanan**   here the aristocratic and noble families
of Iran during the period of languish, as this class played a considerable role in the preservation and safe keeping of Iranian wealth. Researchers have described Iranian society during the Sassanid period as a purely aristocratic society and recognized only the upper classes as representative of that society. It is evident that in Sassanid Iran the nobility and big landowners and Dehghanan, were not only the pillars and protectors of the state, but were also considered as the social backbone and the essence of the national character, culture and literature of Iran.

Following the Arab conquest, the Sassanid state collapsed, but the Dehghanan and the Iranian nobility survived. Although Islam did not accommodate class distinctions and aristocratic privileges, this class retained its distinguished status in society and continued to enjoy part of its traditional privileges during the first centuries of Islam. The significance and influence of the nobility in the Islamic period depended upon the political legacy that for centuries constituted the basis of Iranian domination over western Asia. This influence over the spirit of the nations that constituted the Sassanid empire was such that even after the collapse of the empire, this class continued to enjoy respect and status among the people for several centuries after the spread of Islam, drawing mainly on its social legacy. In the description of the historical events of Iran in Arabic books that draw on Sassanid sources, there are repeated references to titles such as *Ahl al Buyutat, al-Uzama* and *Al-Ashraf.* According to Christensen, these titles are literal translations of Pahlavi titles *Vaspouhran, Vozorgan* and *Azadan.*[36] Traces of these classes could be seen even in the third and fourth centuries of Hijra.

---

[35] *Mo'jam-ul-Boldan*, vol. IV, p. 225.
[36] Christensen, p. 105.

The Sassanid shahs did not entrust the affairs of their *divans* except to noble and aristocratic families and clans, and such functions usually became hereditary within those clans. A number of these clans continued to discharge in the Islamic era the functions that they had performed in Sassanid *divans*. Ibni Hawghal, who lived in the fourth century, writes about Fars: 'In Fars there exists a good tradition and a popular practice, and that is respect for old families, and looking up to those who enjoyed hereditary titles and privileges; in this region there are clans that have inherited the functions of the *divan* from ancient times to the present.' He has enumerated a number of ancient clans of Fars, such as Habib, Safyeh and Marzban. Writing about the clan of Marzban, he says that it was the oldest and largest of the Iranian clans of Fars, and had performed the functions of the *divan* since very ancient times.[37] Estakhri has also referred to this issue and has described a number of clans.[38] In addition to the clans of Fars, many other aristocratic clans of the Sassanid period survived in other parts of Iran, and a number of them such as the Samanian in Khorasan and the Ziarian in Gorgan were able to establish their own states in the Islamic period, because of their traditional social status and legacy.

Considering that Islamic teachings were not conducive to aristocratic life and class structure, the traditional aristocratic classes in Iran were gradually absorbed into the population at large within a few centuries after the emergence of Islam, and they completely disappeared in the later centuries. But the Dehghanan who were considered the pillars of the social fabric of Iran, survived for a longer time and continued to represent the glory of their national and historical heritage. In any event, the nobility and the Dehghanan of Iran are among the factors that contributed to the preservation of part of Iran's ancient heritage.

The national heritage of each nation is preserved mainly within its ancient clans and noble families; this is because the nobility is generally considered the most prominent manifestation of the

[37] *Sourat al Ardh*, vol. II, pp. 292-4.
[38] *Masalek-ul-Mamalek*, pp. 147-8.

national character and the depository of a nation's historical and cultural heritage. This holds true in the case of Iran as were. In the first centuries of Islam, those who were interested in Iran's history and its heritage, relied on this class as one of the most important sources of information and knowledge. Also, most of the books on Iran's heritage that have reached the Moslems have either come from this class or from the Moobadan. Mas'oodi obtained a precious book of history containing the paintings of Sassanid shahs from one of these families in Estakhr in Fars. It appears from what Tabari has narrated of the trial of Afsheen that the interest and passion for collecting books and decorating them was practised in Iran since ancient times by Zoroastrian families.

Afsheen descended from a Zoroastrian family and was considered one of the prominent commanders of Islam during the time of Mo'tasem, the Abbasid Caliph. The Caliph subsequently turned against him and ordered his capture and imprisonment, he set up a counsel of the dignitaries of state to prosecute him, and among the offences he was accused of was that he had in his possession a blasphemous book that was decorated with gold and precious stones. Afsheen responded in his defence that the book on Iranian literature and culture had been passed on to him from his forefathers, and he only enjoyed its literary and cultural contents and avoided its blasphemous material. Regarding its elaborate decorations he explained that since the book had been given to him in that state by his father, he did not see the need to remove the gold and precious stones.[39]

The Dehghanan and the nobility of Iran were not only influential in safe keeping their own historical heritage, but also played a significant role in the dissemination and growth of Arabic literature, as well as the revival of Iranian literature after the spread of Islam. In order to understand this, it is sufficient to consider the efforts made by this group in the second and third centuries of *Hijra*, whether at the court of the Caliphate or in the autonomous and semi-autonomous Iranian states.

[39] For more details this historical trial, see *Tarikh Tabari*, section 2, pp. 1307-11.

**The Sho'ubiah**   Researchers have also commented on the significant efforts of a group of Iranian Moslems who were known among the Arabs as the Sho'ubiah. The Sho'ubiah referred to those who had converted to Islam and were devoted to it, but did not heed to Arab claims of superiority, which after the initial phase of Islam had gradually emerged as an indisputable fact for some people.

One of the positive achievements of Islam was to eliminate all barriers and titles that separated the different groups and often led to conflicts among them. However, this was short-lived, as old prejudices re-emerged in new forms after the death of the Prophet. When in the wake of Islamic conquests, government was secured for the Arabs, they no longer wished to equate themselves with the other Islamic nations and to place themselves at par with them. Among the factors that encouraged this attitude was the fact that the Prophet was an Arab. Other factors included that the Arabic language commanded respect and appreciation as the language of religion throughout the Islamic world, and all significant affairs of the Islamic state in the Amavid period, were controlled by the Arabs. This gave them absolute authority and drove them to self-centrism and self-praise. As a result, they referred to non-Arab Moslems as `Mawali', which although not quite the equivalent of slave was far from the sense of free men also.

The Sho'ubiah did not accept this claim of superiority from the Arabs and they considered Islam to be distinct from such prejudices. In response, they spoke of their own historic glories and their distinguished cultural heritage, they boasted about the superiority of Iranians in science and knowledge and their competence in government, and expended great effort in the conservation of Iran's cultural heritage and the translation of Iranian books into Arabic and their dissemination among the Arabs.

As will be discussed later, most of those who evinced a keen interest in Iranian literary works or translated them were referred to as the *Sho'ubiah*. Although most of their intellectual works have perished, but whatever little is available indicates that this group had a great impact on Arab historical development and the preservation and dissemination of Iranian scientific and literary works.

**Dispersed Books and**
**Papers Rediscovered**

In a number of Islamic sources there are references to treasuries and archives where ancient Iranians preserved their scientific and cultural works. Such accounts may be traced to the fact that in the first centuries of Islam, scholars searching through old buildings occasionally came upon books or writings belonging to ancient periods in Iran, or they found such references in Iranian books of history. However, the available information about these treasuries and archives does not permit one to offer a definitive opinion about them and their characteristics. Nevertheless, it can be can be deduced from the collective information that during the initial years after the collapse of the Sassanid empire many Iranian books and writings were found in this manner. Ibn-i-Nadeem, Hamzah Isfahani and Abu Reyhan Birooni have described and written about the pieces that were found in a building in Isfahan that Hamzah has compared to the pyramids of Egypt and described it as one of the marvels of the orient. This building was intact during the times of these authors and was known as Sarouyeh. One of the events narrated about this location in the three books, *Seni Molook al Ardh* and *Al-Fehrest* and *Al Akhbar al Baghyah* is related to the collapse of a part of this building and the discovery of a great number of ancient books.

Ibn-i-Nadeem obtained details about this event from informed and reliable persons, and has written: 'In this part books were discovered that no one could read.' From Hamzah's writings, it appears that he himself was a witness to this event; he writes that when people asked him about that strange place, he showed them a book by Abu Ma'shar Falaki entitled *Ekhtelaf al Zijat*,[40] which contained a detailed account of the building. This has been described by Ibn-i-Nadeem and Abu Reyhan as well. According to Hamzah, in the year 350, one room in that building collapsed and fifty cases of writings on skin were found in it, in a script that the people had never seen before, and it could not be ascertained when those books had been placed there. After

---

[40] *Zij* referred to an astrological table to calculate and predict the movement of stars, and the book dealt with the comparison between various such tables developed by different astrologers.

referring to that event, Ibn-i-Nadeem, quoting reliable sources, writes,

But, what I saw with my own eyes is that *Abul Fazl bin Ameed* in forty and some years (meaning three hundred and forty and some years) dispatched here (apparently Baghdad is intended) several cases of various books that he had found in Isfahan. These books were in Greek and when knowledgeable people such as Yohanna and others translated them, it was known that they contained the names of combatants and the amount of their pay.

At the time when Ibni Nadeem wrote this in his *Al-Fehrest*, there were a number of these books in the possession of one of his teachers, Abu Sulayman. Who since these books were in Greek, it can be deduced that they pertained to the period of Alexander's successors or the initial years of the Ashkanid dynasty.

Referring to this location Abu Reyhan says that Tahmoureth (an ancient shah of Iran) had built it to preserve books from destruction, he writes

The evidence for this issue is that in our time in Jey (the original city of Isfahan) and among the ruins, houses were found full of numerous cases of a tree bark known as *Touz* with which they covered bows and shields, all containing writings with a script that no one could recognize, or understand their contents.

Apparently, Abu Reyhan is talking of an event other than the one that took place in the year 350, because he was born after 350 and he has referred to an event that took place in his own lifetime.

As mentioned earlier, the accounts of Ibni Nadeem, Hamzah Isfahani and Abu Reyhan Birooni of the characteristics and the date of construction of this building are based on Abu Ma'shar Falaki's *Ekhtelaf al Zijat*. Abu Ma'shar has provided an elaborate account and both Ibni Nadeem and Hamzah have also described it in detail.

According to Abu Ma'shar, the shahs of Iran selected the best locations to safeguard their books and scientific works because of their concern for science and knowledge; he provides a detailed description of the building called Sarouyeh, and how it was selected, and adds that this building was intact in his time. Abu Ma'shar, says that he borrowed the details about this building from a book that was found among the treasures in the same building. He writes that long before the days of Abu Ma'shar, a part of this building collapsed and a room in the building was stacked with ancient books on different areas of science and knowledge written in the old Persian language. According to him, one of the books that was found, was the *Zij Shahriar* which had a great impact on Islamic astronomy.[41]

The *Tarikh Baghdad* makes a reference to a library in Marv that was shifted to that area during the retreat of the last Sassanid shah, Yazdegerd, to the eastern parts of Iran. Information about this library is confined to an account of it in this book. It reads:

Yahya bin Hasan said that, 'when I was in Reghgheh, sitting with Muhammad bin Taher bin Huseyn at a pool side, and I called one of his servants and spoke with him in Persian, Attabi entered upon us and he also began speaking in Persian. I told him, how did you come to learn this language? He said, I have come to this city three times and I have transcribed the Persian books that are in the treasury of Marv. These books reached here from the days of Yazdegerd and are still here to this day.' He then said, I transcribed of these books what I required, and when I reached Neyshaboor and passed it by several *farsang*, I reached a village called Dodar, I suddenly remembered that I had not satisfied my need of one of the books. Therefore I returned to Marv and I settled there for several months. I told him, Abu Omar, why have you transcribed those Persian books? He replied: can one find thought and insight except in Persian books? Eloquence of expression belongs to us and thought and insight belongs to them.[42]

---

[41]    Refer to *Al-Fehrest*, p. 240. Hamzah, '*Sena Molook al Ardh wal Anbia*', pp. 172-6; *Al Akhbar al Baghyah*, p. 24.

[42]    *Duha-al-Islam*, vol. I, p. 180, quoting *Tarikh Baghdad*, vol. VI, pp. 157-8.

# Impact of the Sassanid Administrative Organization on the Caliphate

One of the important elements of Iranian heritage that survived the Sassanid empire was its administrative structure and institutions. During their governance spanning several centuries Iranians had made advances in the field of state administration and had established effective codes and practices for administering their vast empire. All states that succeeded the Sassanids in these and neighbouring territories emulated their example. The Caliphs of Islam understood, more than any other, the importance of the Sassanids and the significant heritage that had survived them, and used that heritage in establishing and developing their own institutions.

With the emergence of Islam, the Arabs were able for the first time in their history to establish a powerful state that extended over vast territories of the present-day Middle East. To administer such a vast state, the nomad holy warriors had neither the requisite knowledge nor experience, hence they were compelled to emulate others. As the Sassanid empire had ruled over and administered these same territories for more than four centuries, and the Iranians were the only ones among all Islamic nations who had knowledge and experience of the intricacies of government and administration, it was not surprising that the Caliphs drew upon the institutions of the Sassanids to develop the structure, organization and procedures of the institutions of their own state.

## The Sassanids as Viewed by Islamic Writers

Arab authors and Islamic historians have unanimously praised the Sassanids for their sound judgement and good practices. They have narrated numerous, though exaggerated, accounts of the fairness of Sassanid shahs and their concern for their subjects. They have also projected the Sassanid empire as the best model for all states of the orient, primarily because of the distinguished heritage it had left behind. While enumerating the superior qualities of each nation, Jahiz has identified the virtues of the Sassanid shahs to be politics and statesmanship.[1] Ibn-i-Sa'eed Andalosi writes, 'The biggest virtue of the shahs of Iran, for which they became universally renowned, was good policy and sound judgement; and they were not rivaled in their patience, refined attitude and balanced government.'[2] Jahiz has described in his holy book *Al Taj*, the class of 'companions to musicians and singers of the Courts, beginning with the Court of the shahs of Iran,' indicating that 'they were the pioneers in this area, and we have learned the art of government and statesmanship, and the protocols of the Court, and concern for the subjects, and such matters from them.'[3] Other Arabic authors have also presented similar accounts. In his praise of Iranians and the Sassanid empire, which he has described as the political model for oriental states, Christensen has quoted two statements, one from the history book by Abul Feda', and the other from a translation by Carra de Vaux under the title *Aberge des Merveilles*[4] which further clarify the views of Arabic authors and their praise for Iranians and the Sassanids.[5]

---

[1]  *Rasa'el Jahiz*, p. 47.
[2]  *Tabaqhat-al-Omam*, p. 24.
[3]  *Al Taj fi Akhlagh al Molook*, p. 23.
[4]  Carra de Vaux, *Abrege des Merveilles*, pp. 128-9.
[5]  Christensen, p. 507. The phrase that Christensen has translated from this book can be transcribed as follows:

All other states acknowledge the superiority of the Iranians, and have praised with fascination their refined methods of government, and their superior practices in war, and their capabilities in harmonizing the colours, and preparing foods and medicines, and good attire, and organization of their provinces, and their concerns for placing each thing in its proper place, as well as poetry, and proper speaking, and their cleanliness and perseverance, and their glorification of their shahs. The superiority of Iranians in all these matters is not challenged by anyone, and in their books of history,

**The *Divan* in**          *Divan* is a Pahlavi term used to denote state
**Iran Before Islam**   administration. In the Sassanid period the institutions that were entrusted with the various
functions of state, such as *kharaj* (finance), *sepah* (army), and *chapar*
(mail) were called *divans*, and the central *divans* were the equivalent of
modern ministries. As the Caliphs adopted Iranian administrative procedures and practices, this word was incorporated into the Arabic language as *divan*, and was first used in the Islamic Caliphate to designate
the office of '*Jam' wa Kharj*' or the office in which the names of the
*Mojahedeen* were registered.[6] As the structure of state administration
in the Caliphate expanded, the scope of use and meaning of this word
also expanded until it acquired the same scope and context that it had
in the sassanid period; in other words, it encompassed all the institutions and offices that were responsible for the affairs of the Caliphate.

It cannot be said exactly when the *divan* was first established in
Iran, but it evidently predates the Sassanids. It is clear from historic
accounts that the Achamenian monarchy also had a relatively structured administrative organization. Among the deeds attributed
to Dariush the Great (521-481 BC) were the restructuring of the
administration of state, organization of the affairs of state, building
public roads and establishing *chapar khanehs* (mail stations). In a
number of accounts there is reference to a library or special archives
in the Achamenian court, Plutarch, the Greek historian, has written
about the *dabirs* (administrators) in the court of Khashayar Shah.[7]

Arabic books of history contain scattered accounts of the internal
organization of Iranian states before the Sassanids and prior to the
conquest of Alexander, which no doubt were based on older sources.
For example, Hamzeh Esfahani writes in the biography of Lohrasb,
one of the Kiani shahs (an ancient Iranian dynasty): 'He was the first
to establish a *Divan* for *Sepah*.' He has also written about Dariush,
the son of Bahman, that he was the first shah who established *chapar
khanehs* on the main roads and equipped them with special horses.[8]

---

there are numerous examples for those who wish to emulate them in good
government.

[6] The Introduction of Ibni Khaldoon, p. 243.
[7] See chapter 5 for these tales.
[8] *Sena Molook al Ardh wal Anbia'a*, pp. 31-4.

The writings of Tabari, reveal that *chapar khanehs* were common in Iran even before Dariush.[9]

One can conclude from such accounts and those by the contemporaries of the Achaemenian monarchy, that the courts of the Achaemenian shahs had different *divans* for the administration of the affairs of state under the supervision of special *dabirs*, and even in certain areas such as *chapar khanehs*, there was not much difference in structure and organization from what existed later in the Sassanid or Abbasid periods.[10] Historical accounts indicate that, among the property destroyed by Alexander after he captured the treasuries of Dariush, the last Achaemenian shah, were the records of the state *divans*, which were burnt at his command.[11]

**A Look at the Organization of the Sassanid Empire**

There is more information about the internal structure of the Sassanid empire, as the material that reached the Moslems from the Iranians and became the basis for the administrative structure of the Islamic Caliphate, came from the Sassanids. The Sassanid empire throughout the history of its existence was sandwiched between, and perpetually threatened by two powerful and dangerous adversaries—the nations of Central Asia to the east and the Roman Empire to the west. Therefore, the Sassanid shahs were compelled to base their reign on a strong centralized government so that they could face those threats from a position of strength. To achieve this, they pursued a two-pronged policy. On the one hand, they consolidated and centralized their rule, and developed strong links between the provinces and the seat of their government; and, on the other, they established an official national religion and eliminated religious differences and conflicts that had emerged earlier as a result of lack of a clear national spiritual consensus. Thus, they made themselves the protectors of the national religion, and made the national religion their strongest pillar of support.

The concern of the Sassanid shahs for the centralization of their

---

[9] Tabari, section 1, p. 692.
[10] Christensen, p. 123.
[11] Tabari, section 1, p. 701.

government and the military dimension of their rule is evident from a letter that has been attributed to Khosrow Parviz in historical sources. When Shirooyeh imprisoned his father Khosrow and usurped his throne, he wrote a letter to Khosrow and listed his sins, including his greed for wealth, which made him inflict very heavy taxes on his subjects. In a letter to Shirooyeh, in which he responded to each of his accusations, Khosrow writes,

As to your claim that we incessantly engaged in amassing wealth and property, then be aware, you ignorant, that after the will of God, the state can be kept with wealth and might alone, and particularly the state of Iran which is surrounded on all sides by enemies; and repulsing them is not possible without a disciplined army and abundance of arms; and that cannot be maintained except with wealth. Our predecessors had accumulated much wealth and arms, but Bahram and his followers did not leave much of that behind.[12]

In the Sassanid period, the integration between the monarchy and religion was such that each was considered vulnerable without the other. Among the sayings that have been attributed to Ardeshir Babakan, is an advice to his son 'Beware my son that religion and the monarchy are as two brothers, one cannot be independent of the other; religion is the base of the monarchy and the monarchy is its protector. What has no base will be destroyed, and what has no protector will perish.'[13]

The two principal policies of the Sassanids—maintaining a centrally integrated and powerful army and a unified religion—were pursued throughout their reign. According to Christensen,

If we consider the first policy as a continuation of the legacy of Daryush the First, we must definitely attribute the second to the innovation of the Sassanid period, which like the establishment of the official religion of Shi'ism thirteen centuries later, must be considered as the outcome of a slow process of transformation that occurred in Iranian society.[14]

[12] *Tarikh Ibn-i-Athir*, vol. II, p. 363. The details of this letter can be seen in Mohammad Mohammadi-Malayeri's book *Translation and Transcription from Persian in the First Islamic Centuries*, Beirut, 1994, pp. 148-90.

[13] *Morooj-al-Zahab*, vol. XII, p. 162.

[14] Christensen, p. 92.

The creation of such favourable conditions could not have been possible without an organized administrative structure, an area that the founders of the Sassanid empire did not neglect. Ardeshir Babakan, the founder of the Sassanid empire, was one of the renowned and prominent personalities of this dynasty. His greatest achievements were the establishment of a new legal code and a new administrative structure, transformation of the class structure in the country, and basing his government on a new infrastructure. Prior to his time Iranian society was divided into three classes; he established a new class, entrusted with the responsibility of administering the state. This new class of *dabirs* was the equivalent of the present-day civil service.

Historians have praised Ardeshir as a legislator. According to Dinevari, he 'perfected the Code of the shahs, structured social classes and united everyone onto one path; he looked after all functions big and small, and placed each issue in its rightful place'.[15] Descriptions about him reveal that he was renowned for his organizational skills and the meticulous administration of his empire. It is written about him,

As Ardeshir rose from his sleep in the morning, he was made aware of all events that had taken place in his empire during the night, and when at night he went to his bed, he was aware of all events that had occurred during the day, such that, they said an angel descended from the heavens and informed him.[16]

The successors of Ardeshir respected the codes and practices that he had established and deviation from them was not permissible. Another Sassanid shah, whose initiatives in reform had a great impact on sustaining the reign of this dynasty, was Khosrow Anooshiravan. He was crowned at a time when the Iranians were disintegrated and the manifestations of languish among them and within their empire had become evident as a result of the emergence of the Mazdak sect and the factors that had led to its emergence. The capability of this ruler saved the Iranians from disintegration and strengthened

[15] *Al-Akhbar-al-Tewal*, p. 47.
[16] Bihaghi, *Al-Mahasen wal Masawe'*, p. 103.

the institutions of their state. He initiated numerous reforms that are amply covered in the history of Iran. It is said that 'he revived the code of Ardeshir, and implemented it, and compelled others to follow it'.[17]

The tributes that Islamic authors have paid to the Sassanids for their statesmanship are not far from reality. The Sassanid empire, as judged by its heritage, and except for the last phase of its existence, deserved such praise. The best manifestation of the stability of an institution of state is that it withstands and overcomes extraordinary circumstances such as war or civil unrest. The Sassanid empire demonstrated through its capability to survive for several centuries a major part of which was spent in fierce battles with eastern and western foes, that at least for some time after Khosrow Anooshiravan, it had such institutional stability.

### The Number of *Divans* in the Sassanid Court

Through no direct information is available about the number of *divans* in the Sassanid court, historical sources provide accounts that accumulatively clarify the administrative system and the distribution of tasks in that period. Ibn-i-Moghaffa', one of the most informed personalities of Iranian history, has enumerated the different seals of one of the shahs of Iran that were used for different state functions—one for coded correspondence; another for regular letters, or the Imperial Secretariat; a third for the allocation of titles and lands; and one for taxes.[18] Christensen has attributed each of these seals to a particular *divan*, and has argued that these references do not embrace all the *divans* of the Sassanid period, and that logically one can say that apart from these *divans*, there were other *divans* for the army, post, minting, weights and measures and perhaps the imperial holdings, etc. According to him, the *divan* of Kharaj, which was considered in the Amavid and Abbasid periods as the most important *divan*, was divided into several departments.[19]

---

[17] *Tarikh Ibni Batrigh*, Manuscript at the Eastern Library, Beirut, p. 130.
[18] Quoting from *Balazori* in *Fotooh-al-Boldan*, p. 464.
[19] Christensen, p. 388.

Apart from the writing of Ibni Mughaffa', other accounts are available about the *divans* and the seals of the Sassanid shahs, and if one concurs with Christensen and considers each seal to represent a particular *divan* then their number increases further, and what Christensen has deduced can also be confirmed through these accounts. Mas'oodi has enumerated the seals of Khosrow Anooshiravan as follows: for taxes, for property, for decrees to allocate property and for *chapar khanehs*.[20] Dinevari has given a substantive description of the *divan* of *sepah* during the reign of Khosrow Anooshiravan, and Tabari has also referred to this *divan*.[21] According to the author of the *Tarikh e Gozideh*, the first person to establish the *divan* of Petitions was Anooshiravan.[22] Mas'oodi has listed the seals of Khosrow Parviz—for letters and *farmans* (decrees), for notes of intimation, for *chapar khanehs*, for *barats* (a type of credit document), for pardons of criminals, for imperial treasuries and inventory of official costumes and ornaments, incense and fragrances, for the *farmans* of execution and the 'sealing' of the necks of criminals, and for correspondence with foreign monarchs.[23] Mas'oodi has referred to other seals as well but as they were not used for state functions, they will not be discussed here. From the accurate description that Mas'oodi gives of each of these seals such as material, colour, design and writings carved on them, it appears that the principal bases of this account were either official Sassanid sources or what was found in the treasury and the archives of the Sassanid court.

To distinguish the principal *divans* from the secondary ones, it is prudent not to rely on these narratives, because in Arabic often the same terminology who used to refer to some of the minor branches of a *divan* thus making it difficult to differentiate them. For example, in his coverage of the Nowrooz festival and the precious gifts that were sent to the shah from various regions, Jahiz writes, 'A special *dabir* wrote the names of those who had brought the gifts and the rewards that the shah designated for each, so that they would be recorded

---

[20] *Morooj-al-Zahab*, vol. II, p. 204.
[21] *Al-Akhbar-al-Tewal*, pp. 74-5, and Tabari, section 1, p. 464.
[22] *Tarikh e Gozideh*, p. 110.
[23] *Morooj-al-Zahab*, vol. II, pp. 228-30.

in the *divan* of *Nowrooz*.'[24] A letter of Tansar, makes a reference to a *divan* in which privileged clans such as the Bozorgan and the Vaspoohran were listed.[25] Also, Arabic geography books occasionally mention the names of *divans* in which *Ateshkadehs* were registered. Estakhri in his narrative on the *Ateshkadehs* of Fars (quoted in chapter 1) says, 'the *Ateshkadehs* of this region are so numerous that we cannot obtain their number except from the *divan*'. As will be discussed later there were also specific *dabirs* during this period for the administration of the affairs of the *Ateshkadehs*, and this *divan* must have been managed by them. It is, however, not clear whether each of these was an independent *divan* or that they were part of other *divans*.

**Permeation of Iranian Institutions into Islam**　　When Islam spread out of the Arab Peninsula and non-Arab masses came into the fold of Islamic society, Islam lost its original and simple form over time and acquired the framework of a state religion that had to rule over vast territories and different nations. It was at this stage that the forefathers of Islam realized that to govern such a state, the simple and primitive structures that they were familiar with were not adequate and they had to give their state an organization that was worthy of it.

After the collapse of the Sassanid rule, a part of the institutional structure of that state and particularly the *divans* of *kharaj* and other financial institutions survived. These *divans* continued to function under the supervision of Iranian *dabirs* and maintained their Sassanid character. Other *divans* that were no longer needed or were not suited to the new environment were discontinued and new *divans* were created in the Islamic state based on their model. These *divans* were established either by Iranians who had embraced Islam and lived at the centre of the Caliphate in Madina or in Damascus, or by the envoys of the Amavid Caliphs who served in Iran, such as Ziad bin abi Sofyan and Hajjaj, and others who had knowledge of Iranian organizations. It should be born in mind that these *divans*

---

[24] *Al-Mahasen wal Addad*, p. 369.
[25] *The Letter of Tansar*, Minavi edn., p. 20.

did not emerge in the Islamic period with the same complexity and sophistication that they had in the Sassanid period, rather they emerged in a simple and primitive form, and later as the Caliphate expanded and progressed and its administrative organization grew and developed, they also evolved, until in the initial years of the Abbasid Caliphate maturity peaked.

During the days of the Prophet and Abu Bakr, the first Caliph, the expansion of the territories of the Islamic Caliphate and its revenues had not yet reached the level that would necessitate the establishment of institutions to record and register the affairs of state. During that period Islam was no more than a religious movement and had not yet developed into a state and a government. Gradually, following the conquest of more territories and growth in the Islamic community, the significance of Madina, the seat of the Islamic state, grew and the city became the religious and political centre of a large part of the known world. As Islam grew, its revenues from war booty and *zakat* and *kharaj* multiplied and the envoys of the Caliphs remitted increasing amounts of revenue and merchandise from different corners of the land, these developments compelled the leaders of the Islamic Caliphate to structure their affairs, establish records, and maintain accounts of revenues and expenditures. Despite the scepticism of first generation Moslems about deviation from their traditional practices, they undertook to learn from others what they themselves had no knowledge and comprehension of. And as was mentioned earlier, they adopted the Sassanid state as their model and replicated it to fulfil the needs of their simple administration, whenever and, however, it was required.

Ibni Teghtegha provides a detailed and valuable account of the establishment of the first *divans* of the Caliphate.

The first generation of Moslems were the fighters, and their war was a holy war and not a worldly one. Among them were those who expended part of their own wealth for the good path, and did not expect any reward for their strife for Islam and the Prophet, except from God. Neither the Prophet nor Abu Bakr assigned any remuneration for them; however, when they went to *jihad* and brought back fortunes as booty, each received the reward that was assigned to him by Islam; and as more fortunes reached Madina from outer regions, they were brought to the Mosque, and the Prophet divided them among the fighters as he saw fit. During the Caliphate of Abu Bakr, affairs progressed in that same manner. However, when the fifteenth year of the Hijra arrived, Omar, who by now had assumed the Caliphate, noted that new territories were falling to the holy warriors, and the treasures of the shahs of Iran were captured and load upon load of gold and gems, and precious garments were reaching Madina; he therefore thought to reward all the Moslems and to distribute that fortune among them. But, he did not know how to accomplish that task, and how to account for all that fortune. At that time, one of the Marzbans of Iran was in Madina, and when he saw Omar's confusion, he told him that the shahs of Iran had what they called the *divan*, and they recorded in it all the revenues and the expenditures of the state, and nothing existed outside of the *divan*. Each functionary of the state had a pay, and his name was registered there, and no mistake could be made; Omar took note of this matter and asked for further details about the *divan*; Marzban provided more details, and Omar found the *divan* useful, and undertook to establish one, and he assigned a pay for every Moslem.[26]

Besides what Ibni Teghtegha has written several historical sources provide additional information. The *Nehayat al Erab* of Souli has dealt with this issue in depth,

At the time of the Caliphate of Omar, Abu Hararah (one of the companions of the Prophet) had brought fortunes with him from Bahrain. Omar asked him, how much have you brought? He said, five hundred thousand *dinars*. Omar was amazed with this figure, and said: Do you understand what you say? He said, yes, five times one hundred thousand. Discussions followed, then Omar ascended the Menbar and said: You people, a large quantity of wealth has reached us; if you wish, I will distribute it among you by weight; or if you prefer, by number. A man stood and said: O' Amir al Mo'meneen; I have seen the Iranians who have a *divan* for this purpose; you also establish a *divan* for us.[27]

From what Souli has written in the *Adab al Kateb*, it appears that this man was Hormozan, one of the Marzbanan of Iran who lived at that time in Madina.[28] Souli has also referred to the establishment

---

[26] *Al Adaab al Soltanyah*, p. 101.

[27] *Nehayat al Erab*, vol. VII, p. 197.

[28] *Adab al Kateb*, p. 190, compare with fn. 4 on p. 197, vol. VIII, *Nehayat al Erab*.

of the *divan* in another narrative. When Omar wished to dispatch an army to some place, Hormozan who was with him said to him, 'This is a group of fighters, each of whom has been given a sum of money, if one of them goes astray, how will it be known? Therefore, it is better that for this undertaking a *divan* be established and the names of all be registered in it.' Omar asked him for the details of the *divan* which he provided.

Other accounts also deal with this issue. Although these accounts vary slightly in details, two points are common: the first Islamic *divan* was established during the time of Omar, and this was done on the advice of Hormozan, one of the greatest Iranians.

**Hormozan**   The history of this period often mentions the name of Hormozan. He was famous in Madina for his knowledge and intellect, and whenever the Arabs faced a problem they consulted him. Birooni has narrated a tale about the origin and evolution of recording of dates in Islam that clearly illustrates this. According to Birooni, Omar was given a deed that carried a due date in *Sha'ban*, Omar wanted to know which *Sha'ban* was mentioned in the deed, the present month or the following *Sha'ban*. Omar summoned the companions of the Prophet to seek their opinion on this matter which had caused such confusion. They decided to some problem by following the ways and practices of the Iranians. They then consulted Hormozan and asked him to solve the problem. Hormozan offered a solution as detailed by Birooni.[29]

Understanding the personality of Hormozan has great significance for the history of Iran and the history of Islam, and therefore a few words are in order. Hormozan was one of the renowned commanders of Yazdgerd, the last Sassanid shah, and thus enjoyed a distinguished position in Sassanid Iran. The governorship of Mehregan Kadeh (in Lorestan) and the district of Ahvaz belonged to his clan, and the governorship of Shush belonged to his brother Shahriar. His clan was considered among the finest in the Sassanid era. Hormozan carved a name for himself in the history of Islamic conquests, as he vigorously

---

[29]   *Al Akhbar al Baghyah*, p. 30.

defended the territories that were entrusted to him and put up a stiff resistance against the invading Arabs. Despite the fact that all his efforts failed and he was compelled to surrender, he rendered important and valuable services in the newly established Islamic society after his surrender.

Hormozan first thought against the Arabs in the battle of Ghadesiyeh, and after the Iranians were defeated in this battle, he proceeded with his forces to Khouzestan, where his command was based. From there he continued to fight the Arabs, who had reached Dashte Meeshan and checked their advance. Oghbah bin Ghazwan, the Arab commander, called for support from Sa'd, who dispatched Na'eem bin Moghren to his assistance. Meanwhile, the Arab commanders succeeded in soliciting the allegiance of groups of Arabs from Bani Kolaib, one of the tribes under the jurisdiction of Iran, which had earlier settled in parts of Khouzestan and as the Iranians were unaware of this change of allegiance, the Arabs took Hormozan by surprise. Unable to put up a stiff resistance, Hormozan sought peace and Oghbah accepted his offer. An agreement was reached under which Hormozan would maintain Ahvaz and Mehregan Kadeh and the Arabs would keep what they had already captured. In the meantime the Arabs had conquered parts of Khouzestan—Souq al Ahwaz and Nahr Tiri and Manazer.

This arrangement continued for some time, until a dispute broke out between Hormozan and a number of Arabs of Wa'el and Kolaib over the boundaries of their possessions, Salma and Harmalah arbitrated on behalf of the Arabs and gave the right to the Arabs. Hormozan saw the decision as one-sided and refused to accept it, he broke the pact with the Arabs, mobilized an army and rose in defiance. The Arabs reported the situation to Omar who dispatched a large army to assist them. When Hormozan saw the enemy well prepared for battle, and realized that he was unable to confront them, he left for Ramhormoz and again made peace with the Moslems. This peace was short-lived, and soon he was engaged in a fierce battle with Na'eem bin Moghren, following which Hormozan left Ramhormoz and went to Shushtar. In Shushtar, Hormozan mobilized loops and made preparations to comfort the Arab invaders. When the Arabs learnt of these developments they headed for Shushtar from every direction. Omar dispatched Abu Musa to their assistance with a large army, and they encircled and besieged the city. The siege continued for several months, but the resistance put up by Hormozan prevented the besiegers from capturing the city. Eventually, they infiltrated into the city through a secret passage, imprisoned Hormozan and sent him to Madina.

It is written that when Hormozan was taken to Omar, the latter asked him: How do you see the outcome of treason and the will of God? Hormozan said: O' Omar, before Islam, God had left you and us to ourselves, and therefore we remained superior to you, but now that God is on your side, you have become victors over us. Omar wanted to put Hormozan to death because he was furious with him, but Hormozan made a shrewd move and managed to save himself. When Hormozan heard of Omar's intention to kill him, he asked for water, but hesitated to drink it; upon being questioned he said: I am afraid that you will kill me while I am drinking. Omar gave him *aman* and vowed not to kill him as long as he had not drunk the water. Hormozan poured the water on the ground and said: Thus I am in safety. Omar lost his temper and was about to break his vow, but several companions of the Prophet who were present in that council stopped him from breaking his promise. Hormozan embraced Islam and stayed on in Madina.

When Hormozan lived in Madina, he was highly regarded in Islamic society and the Caliph also respected him, such that when it was decided to give several Iranian aristocrats and Dehghanan in Madina a share of the booty, Omar gave Hormozan precedence over the others and allocated to him a fixed remuneration of 2,000 *derhams*, which was twice as much as the others share.[30] According to Estakhri, he also developed kinship with the clan of Ali bin Abi Taleb.[31] Hormozan lived in Madina till his death. When Omar was killed, his son Ubaidullah invited Hormozan to show him his horse and attacked Hormozan from behind and killed him.[32] Among the

[30]    *Fotooh-al-Boldan*, pp. 457-8.

[31]    *Masalek-al-Mamalek*, p. 140.

[32]    For more information about Hormozan, refer to *Tarikh Ibn-i-Athir*, vol. II, pp. 423-30, *Fotooh-al-Boldan*, pp. 380-1.

books that Mada'eni has written on Islamic conquests, was a book
called the case of *Hormozan*, which Ibni Nadeem has referred to.[33]
Apart from this reference, there are no other references.

**Administrative Institutions** As explained earlier, in the first pe-
**of the Amavid Period** riod of Islam, which is known as the
period of Khulafaa' Rashedeen, one
*divan* was established to maintain the records of *Bait ul Mal* (treasury), to manage its affairs, as well as to record the names of Moslems
and those who went to *jihad* so as to decide the reward that they
would receive from the booty of war. Despite being primitive, in
form, this *divan* performed the functions of two complex *divans*,
which were established in the later periods with various branches
each, viz., *kharaj* and *sepah*. During this period, the political and
social life of Islam was not yet mature and its foundations were not
yet consolidated, but the necessary elements for the establishment of
a powerful state were already in place. The geographical growth of
Islam as well as the dawn of an era of stability and peace, highlighted
the need for an elaborate organization to administer the state.

The Caliphate of Mu'awiah ushered a new era in the history
of Islam. From this period onward, the Islamic Caliphate that had
emerged primarily as a religious leadership, transformed itself into a
government and became a monarchy. The Khulafaa' Rashedeen did
not distinguish themselves from other Moslems, and were content
with their uncomplicated life, in conformity with their simple and
pious nature. But Mu'awiah elevated himself above others, and in
imitation of the shahs of Iran, established a royal court for himself,
his successors followed his example and added to its grandeur. This
transformation, which was a turning-point in Islamic government,
did not take place easily in Arabia, where the people found such
a lifestyle alien. The Arabs who were unfamiliar with such pomp
and opulence, and were accustomed to a different attitude from the

---

[33] *Al-Fehrest*, p. 103. For a clarification of this issue, see the article by
Mohammad Mohammadi-Malayeri, 'Hormozan and the First Encounter of
the Arabs with the *Divan* System of Iran', *Maghalat va Barresiha*, vol. 12-9,
Tehran, 1351.

Prophet and his successors, were not favourably inclined towards such a transformation. Even one or two centuries after the time of Mu'awiah, pious Moslems were unhappy about the opulent lifestyle of their leaders. During Ma'moun's time, a pious man passing in a boat on the river Dejlah, saw the palace of Ma'moun and cried '*Wa Omarah!*' Hearing this, Ma'moun summoned him and asked him what he had meant. The man replied that he saw a building similar to the palace of the Sassanid shahs, which led him to pass that remark.[34] This conservative attitude of the Arabs created numerous difficulties for Mu'awiah, for example, events related to the establishment of the *bi'ah* for the Caliphate of Yazid. As is known, the appointment of a successor and obtaining the *bi'ah* for him and making the Caliphate hereditary had no precedence in Islam, and it led to much agitation. The actions of Moghairah bin Sho'bah and others and the important events that followed are clear indications that the Arabs did not readily accept this development. Being a shrewd and competent man, Mu'awiah was able to surmount these difficulties and pave the way for the Caliphate of Yazid.

With the increasing demands brought on by expansion and evolution, government practices in Islamic territories witnessed various advancements; the Amavid Caliphs expanded the institutions of state and added to them. It must be born in mind that these new institutions were created gradually and in response to the demand for them. It was at this time that the Caliphs or their envoys in the provinces drew upon the traditions of their predecessors in order to satisfy their needs, and they often followed the Sassanid empire as their model. For example, one of the *divans* that was established in the days of Mu'awiah was the '*divan* of *zamam* and *khatam*' (register and seals). This *divan* was entrusted the responsibility of the registry and safe keeping of the *farmans* issued by the Caliph. Each *farman* was brought to the *divan* and copied, the copy was tied and sealed with wax by the Chief of the *divan*, and was archived,[35] the original was dispatched to the address. The reason for establishing this *divan* was that when Mu'awiah sent a draft to Omar bin Zobeyr through

[34]  *Oyoon-al-Akhbar*, vol. I, p. 314.
[35]  *Al Fakhri fil Aadaab al Sultaniyah*, p. 130.

one of his envoys for 100,000 *derhams*, Zobeyr forged the draft and changed the figure to 200,000 and received that amount. When Mu'awiah learnt of this, he established a *divan* to maintain a copy of all his *farmans*, and to avoid fraud in the future, this *divan* was named the *divan* of *zamam* and *khatam*.[36]

Balazori quoting Mada'eni, writes: 'The first of the Arabs who copied the Iranians and established for himself the "*Divan* of *zamam* and *khatam*" was Ziad the son of Abu Sofyan.'[37] Ziad held the governorship of Fars for a number of years before Mu'awiah, and even during the Caliphate of Mu'awiah, and Mada'eni, had a good knowledge of the events of the first century of Islam, particularly those related to Iran; therefore, it is likely that in establishing this *divan*, Mu'awiah was following Ziad's example. Although in a number of narratives the establishment of this *divan* has been attributed to Mu'awiah, this does not contravene Balazori's, account because these narratives were referring to the establishment of the *divan* in Damascus, the capital of the Caliphate.

Another institution of the Amavid Caliphate was the *divan* of *chapar khaneh*, which in Islam was known as the *divan* of *barid* (post). The establishment of this *divan* has also been attributed to Mu'awiah. Records reveal that when the Caliphate became secured for Mu'awiah, and all obstacles had been surmounted, he expressed a need to develop a mechanism by which he could expeditiously become aware of events in his state, therefore he brought together a number of Iranian Dehghanan and Roman envoys and explained to them his need and they see the *divan* of *barid*. As noted earlier, this *divan* had existed in Iran since ancient times and even during the rule of Dariush I, it had consisted of an extensive network. In the history of the Amavid period there is an occasional reference to the *divan* of *ensha'*, but it is not clear whether this was an independent *divan* or whether it was a part of the *divan* of *zamam*. There is also a reference to *divan mostaghallat* (property). It needs to be clarified that the scope and context of these *divans* was not uniform throughtout the entire period. For example, the *divan* of *barid* was dissolved after

[36] Souli, *Adab ul Kateb*, p. 143.
[37] *Fotooh-al-Boldan*, p. 464.

Mu'awiah, until Abdul Malek revived it and restructured it, hence a number of writers have attributed the establishment of this *divan* in Islam to him.[38]

**The Abbasid Caliphate: A**          The passing of the Islamic Ca-
**Great Transformation in Islam**     liphate from the Amavids to the
                                       Abbasids, was another turning-
point in its historical evolution. In the first period of the Abbasid Caliphate, which scholars have described as the period of Iranian influence and which continued till the end of the Caliphate of Al Watheq bil Lah (132-232), the Islamic Caliphate reached its zenith in progress, power and influence. Following years of conquest, instability and agitation, the Islamic society witnessed a period of stability and peace. During this period, the Abbasid Caliphs, and in particular their Iranian *wazirs*, perfected the organization of the state and the codes of government and statesmanship, and succeeded in making the central government stronger and more capable. By emulating the preceding shahs, they strove to increase the grandeur of the court of the Caliphate, and tried to surpass one another in adopting Iranian customs and codes of behaviour. History and culture, which until then had not acquired the status and significance that they deserved in the court of the Caliphate, progressed immensely, and men of power concentrated on them and encouraged scholars to translate and produce literary and scientific works, thus paving the way for the advancement of science in the Islamic world.

The collapse of the Amavid Caliphate and the emergence of the Abbasids must not be perceived as a mere change in government in the history of Islam. This development was viewed as one of the most critical turning points in the evolution of the Islamic Caliphate, even by the contemporaries of the Abbasids. There were numerous distinctions between the Amavid and Abbasid Caliphates which were due to the differences in the foundations of these two states and the nature of their respective founders. Moslems had been ruled for more than a century by the Arabs who constituted only one of the

---

[38] *Sobhi-al-A'asha*, vol. IV, p. 368, *History of Islamic Civilization*, vol. I, p. 220.

member nations of Islamic society. While maintaining the overall Arabic character of the Caliphate, Islamic society came under the influence of another of its member nations, viz., Iranians, in the area of administration and government, and entered a new phase in its evolution.

As mentioned earlier, the contemporaries of the Abbasid state were well aware of this distinction and significance. Jahiz describes the Amavid state as pure Arab, and the Abbasid state as Khorasani-Iranian.[39] Birooni refers to the prophecies of Zoroastrian astrologers about the return of the rule of the Iranians, and their application by some to the state of the Deylamis. He says: 'I do not know how they have considered the state of the Deylamis as the awaited state, when their justifications apply more to the state of the Abbasids; a state which is both an eastern state and a Khorasani state.'[40] The Abbasid Caliphs, particularly in the first period, were only too aware of this fact, and consequently they remained dependent on the Iranians and perceived them as the protectors of their state. Addressing the people of Khorasan, Mansour, the Abbasid Caliph said: 'You the people of Khorasan are the followers, companions and perpetuators of our movement'. Ebrahim Emam, who launched the Abbasid movement, wrote in a letter to Abu Moslem Khorasani, 'If you can eliminate every Arab speaker in Khorasan, do so! Anyone taller than five *vajab*, that you suspect, eliminate! Do not overlook harmful Arabs as they are close enemies; destroy them and do not leave any house of theirs standing.' While delivering a sermon to the people of Khorasan, Ghahtabah Ta'i, one of the prominent commanders of the Abbasids, and himself an Arab, said:

You people of Khorasan, this land belonged to your ancestors. They were victorious over their enemies because they were noble and just; but as they changed their ways and they became unjust, God was angry with them, ended their sovereign rule, and placed over them the people that were the most inferior in their eyes, who conquered their country and took their sons into captivity. These also, as long as they refrained from tyranny and the breaking of vows, and rose to the support of the oppressed, they maintained

---

[39] *Al-Bayaan wal Tabyeen*, vol. III, p. 206.
[40] *Al Akhbar al Baghyah*, p. 231.

their dominion; but as they also changed their ways and became cruel, and began to oppress the pure and pious men of the Prophet's clan, God chose you to avenge them, so that with your hands these people would be brought to justice, and by doing so, made the punishment of their sins ever harder.[41]

A basic distinction between the Amavid and Abbasid Caliphates was that the Amavids, or at least most of them, fostered ethnic Arab feelings of superiority and sowed the seeds of discord among the different Islamic nations. Islam, as noted earlier, eliminated ethnic privileges and made individual superiority a function of factors other than race and ethnicity. During the Amavid period, this fact was forgotten and the Arabs, who controlled the affairs of the Caliphate, considered themselves superior to others and viewed non-Arab nations with degradation and contempt. Rather than checking such attitudes and building the foundations of their Caliphate on the principle of the equality of Islamic nations, the Amavid Caliphs were themselves victims of bigotry and further inflamed these differences. In the Islamic community of nations, only the Iranians did not accept and resisted ethnic Arab superiority based on ignorant bigotry. Inspired by their historic legacy and cultural heritage and their love for Islam, they strove to discredit these claims with reason and logic, and lead Islamic society on the path of equality and brotherhood. They took an important step to steer Islam in the right direction and to ensure its progress. Consequently, a number of scholars have considered the victory of the Abbasids over the Amavids as the victory of Islam.[42] The Iranians, who perceived the Amavid Caliphate as the cause of such differences, spared no effort in bringing it down. In fact, most of the obstacles faced by the Amavids in this region were either instigated by the Iranians or supported by them. When Mokhtar decided to raise the banner of resistance, he exploited these sentiments of the Iranians; Ebrahim Emam decided to mobilize the people, and for this he selected Khorasan and the people of Khorasan. As history has shown, Ebrahim was not mistaken in his judgement. Iranians who were awaiting the right opportunity, soon launched the Abbasid movement, and ended the rule of the Amavids in Damascus,

[41]   Tabari, section 9, p. 106.
[42]   Nicholson, *A Literary History of the Arabs*, p. 282.

they established the Abbasid Caliphate within the boundaries of Iran and based it in Baghdad near Tisphoon, the capital of the Sassanid empire and the base of its power. The Iranian initiative not only re-established a unified Islamic society but also assumed charge of administering its affairs, and elevated it to such a level that this period was for more prominent than any other period in the history of Islam and is described as the golden age of Islam.

During the Amavid period, development and growth stagnated, as most of the Caliphs were engaged in accumulating wealth and levying heavy taxes rather than attending to the needs of the villages, the peasants became helpless and deserted the villages. The *kharaj* of Iraq that was over 100 million *derhams* before the advent of Islam and was more or less the same during the time of Omar declined to 50 million during the rule of Mu'awiah, and further to 40, and then 18 million during the time of Hajjaj. According to Abu Rasteh, coercive methods like caning and imprisonment were need to collect it. The reason for the decline in the *kharaj* was that most of the settlements of Iran were destroyed and the farmers were dispersed because of the injustice and cruelty of the Caliphs. After Ibn-i-Ash'ath was killed, Hajjaj massacred members of the Iranian nobility, Vaspooharan and Dehghanan, and confiscated their property and wealth. At the time of Hajjaj's death, many of the villages of Iran had perished and the *kharaj* collection was vastly reduced.[43]

One of the main sources of income of the Amavid Caliphs was the Nowrooz gift that they exacted from the farmers. The Nowrooz gift, which was later known as Eidaneh, was an ancient custom in Iran before the advent of Islam, the Dehghanan and those pursuing other vocations offered a gift to the shah on Nowrooz, each according to his ability. These gifts were not considered as taxes, but rather as a customary practice, as there is no mention of the Nowrooz gift or Eidaneh in Islamic accounts of the *kharaj* during the Sassanid period. According to Jahiz, these gifts were registered in a special *divan*, so that according to the value of the gift, the givers could be provided with special assistance from the *khazaneh* during the year, if and when such a need arose, this assistance was generally more than the

[43] *Al A'lagh al Nafisah*, pp. 104-5; *Adab-al-Kuttaab*, p. 230.

value of the gift.[44] After the advent of Islam, the Iranian Dehghanan continued their ancient practice and presented the Nowrooz gift to the Caliphs. The first Caliphs of Islam did not demand this gift; when the Iranian Dehghanan presented the Nowrooz gift to Emam Ali bin Abi Taleb, he decreed that the gifts be considered as their taxes. Waleed bin Aghbah was the first to demand Nowrooz and Mehregan gifts and later Sa'eed bin Abbas also did. When the people complained to Caliph Othman, the Caliph checked him from forcing the Dehghanan to give these gifts. However, the practice re-emerged.[45] The Amavid Caliphs not only demanded this gift like the *kharaj*, but they also increased its amount every year. During the time of Mu'awiah its value reached 50 million *dinars*, or the equivalent of all the taxes that were collected. This practice continued under his successors until it was abolished by Omar bin Abdul Aziz.

The administrative structure of the Abbasid Caliphate was greatly different from that of the Amavid Caliphate. In the Amavid period, although the structure of the Islamic Caliphate had evolved and developed in response to the emerging needs, its institutions were not adequate for the proper administration of the Islamic empire as it continued to expand, and it was inevitable that it would undergo a transformation. The Amavid Caliphate had an Arab character and the Caliphs did not entrust their functions to non-Arabs except in cases of necessity. Although most of the functions of the *divan* were performed by Iranians, the ethnocentrism of the Amavids did limit the Islamic state in the use of the works of other nations, and in particular the Iranians who had significant experience in government and the system of *divans*. Damascus, the centre of the Islamic Caliphate, was close to the Arab populated areas of the Islamic community, and far from Iran, and this also contributed to the limited participation of Iranians in the administration of the state during the Amavid period. At the same time, the policies of the Amavids prevented the different member nations of the Islamic community to come close together, with each contributing to the advancement of this great society to the limit of their talents and capabilities. The dawn of the Abbasid

[44]   *Al-Mahasen wal Addad*, p. 369.
[45]   *Adab-al-Kuttaab*, p. 230.

period must be seen as an outcome of these causes and reasons as also the relative rapid pace of development and transformation that continued in the Islamic world from the dawn of Islam to the end of the Amavid Caliphate.

**The Administrative Organization of the Abbasid Caliphate** During the Abbasid period Iranians had greater access to the institutions of the Caliphate. Not only was Iran's *divan* system adopted, but also the Abbasid Caliphs had no inhibition in imitating the Sassanids in social functions such as customs and codes of behaviour and even the style of attire and other practices. Among the works that have been attributed to Jahiz is a book entitled *Al Taj fi Akhlagh al Molook*, which even if it may not have been authored by Jahiz, was written by a contemporary of his or by someone preceding him. The book describes the personality and ethics of kings and the manner of interacting with them, as well as the codes and customs of the court prevalent at the time. The book clearly reveals the extent to which Iranian customs and practices had impacted the institutions of the Caliphate and had become the model for it. In explaining each subject, the author first discusses how it was in the Sassanid period and then proceeds to describe it during of the Caliphate. A comparison of the two reveals the similarities that existed between the Abbasid court and the Sassanid court.

Describing this aspect of the Abbasid Caliphate and comparing with the Amavid Caliphate, Nicholson has written:

If prior to this period the Arabs played the role of the conqueror nation in the Islamic world and viewed other Moslem nations in a different perspective, now the case is reversed; presently we cross from a nationalist Arab period to a period of Iranian renaissance, and Iranian culture; the elite of the army of this state are from Khorasan; its capital is built in Iranian territory; and the highest positions in the state are occupied by the Iranian nobility.[46]

Von Cromer has more to say on this topic:

---

[46] Nicholson, *A Literary History of the Arabs*, p. 28.

During this period the Iranian impact over the Court of the Caliphate expanded multi-fold, and in the days of Hadi, Rasheed and Ma'moon reached its peak, such that most of their *wazirs* were Iranian; in Baghdad Iranian customs and lifestyle spread and they celebrated the ancient Iranian festivities such as Nowrooz, Mehregan and Ram, and made Iranian attire the official attire of the Court; Mansour himself wore an Iranian hat. At the Court of the Abbassids the same customs and codes of behaviour of the Sassanids were applied, and gold embroidered suits that were characteristic of Sassanid rulers were worn. A coin exists of Motawakkel that portrays this Caliph with an Iranian appearance.[47]

As a result the administrative institutions of the state were entrusted directly to Iranian *wazirs*, and consistent with the needs of the state, they expanded the structure of government by establishing additional institutions, emulating Sassanid models, to the extent that researchers have considered the structure of the Abbasid government as one of the sources of research for the study of the internal structure of the Sassanid state. With the expansion of the structure of government, the number of *divans* in the Abbasid government also increased and the existing *divans* were often divided into several branches. Among the *divans* that were transferred to Baghdad during the time of Mansour when the construction of the city was completed were the *divan* of *kharaj* (finance), the *divan* of *khatam* (seals), the *divan* of *jond* (army), the *divan* of *hawa'ij* (public needs), the *divan* of *ahsham* (livestock), the *divan* of *matbakh ammah* (public kitchen), and the *divan* of *nafaghat* (expenditures).[48] After the completion of Samerreh the *divans* which were transferred there included the *divans* of *kharaj*, *zia'* (land and villages of the Caliphs), *zamam*, *jond*, *shakeriah* (a class of servants) *mawali*, *ghulman* and *barid* (mail).[49]

### Vazar Gafar Madar in the Sassanid State and Wazir A'zam in the Abbasid Caliphate

One of the positions that was established for the first time in Islam during the period of the Abbasid Caliphs was that of *wazir*. The reason for this was the proliferation of the number of the

---

[47] Quoting Brann, *The Literary History of Iran*, vol. I, p. 209.
[48] Ya'ghoobi, *Al-Buldan*, p. 240.
[49] Ibid., p. 267.

*divans* and the expansion of their functions. In the Abbasid period, as in the preceding period, there was a special *divan* for each category of functions of the Caliphate, and each *divan* had a supervisor who was called the *kateb* of that *divan*. In the Islamic Caliphate and until the Abbasid period the expansion of the functions of state and the volume of work of the *divans* had not yet reached the level that called for the establishment of a higher institution to supervise them. In the Abbasid period, however, the expansion of the affairs of the *divans* and the proliferation of their functions prompted the Caliphs to establish a new institution to supervise their affairs and administer them; this institution was the position of the *wazir*, which can be considered as equivalent to the contemporary post of prime minister. According to Christensen, the position of *wazir a'zam* (grand *wazir*) of the Caliphate was a direct replication of the position of *Vazar Gafar Madar* of the Sassanids, and what Moslem authors have written about the position of *wazir a'zam* of the Islamic period is generally applicable to the position of *Vazar Gafar Madar*.

Mawardi has written that, the position of the *wazir a'zam* was comparable in power and authority to that of the Caliph, except in three areas: first, the *wazir a'zam* did not have the authority to appoint his own replacement or his own successor; second, relinquishing the responsibilities of the *wazir a'zam* could only be done by permission of the Caliph and not by the wish of the people, because he ruled in the name of the Caliph and not in the name of the people; and third, the *wazir a'zam* could not dismiss someone whom the Caliph had appointed or modify his responsibilities without special permission. According to Christensen, the second restriction is the product of the Caliphate period that was based on populist grounds. Other than this point, this author believes that the relationship of the Caliphs with the *wazir a'zam* was exactly the same as that of the Sassanid Shahs with the *Vazar Gafar Madar*.[50]

## *Divan* of *Kharaj*: The Financial Institution

The *divan* of *kharaj* was considered the most important institution of the state whether during the Sassanid period or during the Caliphate. When the Moslems gained

[50] Christensen, pp. 102-10.

access to Iran, they heeded to necessity, and maintained many of the financial institutions of Iran, including the practices for the collection of taxes and other dues for the *divan*, and particularly those introduced by Qhobad and Anooshiravan. As a result, the *divan* of *kharaj* continued to function in the same manner as in the Sassanid period. Prior to the conquest of Iraq, the Moslems divided equally among themselves collected from the conquered land. When they conquered Iran, they found complex agricultural and irrigation structures of the fertile plains of Savad (present-day Iraq), the diversity and intricacies of the *divans*, and the institutions of *kharaj* and had difficulties in dismantling them. Omar was, therefore, compelled to abandon the previous practice and adopt a new practice, namely maintaining the lands in the possession of their owners and collecting annual *kharaj* from them.[51]

The Moslems did not follow a single uniform practice in exploiting all conquered lands, because Islamic decrees (*ahkam*) varied depending on the circumstances surrounding the conquest of each land. In some regions one-tenth of the value was levied, and in others *kharaj* was collected. The collection of *kharaj* was also not uniform, for example, in Sham (present-day Syria) *kharaj* consisted of a percentage of annual crop yield, i.e. the revenue of *Bait ul Mal* was determined on the basis of the annual yield of the land. This practice was not common in Iran, because from the time of Qhobad and his son Anooshiravan, all cultivated lands were measured and *kharaj* was determined on the basis of both the surface area and the yield of the land. When these lands came under the rule of the Arabs and they became familiar with such practice, Omar not only decreed that the practice be followed,[52] but he also introduced it in a number of other areas. For example, he instructed Othman bin Haneef to measure an area that had been conquered and to determine *kharaj* for every *jereeb* (1,000 square yards) of vineyards, forests, dates, sugar cane, wheat and barley. This practice continued until the days of Mansoor, the Abbasid Caliph, who, as a result of a substantial

[51] *Ibni Athir*, vol. I, p. 407.
[52] Tabari, section 1, p. 936.

increase in prices, again based *kharaj* on the percentage of yield.[53]

In the *divans*, not only the structures and processes of the Sassanid period were followed, but also their working language remained Persian for almost eighty years, and in some areas, even more than a century after Hijra. It was in the middle of the Amavid period that the working language of the central *divan* of Iran was changed to Arabic. Despite the change in the working language of the *divan*, its basic set-up and rules of business and procedures remained the same as before, without any significant modification.

Apart from the structure of the *divan* of *kharaj*, Iranian coins remained in circulation for a considerable period after the fall of the Sassanid empire, particularly in the eastern territories of the Islamic Caliphate, i.e. Iran and the territories that form a part of it. The Caliphs did not mint Islamic coins until the second half of the first century of Hijra. The first truly Islamic coins were minted during the time of Abdul Malek; prior to that Sassanid coins were in circulation, in addition to *derhams* that the envoys of the Caliph minted based on the Sassanid *derhams*. One of these coins was the *derham Baghli*. According to Beihaghi, this *derham* was minted by Ra'sul Baghl during the rule of Omar, and was based on a Sassanid *derham* without any alteration in its shape. According to Beihaghi, it carried the portrait of the Sassanid shah and the Persian inscription '*Noosh Khor*' under it.[54] Apparently no coin has survived from that period with such characteristics, but the shift from Sassanid coins to Islamic coins in different periods can be studied from other coins that have survived.

As mentioned earlier, in the first years of Islam, the coins that were minted in Iran were the same as the Sassanid coins and did not have any Islamic characteristics. After this period, Arab names began to appear on them, initially in the Pahlavi script and later in Arabic, and their Iranian character gradually disappeared. A considerable number of such coins are available today. The *derhams* of this period include a coin with the carving of an *Ateshkadeh* on one side, and on the obverse the portrait of Yazdgerd, with the name of the envoy

---

[53] *History of Islamic Civilization*, vol. I, p. 213.
[54] *Al-Mahasen wal Masawe'*, p. 502.

of the Caliph in Iran in Pahlavi on one side of the portrait, and on the other side, the Pahlavi phrase '*Farah Afzoud*'. The only trace of Islam is the Arabic phrase '*Besmellah Vali Amr*', inscribed under the portrait of the shah. Among the *derhams* that Sa'eed and Omar, the envoys of the Caliph, minted in Mazandaran, a number of them are similar, with the word '*Tapourestan*' inscribed on them in Pahlavi.

It was mentioned earlier that the *divan* of *kharaj* was translated into Arabic during Hajjaj's time, i.e. nearly eighty years after Hijra. This should not lead to the conclusion that at that time all the *divans* of Iran, whether the central *divan* in Baghdad or other provincial *divans,* were translated into Arabic and Persian was no longer used by the state machinery. On the contrary, there is evidence that there were *divans* in Iran that remained in Persian and maintained their Iranian character for a long time afterwards. Ibni Rasteh, who was from Esfahan and a *dabir* in the *divan* of the Caliph, and who lived towards the end of the third century of Hijra, says: 'The first person at the *divan* of Esfahan who wrote in Arabic was Sa'd bin Ayas, the *dabir* of Asem bin Younes, the envoy of Abu Moslem Khorasani.'[55] This means that the *divan* of Esfahan remained in Persian all throughout the Amavid period and Arabic eras adopted at the end of that period and the beginning of the Abbasid period. According to Ibni Teghtegha, during the time of Sowayd, the grandfather of Mohammad bin Yazdad, the *dabirs* of the *divan* of Marv studied in Persian *maktabs* (schools).[56] The writings of Maghdesi reveal that in the *divan* of Bokhara, letters and appeals to the sultan were written in Dari.[57] Based on such evidence, it can be said that the intervening period between the translation of the central *divan* of Baghdad into Arabic and the translation of other *divans* in Iran was more than a century. It may even be possible that in some distant provinces the *divans* remained in Persian throughout the period of languish and were never translated into Arabic.

The survival of the Sassanid financial institutions had a significant impact on the survival of the Iranian calendar. The Arabic calendar,

[55] *Al A'lagh al Nafisah*, p. 196.
[56] *Al Fakhri*, p. 273.
[57] *Ahsan ul Taqaseem*, p. 335.

a lunar one, was not useful for the calculation of *kharaj* and other functions of the *divan*, which were related to the agricultural cycle and depended on the four seasons of the solar calendar. Hence, the Iranian calendar, a solar calendar, was more appropriate for the functions of the *divan* of *kharaj*. As Birooni has mentioned in the Mo'tazedi months, the survival of the Iranian calendar in the *divan* led to the continued use of names of Iranian months.[58] In the *divan* of Fars, even the days of the month were referred to by their Iranian names. Describing the governorship of Fars, Maghdesi says: 'In Fars, each day of the month has a special name, and the dates of the *divans* are in the same manner, and these names are the equivalent of the names of the week in other provinces.'[59]

Among the traditions that survived with the financial institutions in Islam was the Nowrooz festivities which at all times designated the beginning of the *kharaj* (or the financial year). Another was the many Persian words and phrases that were common in the *divan*, which acquired an Arab character over time. However, the most important tradition that survived was that these financial institutions continued to be administered by Iranian *dabirs*, or *kottab* as they were called in the *divan* of the Caliphate, and these *dabirs* were the single most important source of Iranian cultural influence on Arab literature and culture.

In the end it is necessary to mention that the impact of Sassanid institutions after the fall of that empire was not only confined to the Caliphate, but other states that emerged in the eastern regions of the Islamic empire several centuries later also adopted Sassanid ways to administer their affairs and they were advised on these matters by Iranian *wazirs* who kept their Iranian heritage alive. This is substantiated by an examination of books on government in the

---

[58] *Al Akhbar al Baghyah*, p. 68.

[59] *Ahsan ul Taqaseem*, p. 441. In the Iranian calendar and the peoples who followed the Iranian calendar, such as the people of Kharasm and Soghod, and also in the ancient Egyptian calendar, the week did not exist, and everyday of the month had a name. Birooni considered the use of the week to have originated with the peoples of Western Asia, and particularly the people of Syria and neighbouring territories, where the Prophets have appeared and informed of the creation of the world in seven days.

Islamic period, like the *Siasat Nameh* of Khajeh Nezam ul Mulk and the *Qhaboos Nameh,* and their comparison with what was available of the Sassanid works. Inostranzev has argued that these books of the Islamic period on this subject are reliable and useful sources of information for the study of the Sassanid state and its internal structures and institutions.[60] Discussing the transfer of civilization from one nation to another, Ibni Khaldoon says: 'And thus the civilization and culture of the predecessors pass to the successors, as the civilization of the Iranians passed to the Arabs of Bani Umayyah (Amavids) and Bani Abbas (Abbasids), and the civilization of Bani Abbas passed to the Daylamis and from them to the Turks, and then to the Saljuks.'[61] Apart from the states that arose in the eastern regions of the Islamic empire, states that arose in other regions also witnessed the impact of Iranian customs and way of life. This can be seen from the study of the internal structure of the Fatimid state and other states that emerged in Egypt, because these states also adopted the structure of the Abbasid state as their model, and thus the Iranian *divan* system found its way into their structures as well.[62]

---

[60] Inostranzev, p. 60.
[61] The Introduction of Ibni Khaldoon, p. 174.
[62] *Sobhi-al-A'asha*, vol. III, p. 453.

# THREE

# Iranian *Dabirs* Before Islam and After

As mentioned earlier, in the initial years of the Abbasid Caliphate the class of *dabirs* or *kottab* had become one of the significant classes of Islamic society and was considered among the vital pillars of government. As the position of the *kateb* at the court of the Caliphs had almost the same scope and context as the position of the *dabir* in the Sassanid court, this element of government of the Caliphate was clearly influenced by the model of Sassanid organization, and in fact was a replication of it. Therefore, it is pertinent to first discuss the *dabirs* of the Sassanid state, before reviewing the *kottab* of the Caliphate.

**The Position of the *Dabir* in the Sassanid Period**
Before the Sassanids, Iranian society was divided into three classes: the clergy; the army; the farmers and artisans. During the Sassanid period, a fourth class, i.e. *dabirs*, was established, and each of these four classes was further divided into subclasses. The class of *dabirs* was divided into various categories on the basis of the functions that they performed. In the *Letter of Tansar*, there is a reference to *Kottab Rasa'el, Kottab Mohasebat, Kottab Aghzieh va Sejellat va Shorout*. Physicians, poets and astronomers were also included in this class.[1] Kharazmi has divided the *dabirs* of the Sassanid empire into the following seven groups:

1. *Dad Dibahr*—*Dabir* of the judiciary and judicial decrees.
2. *Shah Amar Dibahr*—*Dabir* of taxes and national revenue.
3. *Kazak Amar Dibahr*—*Dabir* of the special revenues of the shah.
4. *Kanz Amar Dibahr*—*Dabir* of the treasury.
5. *Akhor Amar Dibahr*—*Dabir* of the imperial stables.

[1] *The Letter of Tansar*, Minavi edn., p. 12.

6. *Atash Amar Dibahr*—*Dabir* of the affairs of fire temples.
7. *Ravanegan Amar Dibahr*—*Dabir* of the *owghaf* and charities.[2]

A number of historical sources refer to *dabirs* other than those listed here. Among the names of the noblemen who met after the death of Yazdegerd to discuss how to prevent Bahram Goor from ascending the throne of Iran, Dinevari has mentioned the names of three *dabirs*: Goodarz, *dabir* of the *divan* of *sepah*; Joshnas Azarbish, *dabir* of the *divan* of *kharaj*; and Fana Khosrow, *dabir* of *owghaf* and charities. The first title, i.e. the *dabir* of the *divan* of *sepah*, is added to Kharazmi's list.[3] According to Ferdowsi, the men who spoke against *Bahram* at that meeting was Goshasb Iran Dabirbad.[4] The *Fotooh-al-Boldan* also mentions the title of *Saheb al Zamam* for the *dabirs* of the Sassanid period.[5] *Saheb al Zamam* was in-charge of the imperial seals.

The Sassanids considered the *dabirs* among the privileged classes and one of the pillars of the state, and therefore, the position of *dabir* was reserved exclusively for the nobility. Ferdowsi narrates a tale about Anooshiravan and a shoemaker who offered money to the shah to permit his son to attend the *maktab* and join the class of *dabirs*.[6] This narrative clearly reveals the significance of this class

---

[2] *Mafatih-al-Oloom*, p. 5.

[3] *Al-Akhbar-al-Tewal*, p. 55.

[4] *Shahnameh*, Khavar edn., vol. IV, p. 211. *Iran Dabirbod* was a title given to the chief of the *dabirs*. The word *Dabirbod* appears repeatedly in Arabic books. Mas'oodi has interpreted this title as '*Hafez-ul-Kottab*' in Arabic. Several contemporary Arab researchers have misread and misunderstood this expression because of their lack of knowledge of the Persian language and Persian expressions. Ahmad Zaki Pasha, the publisher of *Al-Taj*, has read this expression as *Hafez-ul-Ketab* (the keeper of the book), and has assumed that what is intended by *Ketab* is the book of *Avesta*, the Zoroastrian holy book, and that the *Dabirbod* was the one who was entrusted to safeguard this book. This scholar has gone further and has proposed that the origin of *Dabirbod* was the Persian word *dabir* and the Arabic word *yad*, meaning hand, and has written it in Arabic as *Kateb-ul-Yad*. Refer to *Ketab-ul-Taj*, corrections by Ahmad Zaki Pasha, Egypt, p. 77.

[5] *Fotooh-al-Boldan*, p. 464.

[6] *Shahnameh*, Khavar edn, vol. IV, pp. 543-5. A number of authors have

at that time, and the efforts of the Sassanid shahs to maintain the prevailing class structure in society.

The history of the Sassanid period makes frequent references to the class of *dabirs*, and events of this period throw up the names of a number of great men of this class. A manuscript of Nehayat-ul-Erab that at the court of Khosrow, apart from Bozorgmehr Bakhtakan, Shapoor Moobadan Moobad and Yazdegerd Dabir Bod, there were seventy others learned men who were in the permanent service of the shah.[7] Dinevari has referred to Yazdak Kateb; Yazdak was the *dabir* of the *divan* of *sepah* in the army of Bahram Choobin, and when Bahram defied the shah, he left him to join the court of Hormoz.[8] Tabari and Dinevari have identified the man in-charge of the *divan* of *rasa'el* at the court of Khosrow Parviz as Yazdan Jashnas or Asfad Jashnas; there are references to Havari or Havabi among the *dabirs* of this *divan* during the rule of Khosrow Parviz. In the days of Bahram, Narsi, the son of Shapoor, was considered among the learned and wise *dabirs*; during the time of Ghobad, Sookhran and Zarmehr were among the distinguished *dabirs*;[9] and Mehr Azar Jashnas, the son of Shirouyeh, was one of the competent and efficient *dabirs* of the Sassanid state during the rule of Ardeshir.

| | |
|---|---|
| **Arab *Dabirs* at the Court** | In order to administer the affairs of |
| **of the Sassanid Shahs** | the satellite Arab state of Hirah,[10] and |

---

interpreted Ferdowsi's verses that attending the *maktab* and getting education by the common people was forbidden. This is baseless. What was forbidden and required the permission of the shah was not education, but promotion to the position of *dabir*, which was confined to the progeny of those who belonged to the same class, in accordance with the class structure of Iranian society.

[7] Browne, *J.R.A.S.*, 1900.

[8] *Al-Akhbar-al-Tewal*, pp. 86-90.

[9] *Tarikh Ibni Batrigh*, manuscript available in the Eastern Library, Beirut, p. 119.

[10] Shapoor the first created the state of Hirah around AD 240 on the banks of the Euphrates comprising parts of modern Iraq. The objective was to manage the affairs of the Arab residents of the region, maintain peace in the area by keeping in cheer the Arab nomads in the desert who raided the

to translate the correspondence that reached the Sassanid court from the Arab-speaking parts of the empire, there were special *dabirs* at the Sassanid court who were normally selected from among the Arabs of Hirah. The first Arab known to have held the position of *dabir* at the court of Shahpoor was Loghayt bin Mo'bed, or Loghayt bin Ya'mar, who belonged to the clan of Ayad. In Arabic literature, there exists a long poem attributed to him, in which he alerts his clan of Shapoor's might and grandeur, and his decision to wage war against him. Mas'oodi writes that when a group of Arabs from Ayad bin Nezar's tribe attacked a part of the territory of Iraq which was under the control of Hareth bin Agharr and captured it, Shapoor dispatched a force to deal with them. Loghayt was in the army of Shapoor, and he sent that poem to his clan from there.[11] Not much information is available about Loghayt and his deeds at the court of Shapoor.

Eminent Arabs who became *dabirs* at the Sassanid court were the family of Hammad bin Zayd, the *kateb* of No'man Al Nasri, the shah of Hirah. Hammad was a Christian and his relatives who served the *divan* were Ziad bin Hammad, Adi bin Zayd and Zayd bin Adi. Although the origins of this family were traced to the Arabs of Hirah, they lived in Iran and grew up among Iranian families and were therefore familiar with the Persian language and culture. No'man the Third, the son of Monzer the Fourth, who was known among the Arabs as Abi Qabus (AD 580-602 or 585-607) was educated by Adi bin Zayd because of his proficiency in Persian that he had acquired under the tutelage of Adi. He named his son Kavoos, and acquired his title from his son's name.

As mentioned earlier, Hammad bin Zayd, the founder of this clan, was the *kateb* of No'man al Nasri, the shah of Hirah. Hammad was at the Sassanid court named Farrokh Mahan, who had a great influence

---

villages and settlements of Iraq. The rulers of this state who held the title of shah, were generally appointed from among the people of Hirah, and this practice continued until after No'man bin Monzer known as Abi Qabus. Khosrow Parviz entrusted the rule of the state to one of his commanders, and this arrangement continued until the Islamic period.

[11]   For more details, refer to, Ibni Doraid, *Al-Eshteghagh*, Wustenfeld edn., *Al-Moghtabas* periodical, 3rd year, pp. 774-8; *Morooj-al-Zahab*, vol. II, pp. 176-7.

on the education of Hammad's children. Abul Faraj Esfahani has provided a useful account about this family. According to him, Farrokh Mahan taught Persian to Ziad, Hammad's son who was already fluent in Arabic, and he employed him in the *divan* of *chapar* (mail). Ziad remained in that position until the death of No'man al Nasri. After No'man's death and until the Sassanid shah selected Monzer bin Ma'-us-Sama' as the shah of Hirah, Ziad was responsible for the administration of that territory with the support of Farrokh Mahan.

Abul Faraj Esfahani, adds that when Ziad went to Hirah, he left his son Adi in the use of Farrokh Mahan, who sent him with his own son Shahan Mard to the *maktab*, where he learnt to read and write in Persian, and became fluent in Arabic. Farrokh Mahan commended his skills to Khosrow Parviz, who appointed him along with Farrokh Mahan's sons in at the *divan*, and entrusted the affairs of Hirah to him.[12]

Relations between the Arab *dabirs* of the Sassanid court and the rulers of Hirah were not always cordial, and because of their internecine rivalries, they conspired against each other, often resulting in bloodshed. This rivalry was due to the fact that the Arab *dabirs*, because of the position that they enjoyed in the Sassanid state, interfered in the affairs of Hirah and influenced the appointment and dismissal of the shahs of that territory, and this was not tolerated by the *shahs* of Hirah, particularly those who could not bear competition.

One such conflict which also impacted the policies of the Sassanid empire, broke out between Adi bin Zaid and No'man bin Monzer, the shah of Hirah. Monzer appointed Ayas bin Qhabisah Ta'ee as his successor before his death, so that he would take care of the affairs of the state in the interim period until the Sassanid shah would appoint a new ruler. However, as the shah was not able to find a competent person, he considered dispatching a military expedition to Hirah and appointing an Iranian ruler. Adi bin Zaid, lobbied the shah who changed his mind and appointed No'man, the son of Monzer, who had been brought up by Adi, to succeed his father.[13] Adi wanted to keep No'man under his control, and through him, enhance his

---

[12] *Al-Aghani*, vol. II, pp. 1-103; *Morooj-al-Zahab*, vol. III, pp. 204-5.
[13] *Al-Aghani*, vol. II, pp. 109-10.

influence in Hirah; but No'man was a determined and capable shah, and was not willing to be controlled by Adi.

According to Tabari, No'man was upset over a letter that Adi had written to him. He invited Adi to Hirah. Unaware of No'man's intentions, Adi obtained the shah's permission and went to meet No'man. As soon as he arrived, No'man captured and imprisoned him. When Khosrow Parviz learnt of this development, he sent a *farman* to No'man to free Adi, but before the *farman*, reached No'man he had already killed Adi. He gave the envoy of the shah a handsome reward with the instruction, to report that Adi had died of natural causes.[14]

After Adi, the affairs of the *divan* were entrusted to his brother,[15] but as he was assigned other tasks, Zaid, the son of Adi, was appointed to the *divan*. Zaid had been waiting for an opportunity to avenge his father. He succeeded in turning the shah against No'man. Khosrow summoned No'man to Tisphoon, and when he reached the capital, the shah ordered that he be crushed to death by elephants.[16]

No'man was eulogized by Nabeghah Zobyani, and he became a renowed figure in Arab literature. Hend, his wife, converted to Christianity and built a monastery in Hirah that was named after her; this monastery was still standing in the days of Tabari.

The salaries of the Arab *dabirs*, who were responsible for the affairs of Hirah, was paid by the Arabs of that region. According to Tabari, the Arabs paid the salaries in kind such as, two colts, fresh and dried dates, *kashk* and leather.

According to Abul Faraj, the author of the *Al-Aghani*, the first person in the *divan* of *Kasra* to use in Arabic was Adi bin Zayd. If one accepts this, it must be added that prior to this date, there was no special *divan* to administer the affairs of Hirah, and they were undertaken as part of the affairs of the state.

| **Emergence and Development of the Function of *Kitabah* in the Period of the Caliphs** | During the period of the Prophet and the Kholafa' Rashedin the position of *kateb* or *dabir* was not |
|---|---|

---

[14] Tabari, part one, pp. 1020-4.
[15] Ibid., p. 1024.
[16] For more details, ibid., pp. 1024-9.

considered to be of particular importance. In those days whenever the Caliphs or their envoys wanted to record or keep an account of something, a member of the community who could write was summoned to perform the task, without this being considered as a distinct function. When Omar dispatched an Arab army to Nahavand to fight the Iranians, he entrusted the task of keeping account of the spoils from the war to Sa'eb bin Aghra' who knew how to read and write. Omar told him, 'If God makes you victorious, divide the booty that you obtain among the fighters and keep the *Khoms* (fifth), and if this army perishes, you too keep with them as the heart of the earth is better than its back.'[17] In this campaign, although Sa'eb bin Aghra' was individually in-charge of all the tasks which were performed by a number of *dabirs* in the *divan* of *sepah* and *divan* of *mohasebat* during the Sassanid or Abbasid periods, such tasks were not considered as specific functions, which would distinguish him among other *Mojahedeen*. Perhaps, he did not even receive any additional pay for this.

Because of the simplicity of the institution of the Caliphate on the one hand, and the limited number of Arabs who could read and write on the other throughout the period of the Kholafa' Rashedeen, the task of *kitabah* remained limited and simple. When, the Caliphate fell to the Amavids, and they undertook to establish and expand the *divans*, they were compelled to assign to particular persons the responsibility to administer the affairs of those *divans*, and to transform that responsibility into a distinct profession. Thus, the position of *kateb* became an official position in government, and with time, as the functions of state expanded, it gained in scope and significance, such that the class of *kottab* became one of the distinguished social and political classes of the Caliphate. Despite its significance, the growth and development of this class remained limited in the Amavid period as compared to the Sassanid or Abbasid periods.

There were several reasons for this apart from the relative simplicity of the Amavid administrative structures and processes, writers in general did not enjoy much social status in the Amavid period, on the one hand, and on the other, the working language of the most

---

[17] *Tarikh Ibni Athir*, vol. III, p. 10.

important *divan*, i.e. the *divan* of *kharaj* and its branches remained Persian and Roman in the second half of this period, and Arab-speaking *dabirs* did not have a role in the functions of the *divan*. The translation of the *divans* of *kharaj* of Iran and Syria into Arabic, was a major stride in the development of the profession of *dabir* in Islam, following which many, Arabic-speaking Moslems rose as competent and efficient *dabirs*, and as their control over the financial institutions of government expanded, they also enhanced their influence over other parts of the administrative organization of the Caliphate, and strengthened their position and status within the state.

The Abbasid Caliphate removed the other constraint on this profession, namely that of clout and social standing. As Iranian *dabirs* in the Abbasid era assumed charge of the affairs of the Caliphate, they not only succeeded in changing the prevalent social attitudes towards *Ahli Ghalam* (writers and authors), but also ensured public respect and appreciation for them. Through these efforts had begun towards the end of the Amavid period, their efforts came to fruition only in the Abbasid period. The best example of such efforts by Iranian *dabirs* is a letter by Abdul Hamid Kateb to the *dabirs* of his period, reminding them of the significance of the position and the functions of *dabirs*,

The country obtains organization at your hands, and the affairs of kings are put in order by you; may God improve their reign with your wisdom and insight; may their revenues be collected and their country be constructed. Kings with all their glory and rulers whether big or small will be in need of you for their affairs, and their difficulties will not be resolved except by you. Thus, you are to them as their ears and eyes and tongues and hands, with which they hear and they see and they talk and they overcome their enemies.[18]

From the beginning of the Abbasid period the significance and influence of this class of functionaries in the Caliphate continuously increased, and it was not long that from within this profession emerged the position of *wazir a'zam* that after the Caliph was considered the highest within the Islamic state.

---

[18] *Sobhi-al-A'asha*, vol. I, pp. 85-9.

**Iranians as *Dabirs* and *Wazirs***    An important issue that must be borne in mind about the *dabirs* and *wazirs* in the different periods of Islam is that this category of functionaries was often selected from among Iranians. It is interesting that even during the rule of the Amavid Caliphs who had no sympathy for non-Arab elements and strove to give the Islamic Caliphate an Arab character, Iranians were able to find their way into the Caliphate and assume control of the *divan*.

A persual of the ancestry of the *dabirs* of this period reveals that most of them were from non-Arab ethnic backgrounds, such as Abdul Rahman bin Dorraj, the *dabir* of *mu'awiah*; Abul Za'aiza'a was in-charge of the *divan* of *rasa'el* during the days of Abdul Malek; Na'eem bin Salama managed the *divan* of *khatam* during the same period; Layth bin Abi Farwa and Esma'il bin Abi Hakim both *dabirs* of Omar bin Abdul Aziz; Salim bin Abdullah, the *dabir* of Hesham; his son Abdullah bin Salim was the *dabir* of Walid bin Yazid; Omar bin Hareth was in-charge of the *divan* of *khatam* during the days of Yazid bin Walid; Othman bin Ghaith managed the *divan* of *rasa'el* under Caliph Marwan bin Mohammad; Abdul Hamid bin Yahya, the most distinguished Arab *kateb* who had developed his own unique style, and Ibni Mughaffa' his companion and colleague whose writings are among the finest in Arabic prose.

The Amavid Caliphs were concerned about the increasing control of Iranians over their Caliphate, and one of the objectives of Abdul Malek and Hajjaj in the translation of the *divans* of Iran and Syria was to break the control of non-Arab *dabirs* over the *divan*, and place it under the supervision of Arabs. As historical events have shown, this strategy ended in failure as within a short period Iranians became fluent in Arabic and extended their influence over the Arab *divan*. Solayman bin Abdul Malek is quoted as having said: 'Amazing are these Iranians, that when they were ruling they were in no need of us, but when the reign became ours we could not remain needless of them.' He also said, 'Are you not amazed with the Iranians, that we have become in need of them in all things, even in the learning of our own language?' The Amavid Caliphs were concerned about this as despite all their efforts, they could not avoid dependence on Iranians in the administration of their state. The *wazirs* in the Abbasid period, however, perceived this as a natural phenomenon, and the result of several centuries of Iranian experience in government and the Arabs' lack of experience in this area. In the presence of Yahya Barmaki, an Iranian debated with an Arab and said: 'We never were in need of you in our affairs or our language, but when you have become the rulers you are in need of us in your affairs and your language.' Yahya told the Arab, 'tell him wait until we rule for a thousand years like you did, then we also will not be in need of you'.[19]

To have a better understanding about the *dabirs* of the Abbasid state it is important to study the identities of prominent *dabirs* and *wazirs* of this state in the different periods and review what their contemporaries have written about them. Commenting on *divans* and *dabirs* of the Caliphate during his period; Estakhri writes: 'The administrators of the *divans* and those who are the pillars of politics whether *wazirs* or other functionaries, are Iranians'. After enumerating a number of prominent families of Iranian *wazirs* such as the Barmaki and Zur Riasatain, he says: 'Those in charge of the affairs of the Caliphate are also among the Iranians that during the Sassanid period came to the land of Sawad and settled in Iraq'.[20] While discussing Khorasan he says: 'All the commanders and *dabirs* of the Caliphate in Iraq and its commanders in Khorasan are from this region; also prominent leaders and scholars and *faghihs* have risen from this area'.[21]

**How Most Functions of the** *Divan* **were Entrusted to Iranians** Scholars who have studied the socio-political conditions of the Abbasid Caliphate have alluded to the fact that most functions of the *divan* were entrusted to Iranians and have given reasons for this.

In the foreword to this book it was mentioned that following the establishment of the Islamic state, the Arabs were unfamiliar with the intricacies of statesmanship and politics, and did not have the knowledge or culture that the administration of such a vast state

[19]  *Adab-ul-Kuttaab*, p. 193.
[20]  *Masalek-ul-Mamalek*, p. 146.
[21]  Ibid., p. 262.

required. It was also mentioned that, among the Islamic nations, there was none other more worthy of this task than the Iranians, who had governed these territories for centuries and had acquired vast experience in this regard. As a result, many functions of the *divan* continued to be performed by Iranians out of necessity. The Arabs did not have much competence in the management of the affairs of state or of the *divan*, whether during the Amavid Caliphate, when they had unchallenged authority or in the Abbasid period when their authority was limited. Ibni Khaldoon, a prominent Arab writer, has authored a paper entitled 'When Arabs dominate an area, it will soon head towards destruction', in which he has identified their bad management and lack of familiarity with organization and discipline as one of the causes of this. Ibni Khaldoon has cited a number of historical examples to substantiate this. In another paper entitled 'That the Arabs are the Furthest Nation to Politics and Statesmanship' he writes,

The Arabs are more primitive and nomadic than other nations, and because of their simple and rugged lifestyle, have less feeling of need for each other, and therefore accept authority and discipline, which are the basic requirements of politics and statesmanship, with more difficulty. According to this author, the only way in which the Arabs can establish a state and govern, is through religion that compels them to adhere to divine dictates. This is why when religious conviction weakened in them, they returned again to their nomadic lifestyle, and were sidelined in politics and government, and no bonds remained between them and the state except that they were from the same race as the Caliphs; and as this position also withered, they lost all remaining relationship to it and even forgot their origins.[22]

Ahmad Amin has explained why the position of *wazir* was often entrusted to Iranians:

The skill of writing that the Caliphs considered the pre-requisite for the position of *wazir*, was one of the main reasons that made this position often exclusive to Iranians. The Arabs possessed eloquence of speech rather than eloquence of prose or writing skills. Perhaps this is the reason why they have extracted the Arabic word for eloquence from the root '*lisan*' meaning

[22] The Introduction of Ibni Khaldoon, pp. 149-52.

tongue, and they call that who has eloquence in expression as '*Lasen*', while there in no such word extracted from the root of '*kitabah*' meaning writing.

He continues: 'The truth is that the art of writing is stronger among the Iranians than the Arabs, and even in the Amavid period, the most renowned writers like Abdul Hamid and Salem were Iranians'. The Arabs were always proud of the sword and the tongue, but not the pen. Yazid bin Mu'awiah enumerated the virtues of his clan to Ziad bin Obayd, 'We elevated you from the clan of Thaghif to the glory of Qoraysh, and from Obayd we related you to Abu Sofyan, and from the pen we raised you to the *Menbar* (podium).' He has quoted a number of verses on this subject from Salit bin Jarir al Namri, from the book *Al Wozara' wal Kottab*, transcribed by Jahshiari.[23]

The complexity of the *divans* of Iran also explains why the functions of the *divan* in the Caliphate remained with Iranian *dabirs*. Estakhri has described the complexity of the *divan* of *kharaj* of Fars province, which was unparalleled in complexity. This complexity was due to the diversity of the sources of income and the differences in the practices applicable to each of them, which necessitated the maintenance of various account systems in the *divan*. Needless to say that the administration of such *divans* was not possible except by experienced *dabirs*, and for this reason their administration for several centuries after the collapse of the Sassanid empire was the responsibility of the same families which had administered them before the advent of Islam, and in effect these positions became hereditary within those families.

**Iranian *Wazirs* and Arab Caliphs**    Much has been said about the scientific and social movement of the Abbasid period; in order to uncover the underlying causes of this movement and the factors that strengthened it, the administrative structure of the Caliphate and particularly those who headed and managed it should be studied in greater depth. As mentioned earlier, one obvious impact of the class of *dabirs* on the Caliphate was that they popularized some of the customs and practices of the Sassa-

---

[23] *Duha-al-Islam*, vol. I, p. 167. Also refer to *Al Wozara' wal Kottab*, Cairo, 1938, p. 28.

nid court at the court of the Caliphs. One of the practices of the Sassanid court was that each class of functionaries, including the *dabirs*, had their own special dress codes by which they were recognized and distinguished. The *wazirs* of the Abbasid Caliphate followed the same practice and copied their predecessors in their dress codes, they even went further and introduced certain practices of the Sassanid court that did not quite conform with Arab traditions and customs in the court of the Caliphs. According to Jahshiari, whenever Fazl, the son of Sahl, the *wazir* of Ma'moon, who was also known as Zur-Riasatayn, wished to have an audience with Ma'moon, he would sit on a throne carried by a number of noblemen to the Caliph, when Ma'moon's eyes would fall on him they would place the throne on the ground and he would rise and walk toward the Caliph. The noblemen would place the throne where he wished to sit in audience. As Fazl approached the Caliph, he would greet him and sit on the throne. Jahshiari says: 'Zur-Riasatayn copied this custom from the Sassanid court, as one of the *wazirs* of that period would sit on such a throne, and twelve princes would carry him.'[24] Among those who carried the throne of Fazl were Sa'eed bin Moslem and Yahya bin Ma'az. Not only did Iranian *dabirs* follow the traditions of their ancestors, but they also induced the Abbasid Caliphs to follow suit. Mansoor was the first Abbasid Caliph who wore an Iranian hat, and his successors followed his example, clearly inducting the influence of Iranian *dabirs* and *wazirs*.

In his review of *Tarikh Azadi*, Birooni has narrated a tale from *Hamzeh Esfahani* that clarifies to some extent the position of Abbasid Caliphs on the *divan* system of Iran. He writes: Esfahani says: One day the Caliph Motawakkel was on one of his outings, and he noticed one of the plantations that was not yet ready for harvest, and said: Abdollah bin Yahya has asked for my permission to open the *kharaj*, while the plantations are still green; in such a situation, how do people pay their *kharaj*? Those present said: this situation has inflicted great losses on the people, because as such, they can pay what they owe either through loans or by pre-selling their crops, or they have to abandon their land and leave their land, and they have

---

[24] Jahshiari, *Al Wozara' wal Kottab*, pp. 401-2.

consistently demanded justice to address this matter. Motawakkel said: Was this practice initiated in my days, or has it always been such? They said: This was a practice that the shahs of Iran initiated, and always asked for the *kharaj* at Nowrooz, and in this matter they have been the models for Arab monarchs. Then Motawakkel summoned the Moobadan Moobad and said to him: The complications of this situation have compounded, and I am not one to deviate from the practices of the shahs of Iran; but how did they, with all their wisdom and good deeds, open the *kharaj* in this period? Birooni has narrated in detail the explanation given by the Moobadan Moobad about leap years and its observance in the Sassanid period, and its negligence by the Arabs, causing Nowrooz to fall earlier. Motawakkel ordered Ebrahim bin Abbas to collaborate with Moobadan Moobad to push back the Nowrooz to its proper timing. As this exercise was completed during the days of Al Mo'tazed, the successor of Al Motawakkel, this calendar is known as the Mo'tazedi calendar. Birooni has quoted two verses from a poem by Bohtori in praise of Motawakkel and his initiative to correct the timing of Nowrooz.[25]

It would be appropriate to say a few words about the significance of Nowrooz during the Abbasid period, the revival of which was one of the prominent achievements of Iranian *dabirs*. After the collapse of the Sassanid empire, this feast, like many other Iranian traditions, lost its significance within the official organs of the Caliphate, particularly since the Amavid period was not conducive to its continuation. However, Nowrooz regained its greatness and glory within the official organs of the state during the initial years of the Abbasid Caliphate. Not only did the Iranians at the court of the Caliphs celebrate this ancient festival in the traditional manner, but it also became one of the popular feasts of the land and the Caliphs participated in it. Arab literature of this period contains poems and letters that were written in celebration of this feast. Sending presents and congratulatory notes were among the customs of this festival, which were widely practised by the learned and the nobility, particularly by *dabirs* and *wazirs*.

---

[25] *Al Akhbar al Baghyah*, pp. 31-2.

The poems written in Arabic on the occasion of Nowrooz and Mehregan and usually included in congratulatory notes, and the poems that were read by poets on the day of Nowrooz, have been discussed by Hamzah Esfahani in this book: *Al Ash'ar al Sa'erah fil Nowrooz wal Mahrajan*. One of the letters written during this period felicitating *Nowrooz* reads,

This is the day that Iranians hold with pride, and the Arabs follow suit in celebrating this feast with them, and observing their traditions. The Iranians achieved unrivalled greatness in government that was beyond imagination, and which no one could equal. And when their state collapsed, they became the subject of proverbs because of their noble deeds and good name, and others followed their model; they celebrated their feasts, for which they made long preparations.

According to Ghalqashandi, the *dabirs* of the Abbasid period viewed this feast with greatness and paid much attention to its traditions and glory.[26]

**The General Culture of Islamic *Dabirs***   The administration of the *divan* and the affairs of the Caliphate compelled the *dabirs* to enhance their knowledge and experience. Each of the *divans* required a particular field of knowledge that the *dabirs* had to master. For example, the *divan* of *ensha'* required superior writing skills and knowledge of the writing codes; the *divan* of *kharaj* necessitated mastery of mathematics and geometry; the *divan* of *barid* (mail) demanded geographical knowledge. Since the *dabirs* and *wazirs* were constantly in the company of the Caliph and assisted him in all his affairs, it was expected of them that, over and above the technical knowledge pertaining to their own line of expertise, they should have a high level of general knowledge and sophistication, which would broaden their minds and vision as well as strengthen their judgement and determination. A knowledge of history and the biographies of the earlier shahs, the art and traditions of their government, and the mastery of codes of behaviour in the presence of the royalty and nobility, must have been a part of it. Such knowledge and skills constituted a general culture, and in

[26] *Sobhi-al-A'asha*, vol. IV, p. 48.

later centuries was the theme of numerous Arabic books such as the *Oyoon-al-Akhbar* and the *Al Eghd al Farid*. An interesting question is that in the first and second centuries of Islam when such books had not yet been produced what were the sources of information upon which the *dabirs* relied to acquire their knowledge of such matters? How did their preliminary knowledge develop further over time and become the subject of those books?

It is certain that the *dabirs* relied on the heritage of their predecessors to obtain the requisite knowledge and broaden their minds and intellect. This is not only supported by their writings, but also is reiterated by their contemporaries and others who came later. In *Al Dorrat ul Yatimah* Ibni Mughaffa', one of forefathers of Arabic literature and culture, describes the knowledge and eloquence of his predecessors and their works, which, he says, relieved their successors of the burden of experimentation. Praising them, he says,

The ultimate knowledge of our learned men has been the outcome of picking from the tree of their knowledge; and the ultimate good deed for our well doers is to replicate their good example; and the best phrases of our speakers is the reference to their books; it is as if they speak to them and they listen to their words. What we find in their writings is a selection of the thoughts, ideas and sayings of people past; as we have not seen later writings on a subject on which the fore-bearers had not preceded them; not on the glorification of God almighty; and not on contempt for material life and refraining from it; and not on writing on the various fields of science and their classification; and illuminating the path, and the clarification of the elements of knowledge; and not in literature and ethics, such that after them, there remains no domain uncovered for any writer or speaker.[27]

Jahiz, one of the forefathers of Arab literature, mentions in the introduction to a book:

And if all that our predecessors have written and immortalized in their biographies and their books of various fields of wisdom, through which we have seen what was hidden from us, and we have opened doors that were

---

[27] *Al Dorratul Yatimah*, *Al-Moghtabas* periodical, vol. III, p. 189. This book has been repeatedly published as *Al-Adab-al-Kabir* and this phrase is mentioned in its introduction. Also, see the collection of papers of Ibni Mughaffa', corrections by Yousef abu Halgheh, Beirut, 1960, p. 63.

closed to us; and we have covered our deficiencies with their abundance, and we have understood what was not possible to understand without them; if all that did not exist, then our reward from wisdom would be small, and our reach to science and knowledge would be limited.[28]

It would be worthwhile to discuss the writings of Ibni Mughaffa' and Jahiz so as to clarify who were the predecessors whose writings have been useful to this class, and what types of writings they had access to. The history of Arab literature does not shed any light on this because during the Jahili period the Arabs had not produced any work that could be classified as science, and even the art of writing and the ability to read was very limited among them. In other words, they had no books or written literature or recorded history. Even in the Islamic period, until the days of Ibni Mughaffa', the art of writing in Arabic had not been developed to an extent that significant books could be written in various fields of science and literature and ethics; except for some basic works in the area of Islamic *Shari'a*, not much was added to the earlier works. Not only is the range of information and the trend of thought seen in the work of the *dabirs* of this period like Ibni Mughaffa' and Abdul Hamid unprecedented in Arabic works, but also the sciences that became identified with the Arabic language and were later known as literary sciences had not yet emerged in the form of science, and the knowledge of the Arabs in these areas was extremely superficial and scattered.

One may initially assume that Ibni Mughaffa' and Jahiz' reference to the works of their predecessors meant in reality the works of the Greeks; but a review of the history of Islamic culture, reveals that this impression is erroneous. This is because until this period, the degree of familiarity of Moslems with Greek scientific and cultural works was rather limited and it is unlikely that they would be influenced by them, and at no time in their history did the Arabs ever rely on Greek sources to this extent.

The following chapters discuss books in the different disciplines of knowledge and literature that were translated from Pahlavi into Arabic and thus became part of the treasury of scientific and literary sources that Islamic *dabirs* and scholars have relied upon;

[28] The Book *Al-Hayawan*, p. 10.

these translations primarily pertained to subjects that were directly converted to the work of this class of *dabirs*, and with further editing and refinement in Arabic, became known as the literary arts or literature. Some of the fields of Arabic literature have their roots in these translations. In their writings, Ibni Mughaffa' and Jahiz were referring to this genre of Iranian works that were available to the *dabirs* and other scholars at the time. This can be safely said in the case of Ibni Mughaffa' because, he never relied on Arab sources in his writings, and this was the main reason for the differences between his writings and those of Arab authors. Undoubtedly, the sources of information for Ibni Mughaffa' were Pahlavi books and letters, many of which he translated into Arabic.

### The Position of *Dabirs* in the History of Iranian and Arab Civilization

The *dabirs* in the court of the Caliphate had great significance and influence on both Iranian and Arabic civilizations and cultures. This is because they were the most critical factor in the influence of Iranian culture on Islamic civilization, as well as one of the most vital groups responsible for the development and expansion of Arabic literature. They, on the one hand, undertook to translate Pahlavi books into Arabic, thus enlarging the scientific and literary wealth of the Arabic language, and on the other, strove to disseminate these books within Islamic society, thus opening new paths in Arabic and Islamic literature.

An examination of the first literary works that have been handed down from Islamic *dabirs* as well as, a review of what Arab authors have written about their culture and knowledge reveal that they relied on Pahlavi books, or the Arabic translations that were available to them at that time, to obtain information that they required for their work, just as the Sassanid state was their structural and behavioural model, and the manner in which they handled the *divan* and other affairs of the state. From those books they drew guidance in the art of government, procedures of the *divan*, the codes of correspondence, and the codes of ethics and other areas of contemporary knowledge, and benefited from them to expand their intellect, knowledge and social refinement.

It is interesting that in the initial years of the Abbasid era most of the people who translated Pahlavi books were either from the class of *dabirs* or their contemporaries and followers. A number of these *dabirs*, or *wazirs* in this period, even composed some of these works in verse, or encouraged others to compose them in verse, because of their passion for these works. For example, Ahmad bin Yahya Balazori composed the *Ahde Ardeshir* in verse, and Khaled Barmaki, one of the renowned *wazirs* of the Abbasid period, exhorted Aban bin Abdul Hamid Laheghi to render a number of books in verse, including the *Kalileh va Demneh*, the Biography of *Anooshiravan*, the *Blohar* and the *Buzasf*, the *Ketab Rasa'el* and the *Ketab al Hend*. It is said that Yahya and Fazl, the two sons of Khaled Barmaki, each gave 5,000 *dinars* to Aban Laheghi for rendering the *Kalileh va Demneh* in verse.

Just as theologians were the agency for the introduction of Greek philosophy in Islam, and Assyrian physicians intiated the translation of most of the Greek and Indian medical books into Arabic, so were the *dabirs* of the Caliphate the agency for the transfer of Iranian civilization and culture to Islam and the Arabic language and culture. Their efforts bore fruit and within a short period the literature of Iran became integrated into Arabic literature, and Islamic scholars evinced a keen interest in learning it. This is why Iranian literary masterpieces appear in books of Arabic literature in a form different from that seen in Islamic religious books. In religious books Iranian literary works are introduced as works of blasphemy by a nation of atheists and non-believers, on the other hand, the authors of literary books have referred to Iranians as a nation of knowledge and culture, wisdom and intellect, they have considered their heritage as literature and ethics, and attributed to them many noble qualities. In such books, the *amthal* of Buzarjomehr, the wise sayings of the Moobadan and the words of advice of Ardeshir and Anooshiravan have been quoted at par with the wise sayings of the forefathers of Islam or other prominent Arabs, without prejudice or distinction.

## The *Dabirs* of the *Divan* in the View of Jahiz

In his paper Jahiz disparages of the ethics of the *kottab*, and offers much information on the original sources of the knowledge and insight of the *dabirs* of this period. Further, judging from what Jahiz has selected from the range of writings in his criticism of this class, one can understand how his contemporaries among the Arabs and Moslem jurists viewed the *dabirs*. From the writings of Jahiz the following issues can be deduced:

1. Contrary to the scholars of their time who generally recited Arab poetry or quoted the *Hadith* and studied the *Figh*, the *dabirs* read Iranian literary works and obtained their knowledge from them. Jahiz has enumerated such books as the *Hekam wa Amthal* (Maxims and Proverbs) of Bouzarjomehr, the *Ahde Ardeshir*, the *Rasa'el Abdul Hamid, Ibni Mughaffa', Mazdak Nameh* and *Kalileh va Demneh*. He has argued that none of these *dabirs* ever studies and debated the Koran, or learnt the *Tafseer* and the *Figh*, or evinced an interest in reciting the *Hadith* or the *Akhbar*. If anyone of them did so, not only would he find it distasteful and undesirable, but also his colleagues would heap contempt on him and characterize his life as inferior.

2. The *dabirs*, more than their contemporaries, openly questioned religious beliefs, and did not accept common practices and customs without scrutiny. Jahiz has criticized their questioning of the *Ta'leefe Ghor'an va Nasekh o Mansookhe An* and their tendency to disbelieve the *Akhbar*, and he described their reliance on the mind and logic as one of their evil traits.

3. This class did not join the Arab Moslems in eulogizing prominent Islamic men and did not hesitate to initialize them. Jahiz has added that whenever the names of the companions of the Prophet were mentioned, the *kottab* did not cite their attributes, nor did they speak highly of other prominent Moslems such as Sharih, Hassan, Sha'bi, Ibni Jaber and Nakha'i.

4. The *dabirs* and the staff of the *divan*, more than other classes, were partial to Iranian customs and way of life. At their get togethers they would often recall the competence and attributes of Iranians in statesmanship and conquest, and discuss the greatness of the Sassanid shahs and their empire, and they debated on these issues with the Arabs.[29]

---

[29] Three papers by Jahiz, corrections by Fenkel, Cairo, 1344 H.

It is not a matter of debate that the ethics and behaviour of the *dabirs* and the areas of their knowledge were beyond the scope of Arab traditions and were perceived negatively by those who viewed every aspect of life only through these traditions, and considered non-conformity with them either as *Sho'ubiah* or disassociation from Islamic life.

**Why Most *Dabirs* of this Period were Accused of Love for Iran or of *Zandaghah***  A scrutiny of the history of the *Kitabah* in the initial years of Islam reveals that most people of this class as well as their companions and peers were known for their love of Iran; and whenever they were criticized by their contemporaries, they were not only accused of *Zandaghah*, but were also put to death for this crime. *Zandaghah* was an accusation that was usually made against men of thought, particularly those who deviated from tradition. This was not because they were truly *Zendigh* or that they did not believe in Islam, but because, in addition to Arab culture, they had access to sources of other cultures. As a result, whatever they said or wrote fascinated, the learned, but for their contemporaries who only thought in terms of common traditions and also viewed Islam in similar terms, it was *bid'ah* or affiliation to Iran or *sho'ubiah*.

The history of Islam offers much evidence of this. When the enemies of Ibni Mughaffa' wanted to destroy his clout and esteem in Islamic society and demonstrate that he did not believe in Islam, they alleged that when he was passing near an *Ateshkadeh*, he recited two verses which revealed his deep affection for that temple.[30]

When Sofyan, the envoy of Mansoor the Abbasid Caliph, decided to kill him because of political reasons, he was accused of *Zandaghah* and was killed for it. According to Ibni Khaldoon, Haroon al Rashid wished to demolish Eivan Kasra, and he consulted his *wazir* Yahya, the son of Khaled Barmaki. Yahya advised him against it and Haroon accused him of being overcome by his passion for Iran and Iranians.[31] When Asma'i wanted to disparage the Barmaki family, he recited a

---

[30] *Oyoon-al-Akhbar*, vol. I, p. 50.
[31] The Introduction of Ibni Khaldoon, p. 346.

number of verses about them: if *sherk* was mentioned, their faces lit up, and if an *Ayeh* was recited to them, they recited verses from the *Mazdak*.[32]

Mohammad bin Layth Khatib, one of the followers of the Barmakis, was also known as *Zendigh*. Sahl, the son of Haroon and an Iranian *wazir* of this period, who had been given the title *Bouzarjomehr* of Islam because of his knowledge and wisdom, was accused of *Sho'ubism* and anti-Arab sentiments. Ibni Nadeem also described him as such.[33] When Fazl bin Sahl, the *wazir* of Ma'moon, convinced him to change the symbol of the Abbasids from black to green, they attributed this to his affection for Iran. According to Jahshiari, Fazl bin Sahl chose green colour because it was the colour of the robe of *Kasra* and the *Majoos*. When Fazl was engaged in a debate with Na'eem bin Hazem in the presence of Ma'moon about the transfer of the Caliphate to the Alawites, and Fazl spoke in favour of such a more, Na'eem said to him: 'You consent to this matter because when the Caliphate is transferred to the clan of Ali, you will deceive them and transform the state to *Kasraism*.'[34] Ali bin Obaydeh Rihani, a talented writer at the court of Ma'moon, was also accused of *Zandaghah*. He not only produced Iranian cultural works, but also authored several books with Persian titles. Ibni Nadeem has credited him with books like *Mehr Azar Gashasb*, *Keylohrasb*, *Roshana'i Nameh* and *Adab Javanshir* to him.[35]

Mention has been made of the efforts of Aban bin Abdul Hamid Laheghi in the translation of Pahlavi books and their rendition in verse, as well as his relationship to the Barmakis. Abu Nawas recited two verses condemning him and calling him a follower of Mani.[36]

[32]  *Oyoon-al-Akhbar*, vol. I, p. 50.
[33]  *Al-Fehrest*, p. 120.
[34]  *Al Wozara' wal Kottab*, pp. 396 ff.
[35]  *Al-Fehrest*, p. 119.
[36]  *Oyoon-al-Akhbar*, vol. IV, p. 143.

# FOUR

# The Literary Movement of the Abbasid Era and the Translation of Iranian Books

The literary and scientific movement of Islam began in the initial years of the Abbasid Caliphate. The grounds for this movement had been laid to some extent in the earlier periods; but prior to this period the social conditions of the Arabs were not conducive to rapid advances in the fields of science and knowledge. Even if efforts had been made by enthusiasts in these areas, they would not have borne fruit.

As mentioned earlier, the scientific and cultural movement of Islam was the outcome of the efforts of numerous people who came together under the banner of Islam and established an integrated society. As the roots of Islam could be traced to the Arabs and it developed and flourished in the Arabic environment, and since the Koran was in Arabic, Arabic culture and language were the common grounds on which the scientific and literary movement of Islam was based. In order to understand Islamic culture, it is imperative to review the various areas of Arab knowledge during the period preceding Islam and during the first century of Islam, and examine its essence, before it was transformed through interaction with other cultures.

During the Jahili period, the Arabs had acquired simple knowledge about certain areas of life in accordance with the needs of their simple lifestyle, but their knowledge had not yet reached the level that would classify it as science. Science consists of a set of structured principles or facts based on natural and clear causality. During this period, the Arabs had not mastered such knowledge in any areas of life, and if in areas like medicine and astrology they had acquired certain knowledge from experience, their knowledge was simple, unstructured and based on vague and unnatural causality. After the emergence of Islam and for some time after that, the Koran was the only book that the Arabs cared to read and learn. Following the death of the Prophet, the prophetic traditions and the tales narrated about his companions became the basis for interpreting Koranic judgements, and the collection and recording of these narratives were considered a must. With the passage of time, the scope of this knowledge gradually expanded and the ground was laid for that branch of science that came to be known in later centuries as *Shari'a*. During this period the Arabs narrated verses and tales from the Jahili era, which later became part of a different branch of science known as literary sciences or literature.

It must be mentioned that for some time after the emergence of Islam, the Arabs were not yet familiar with the art of writing books, and all their knowledge, whether of the Koran or about their past heritage, was orally transmitted through tales and events. The Arabs initially believed that Islam and the Koran had superseded any knowledge from the past, and therefore they were not appreciative of other peoples, books or scientific works because as far as they were concerned their contents were contrary to the teachings of Islam and the Prophet. As the domain of Islam expanded and other non-Arab peoples entered its fold, such beliefs, which were baseless, were dissipated and the Moslems began to translate and reproduce other works and produced books in Arabic.

**Islamic Culture in
the Amavid Period**
With the passing of the period of the Prophet and the first four Caliphs, the Caliphate passed into the hands of the Amavids, who wished to give it monarchic character. They therefore were keen to understand the administration and government of previous monarchs, to learn from their deeds and their experiences, and listen to tales or read narratives in these areas that would help them in their purpose. This interest exposed the Arab Moslems to the heritage of other nations, and permitted them to benefit from it to the extent that their intellectual capacity allowed. As a result, the ground was laid for the translation of Iranian and other works into Arabic. It has been written about Mu'awiah that, every night, he would listen to

tales of the Arabs and their conquests, the history of Iran and the shahs and how they treated their subjects, and other tales from the past. He would rise before daybreak and his servants would read to him the narratives of kings, their wars and their military arts. Thus, he became acquainted with the tales, narratives and politics of the earlier ages.[1]

Although in the Amavid era Islamic society had made some progress, the overall environment was not conducive to the enhancement of Islamic culture, as the foundations for the development of knowledge and culture had not yet been laid. One day when Abdul Malek saw his son reading a book on *Siyar va Maghazi* (events and meanings), he decreed that the book be burnt and advised him to read the Koran.[2] Omar bin Abdul Aziz, who was considered one of the most pious of the Amavids, found in the treasury of books in Damascus a book on medicine written by a priest by the name of Haroon bin A'yun and translated into Arabic by Maserjuyeh. A group of people sought his permission to copy the book and disseminate it; he contemplated on the matter for forty days before granting their request. This hesitation on the part of the Caliph and that, too, for a useful medical book, demonstrates the conservatism of those who should have taken the lead in promoting science and knowledge in that period.

A trail of the Jahili Arabs who were not too familiar with script and writing was their overdependence on memory. The trove of poetry and tales that was collected as Jahili literature in the Islamic period, had been transmitted verbally from one generation to another until it reached the Moslems. As records show, many poets shared a narrator who memorized the poems and then recited them. In effect, the same task that was done in the later periods of Islam by records and the *divan* was accomplished by narrators during the Jahili period. This practice continued after the emergence of Islam and in the first Islamic century was widely practised by the Arab Moslems. Even during the times of Jahiz, the Arabs viewed this practice with pride. While comparing Arab and Iranian orators and their eloquence, Jahiz favoured Arab orators because whatever that

---

[1] *Morooj-al-Zahab*, vol. II; *Dar-al-Raja'a*, Egypt, p. 332.
[2] Nicholson, p. 247.

the Arabs said was from memory and without any prior record, while the Iranians had acquired their knowledge of science and literature through the written word from ancient times and had continuously added to it.[3] Due to this practice, the Arabs, did not pay attention to recording and safe keeping their works, a basic prerequisite for developing the ability to write books and make progress in the sciences. Some of them even viewed such practice with contempt as revealed by numerous verses in Arab poetry.

Among the Arabic books that have survived after the Koran are the *Alsyrah* written by Mohammad bin Ishaq, and the *Al Ansab* by Ibni Kalbi, the manuscript copy of which is in the British Museum. According to Degouy, and as is mentioned in this copy, its contents are drawn from the forefathers of Islam such as Abi Horayrah, Abdullah bin Omar bin A'as Zohari and Hasan Basri, who had expressed a desire that after their death their books be burnt so, to avoid an erosion of the practice of rote learning.[4] There are other references to men in the first Islamic era who burnt and destroyed their own works because they were not only concerned above declining dependence on memory, but also because of their piety and restraint. Georgy Zaidan has referred to several such men from Kashf-ul-Zonoon wal Bayan like Ahmad bin abul Hawari, Sofyan Thowry and Abu Omar bin Ala'.[5] At the end of his quest for knowledge, one day Ahmad bin abul Hawari received an inspiration from the divine and he carried his books to the shore of the Euphrates where he cried and said: 'You were a good guide to me to the creator, but now that I have reached what I was seeking, I no longer need a guide', and then he washed them in water. There is a similar story about Abu Omar bin Ala'. He had a chamber of books, and when he took to piety and became a hermit, he burnt all his books. Sofyan Thowri expressed a desire that after his death his books be buried as well. When Abu Aoun bin Ata saw his approaching death, he burnt all his books and writings. Such deeds have been attributed to many other men of Islam.[6]

[3] *Al-Bayaan wal Tabyeen*, vol. III, p. 20.
[4] *Encyclopedia Britannica*, 1988 edn., under *Tabari*.
[5] *History of Islamic Civilization*, vol. III, p. 47.
[6] Margoliouth, *Arabic Historians*, p. 97.

According to Goldziher, Moslems refrained from recording the sciences even in the second century of Islam. Because of a lapse of memory, Abdul Rahman bin Harmala Aslami, who died in the middle of the second century, was compelled to seek permission to record what his master Sa'eed bin Habib had dictated to him, but he refrained from doing so till he was granted permission. Braun has explained why the Moslems of this period refrained from recording the *Hadith*. According to him, it was their concern that the papers on which the *Hadith* were recorded would not be treated with the respect that was due to the words of the Prophet, or that the records of the *Hadith* would be considered as important as the Koran and be equated to it. In any case, in the first century of Hijra no advance was made in writing and translation neither in the *Hadith* and *Shari'a* sciences nor in any of the fields of knowledge of that period. However, with the dawn of the scientific movement of Islam, *Shari'a* sciences progressed along with other sciences and scepticism towards writing and recording was dispelled.

**The Golden Era of Islam**   Contemporary historians have described the initial years of the Abbasid Caliphate as the Golden Era of Islam, because at the time the Islamic Caliphate was at the peak of progress in terms of political stability and social and administrative organization. This period also heralded the scientific and cultural movement of Islam. As we have said earlier, this period has also been termed as the period of Iranian influence, because in this period the administration of the affairs of state was in the hands of Iranian *wazirs* and *dabirs* and commanders.

Advancements made by Moslems in the first century, whether in the conquest of new countries and the establishment of a powerful state, or the spread of the Moslems faith, necessitated that corresponding advances be made in science and knowledge and other aspects of life. But the Amavid Caliphate and those who had control over it did not have the capacity to trigger the type of cultural renaissance that was to come in the second century.

But when control of the Caliphate fell to the Abbasids, and the administration of its affairs was entrusted to Iranian *wazirs* and *dabirs*, with the interest that they had in the promotion of science and culture, and the support that they received from the Caliphs some people began to translate books from Persian and Greek and other languages, and as they received substantial reward for their work, this scientific and cultural movement gradually gained a sophisticated status, and the Arabic language that previously lacked scientific and technical capacity, became a rich and strong language, and the Baitul Hekmah that was established by Ma'moon with the supervision of a number of Iranian scholars, became very renowned.

The scientific and cultural progress of Islam was the result of the interaction of Islamic teachings with other cultures that had existed in the region before Islam, and each had covered separated stages of progress. The first Abbasid period is significant because it provided a conducive environment for that interaction. An examination of Ibni Nadeem's *Al Fehrest* reveals that most translations from non-Arabic books, whether Iranian or Indian, Greek or Assyrian, were done in this period. These translations are considered the pillars on which the scientific advancements of Islam were based, and which enabled Moslems to continue the scientific efforts of former nations and contribute to world civilization.

**Arabic Literature and the Cultures of Iran and Greece**  It was earlier mentioned that Iranian and Greek thought had an extensive influence on Islamic literature and science at various periods of Islamic history, and had left a deep impression on Islamic culture. It should be added here that the influence of these two cultures on various fields of Islamic sciences and literature was not identical, and each had a greater impact on particular fields and areas. However, it is not possible to determine the extent of the influence of foreign cultures on various fields of Islamic knowledge. It can be said that the influence of Greek thought was generally in the areas of philosophy, whereas Iranian thought influenced the literary arts, the organizational and administrative sciences of government, the social practices of Islam and a number of other areas.

A number of Western authors who have written on Arab literature and Islamic civilization have exaggerated the extent of influence of Greek thought on Islamic culture, and have extended it to almost all scientific and cultural aspects of Islamic as well as

Arab literature. This is partly because the means of research on the history of Islamic civilization and culture and its development are not as well established as they should be, and consequently not much information is available to researchers in the field. Another reason is that some writers consider ancient Greece as the only source of knowledge and culture in the world, and attempt to relate any advancement made by other nations, and particularly the peoples of the east, to this source. This issue will not be discussed here but it can be refuted *vis-à-vis* Arabic literature and social and political life, because in these areas one does not find any traces of Greek influence. At a time when Arabic literary sciences were emerging and Arabic literature was maturing, the Arabs had not been exposed to Greek thought, and they were not conversant with Greek thought at any time in their history to be influenced by it. In the periods under study, no Greek literary book was translated into Arabic and no Greek literary art found its way into Islam. Taha Hosseyn, a contemporary author and a staunch supporter of Greek civilization, has considered Arab literature, particularly the art of expression, to be influenced by Greek thought. Nevertheless, in his study of the character of Arab poetry, he has argued that Arab poetry is neither epic nor theatrical, but lyric, he has concluded that nations with epic or theatrical poetry have followed the Greek model, and since the Arabs were not exposed to Greek works, they did not have this genre of poetry.[7] Gibb has also exaggerated the influence of Greeks on Islamic culture; nevertheless, he has stated that the Arabs were not familiar with Greek literature.[8]

The issue to be considered here is that the impact of one culture and civilization over another is the product of several years and even centuries of social contact and interaction of thought and literature. Under such circumstances, one can talk of cultural impact between nations, but when such circumstances do not exist one can only express a cautious opinion and not conclude that any trace of similarity between two cultures is necessarily proof of the impact of one over the other. If one accepts that Islamic culture has been

---

[7] *Fil Adab-al-Jahili*, pp. 240-2.
[8] Gibb, *Arabic Literature*, p. 36.

influenced by Greeks in the philosophical sciences, empirical wisdom and related disciplines, it is primarily because the basis of Moslems, core knowledge in these areas was the translations of Greek books and they often followed Greek philosophy in matters of doctrine. As mentioned earlier, there are no traces of Greek influence on the political, social and literary life of the Arabs.

When one accepts that Iranian thought and culture had a deep impact on Arabic literature and related fields, as well as on the political and social life of Islam, it is because Iranians were interested in the creation of political and social life and in laying the foundations of these literary arts; in short, they were the forefathers of many fields. The administrative institutions of the Caliphate were established by Iranian *dabirs* and *wazirs*, and the social environment of Moslems, and the court of the Caliphate, particularly during the Abbasid period, had acquired an Iranian character. When Arab literature was developing, Iranian culture was the most important foreign culture that interacted and integrated with it; Iranians were among the influential factors in the political and scientific development of Islam. In other words, Iranians were the source of the conceptual and literary works that triggered the process of development, and they not only translated of those works into Arabic, but also produced similar works in Arabic. Commenting on the influence of Iranian and Greek cultures on Arab literature, Ahmad Amin has noted:

It is very difficult to find evidence of Greek thought in Arab poetry, or to find an Arab-speaking poet of Greek or Roman origin, who later learned Arabic and composed poetry in Arabic, while numerous Iranians have become renowned Arabic poets. Islamic historians adopted their practice from the Iranians not from the Greeks, and what has limited the influence of Greece on the Arabs was the little information that the Moslems had about the literary life of the Greeks.[9]

There are no two opinions that the best evidence of the cultural development of a nation is its language and the words and expressions therein. Arabic contains many non-Arabic words that have been borrowed from other languages and given an Arabic character. A group of such words have entered this language through

[9]   *Fajr-al-Islam*, p. 160.

translation and adaptation, and another group, as a result of the social interaction of the Arabs with other nations. In other words, whenever the Arabs came across a new thing or a new concept that was not familiar to them and they could not find a suitable word for it, they adopted its original word and used it. A perusal of non-Arabic words in Arabic reveals that most of them, particularly those related to the administrative and social environment and Arabic literature, have been borrowed from the Persian language, and except for rare cases, these words have been largely adapted from Persian expressions. Kharazmi has mentioned many expressions of the *divan* in *Mafatih-al-Oloom* that shed more light on this issue.

**The Forefathers of Science in Islam**   Ibni Khaldoon notes:

The leadership of Iranians in seeking knowledge and the promotion of culture was felt in Moslem society from the first centuries of Islam, and with time became more evident until it developed into one of the recognized features of Islamic civilization.

In a chapter entitled: 'That the Knowledgeable in Islam are Often Iranians' Ibni Khaldoon writes,

It is a strange coincidence that in the Islamic society most of the leaders in the fields of knowledge are Iranians, and rarely can one find an Arab scholar in the theological and physical sciences; and if one is ethnically Arab, his language and learning environment and his teachers are Iranians.

Ibni Khaldoon has offered a detailed explanation of this issue:

When the religion of Islam appeared among the Arabs, they, as a result of their simple and nomadic life, did not possess science or industry, and they learned the teachings of religion orally, and learned their interpretation from the Prophet and his companions. The Arabs knew nothing of teaching and writing, because no one had compelled them to it, and they had not felt the need for it. The period of the companions of the Prophet and their followers thus passed, and only a few of them had learned to read and became known as *Qhorra'*, or readers. And this title was an elated title that distinguished them from the rest of the Prophet's companions, who were generally illiterate. And because from the days of Haroon al Rasheed, the interpretation of the rulings of the Koran had become more complex, and also required knowledge of other areas such as *Tafseer* and *Hadith* and so on, other areas of knowledge emerged that later developed into various fields of science.

Presenting a brief account of the history and development of Islamic and Arab sciences, Ibni Khaldoon says:

And thus, a range of sciences emerged, and to grasp their essence necessitated learning; therefore, they were considered among the professions. We have said earlier that industries and traits are characteristic of peoples with urban civilization, and the Arabs were far from such life; and since in that period the people with civilization were the Iranians and those who followed them, therefore, the sciences and the arts belonged to them.

After identifying a number of prominent scholars and indicating the superiority of Iranian scholars in many fields of Islamic sciences, he adds: 'And thus, the saying of the Prophet (*law ta'allagha l elmu be aknafissama' lanalahu ghawmun men ahle Fares*) proved to be true.' These remarks refer to those Arabs who continued their nomadic way of life even after the advent of Islam, and did not integrate into the urban Islamic society. According to Ibni Khaldoon, when other group of Arabs who had abandoned their traditional way of life in the light of Islamic teachings and interaction with other civilized nations of that period acquired a position of power and authority, they considered engaging in activities such as learning the sciences and the arts to be below their status, and thus they paid no attention to it.[10] Commenting on this, Georgi Zaidan has cited a number of instances of Arab contempt towards those who sought knowledge.[11]

As mentioned earlier, Iranians evinced an avid interest in science and knowledge in this period, and Iranian *wazirs* expended fortunes on encouraging scholarship. Arab literature provides numerous accounts of the passion of the Barmakis and other Iranian families for the sciences and promotion of knowledge. According to Jahshiari, Yahya bin Khaled had established free schooling for orphan children.[12] Because of their abiding interest and concern for scholarship, Iranians maintained their leading position in areas of

[10]   The Introduction of Ibni Khaldoon, pp. 543-5.
[11]   *History of Islamic Civilization*, vol. III, p. 51.
[12]   Jahshiari, p. 212.

scholarship, culture and related fields in Islamic society, and were an authority on Islamic or Arab sciences. It is worth noting that other than the general areas of Islamic sciences, even in areas that dealt with the structure and context of Arabic language, Iranians had acquired prominent positions of authority, despite the fact that Arabic was an alien language for them. In fact, the first books on Arabic language were produced in Khorasan,[13] and the foundations of Arabic grammar were laid by Sibouyeh of Fars province, and the writings that later became known as Arab literature were mostly produced by Iranian scholars.

This scientific endeavour led Ibni Khaldoon to describe the Iranians in Islam as *Hamalat Elm* (carriers of knowledge), and this is substantiated by contemporary scholars on the basis of their research. In 'Arabs and *Ajams*', a chapter in his book *Mohammedanisch Studien*, Goldzeiher notes that in the Islamic government not only did non-Arab elements assume the leadership of state administration, but they also acquired leadership in religious sciences. According to Von Kromer, Islamic sciences like *Qera'ah*, *Tafseer*, *Hadith* and *Fiqh* in the first and second centuries of Islam, were essentially in the hands of non-Arabs and the Arabs largely devoted their energies mainly to their ancient poetry and its expansion. Braun has noted that non-Arabs surpassed the Arabs even in this area, as their scholars were the ones who had developed the historical and literary content of Arab knowledge. He has added that, even if one does not completely agree with Paul de Legard who maintained that 'none of the Moslems who produced any scientific work was a Semite', there is no doubt that the Arabs played a secondary role in both the religious and literary sciences as they viewed knowledge and culture with contempt and considered learning to be futile except for teachers and instructors, when others made all-out effort to learn. According to Jahiz, they considered it inappropriate for anyone from Quraysh to learn anything other than about their glorious past wars.

---

[13] That was *Ketab-ul-Ayn* by Khalil bin Ahmad Farahidi. In 248 of Hijra, a stationer brought it to Iraq from Khorasan, prior to which the book was in the treasury of the Taheris, but was also well known in Baghdad and Basrah. Khalil died in 170 of the Hijra, at the age of 74.

**Translators of Pahlavi works into Arabic**    Ibni Nadeem has listed the name of numerous translators in his index: Abdullah bin Mughaffa'; most of the members of the Nowbakhti family; Musa and Yusof, the sons of Khaled; Ali bin Zyad Tamimi; Hasan bin Sahl; Ahmad bin Yahya also known as Balazori; Jabala bin Salem, the *dabir* of Hisham, the Amavid Caliph; Eshaq bin Yazid; Mohammad bin Jahm Barmaki; Hesham bin Qassem; Musa bin Issa also known as Khosravi;[14] Zadouyeh, the son of Shahouyeh Esfahani; Mohammad, the son of Bahram, the son of Matyar Esfahani; Bahram, the son of Mardanshah who was the Moobad of the city of Shahpoor; and Omar Farrakhan.[15] According to Inostranzev, the translators enhanced in this index can be subdivided into four groups on the basis of the types of books that they had translated. Omar Farrakhan represents a separate group which is the fifth group.

The first group includes those like Abdullah bin Mughaffa' who did not confine their efforts to translating any particular type of Persian books, instead they translated books in various branches of the sciences of their times. Abdullah bin Mughaffa' was not merely a translator, but was an outstanding scholar who had a tremendous impact on his environment. Not only did he translate numerous books on history, logic, literature and legend from Persian into Arabic, but also composed diverse literary works in each field, and secured a special place in the history of Iranian and Arabic civilization and culture. Ibni Nadeem has also mentioned his name.

The second group comprised those who translated Iranian scientific and technical works. This group consists of the Nowbakhti family, the sons of Khaled, Ali bin Ziad Tamimi, and Hasan bin Sahl, they were renowned scholars in astronomy and have been described as such in Islamic books. Nowbakht, the astronomer of the Abbasid Caliph Mansoor, was succeeded by his son Fazl. The book on astronomy produced by the Nowbakhti family were the first of their kind in Arabic, and were among the earliest cultural works of Iran to be translated into Arabic. Musa and Yusuf served

---

[14] In *Al-Fehrest* the word *Kasravi* is distorted to *Kordi*.
[15] *Al-Fehrest*, p. 244.

Dawood bin Abdullah and translated for him from Persian into Arabic. They also translated books on science. Ali bin Tamimi, an authority on astronomy, translated into Arabic the *Zij Shahryar*, an important work of the Sassanid period of astronomy. Hasan bin Sahl, an eminent astronomer, figures among astronomers in Ibni Nadeem's index.

Included in the third group were Balazori and Jabala bin Salem, i.e. those who focused more on the translation of literary books including heroic stories, literary ethics, etc., Balazori rendered in verse the famous Pahlavi book, *Ahde Ardeshir*.[16] Jabala translated the book on Bahram Choobin, and another on Rostam and Esfandiar.[17]

The fourth group included those who translated tales, stories and narratives, but no other types of books. In this group there were seven persons who are listed in Ibni Nadeem's index between Jabala bin Salem and Omar Farrakhan.

Before discussing the fifth category which according to Inostranzev, is represented by Omar Farrakhan, it is important to mention those translators whose names have not appeared in the listing:

1. Ibni Nadeem, the author of *Al-Fehrest*, had translated a book on the codes of war and the movements of armies, the conquering of fortresses and cities, the building of camps, etc., that had been written for Ardeshir Babakan.[18]
2. Salam or Salem, worked with Sahl bin Haroon in the administration of the Bait ul Hekmah in Baghdad. According to Ibni Nadeem, he translated some works from Persian.[19]
3. Eshaq bin Ali was the son of Soleyman, and according to Ibni Nadeem, he translated a Persian book on veterinary medicine including the treatment of animals and the relevant practices.[20]
4. Fazl bin Sahl, the *wazir* of Ma'moon, was also known as Zur Riyasatayn. According to Jahshiari, he translated a book from

[16] Ibid., p. 184.
[17] Ibid., p. 305.
[18] Ibid., p. 314.
[19] Ibid., p. 120.
[20] Ibid., p. 315.

Persian into Arabic for Yahya Barmaki. Yahya was highly impressed by his beauty of expression and mastery of the subject.[21]

5. Zadan Farrokh, the son of Piri Kaskari, translated a book on geography from Pahlavi into Arabic. It contained information on the characteristics of the cities of Iran and the people of each city. Ibni Faghih, an Islamic geographer, quoted from him.[22]

6. Mohammad bin Khalaf, the son of Marzban, was also known as Abul Abbas Domiri. According to Yaqoot, he translated more than fifty books from Persian into Arabic.[23]

**Omar bin Farrakhan**   Omar bin Farrakhan represented a separate group of translators which worked on books other than the ones discussed earlier. Inostranzev has provided useful information about him and his translation of a Pahlavi book: Ibni Nadeem has not mentioned the title of the book that Omar translated, but it seems that he was a translator of historical books, as his name appears in the list of such translators. However, his fame in areas other than history does not support such an assumption. Omar was one of the renowned astronomers of the Abbasid period, and Ghefti has described him as one of the leading scholars and translators of the science of the movement of stars and their laws.[24] According to Ibni Sa'ed Andalosi, Abu Ma'shar Falaki has described him in the book *Ketab Mozakerat*, as one of the four distinguished astronomers, and has invited him with Honain bin Eshaq, Ya'qoob bin Eshaq Kendi and Thabet bin Qorrah Harrani, who were renowned physicians and astronomers of Islam.[25] Ibni Nadeem has also listed him in the category of astronomers. Thus, it is clear that he was famous for his work on science rather than history and literature.

It appears that Ibni Nadeem's translation of Omar Farrakhan, on the basis of which he included him in his list of translators, was not in the fields of science and astronomy, otherwise he would

---

[21] Quoted by him from Ahmad Amin in *Dhoha-al-Eslam*, vol. I, p. 93.
[22] *Al-Boldan*, p. 209.
[23] *Mo'jam-al-Udabaa'*, Margoliouth edn., p. 105.
[24] *Tarikh-al-Hokama'*, p. 24.
[25] *Tabaghat-al-Omam*, p. 56.

have mentioned him in the list after Ibni Mughaffa' and other translators of this genre of books. Therefore, an attempt has to be made to identify the book that Omar had translated. Ibni Nadeem has referred to Omar Farrakhan in a chapter of his *Al-Fehrest*, that focuses on the fields of astronomy, mathematics, music and other sciences, and has mentioned Omar's review of Ptolemei's book (*Batlimus*). Among the list of books by Omar, he has referred to one entitled *Al-Mahasen*. As revealed by the title of this book and other similar books in Arabic, this was not a scientific book, and the fact that Ibni Nadeem has referred to it in this chapter is because he has listed Omar Farrakhan's other books and he could not have omitted this book. *Tarikh-al-Hokama'* refers to a book by this title that is also attributed to Omar.[26] Inostranzev strongly believes that what Omar Farrakhan translated from Pahlavi and because of which his name was listed among the translators, is the same book *Al-Mahasen*, which both Ibni Nadeem and Ghefti have attributed to him.

In ancient Iranian literature, much significance was accorded to the type of books written on the codes of good behaviour and refined attitude, etc., and therefore this area constituted an important field of Pahlavi literature. This kind of behavioural guidance was seen both in books like the *Andarznameh* and the *Pandnameh* as well as in Zoroastrian religious books in which good and bad traits were often contrasted and were distinguished from each other under the heading of *Shayad Nashayad*. As these books were translated into Arabic, and similar books also appeared in this language, they were known by titles such as *Al-Mahasen wal Addad*, *Al-Mahasen wal Masawe'* or *Al-Mahasen*. Omar's *Al-Mahasen* was one such book, and perhaps it was the first of its kind to be translated from Persian into Arabic. This seems likely because Omar Farrakhan originally hailed from Tabarestan and had spent some time in the service of Yahya Barmaki and Fazl bin Sahl,[27] and it was Fazl who had summoned him from Tabarestan and had employed him in the service of Ma'moon, to do translation and write literary works. Keeping in view the interest of Yahya Barmaki and Fazl bin Sahl in the heritage of Iran, it is quite

---

[26] *Tarikh-al-Hokama'*, p. 242.
[27] Ibid.

likely that among the books that Omar translated from Persian was the *Al-Mahasen* and he was the first person to introduce this type of Persian literary books in Arabic literature.[28]

**Some Clarifications**  With respect to the discussion so far, the following explanations are in order:

1. The translations of Pahlavi books during this cultural movement were not exact reproductions of the original text. Some of the translators freely altered the text of the books that they translated according to their own tastes, or those of their readers, or to make the text more suitable to the Islamic environment. Thus, they often changed the original text, particularly of literary books, mailing addictions or deletions as they saw fit. Noeldke has commented on Ibni Mughaffa' and his style of translation, 'We must not consider the work of Ibni Mughaffa' as translation. Ibni Mughaffa' was a writer who followed a particular style of his own, and all his effort was directed at writing books that were suitable to the taste of his readers, who were generally literate and intellectual; therefore, he altered the books that he translated, and he even did not feel restrained on occasions to add material that did not exist in the original text.' To substantiate his point he has referred to several cases in the translation of *Kalileh va Demneh* by Ibni Mughaffa'.[29] This point of view applies not only to Ibni Mughaffa', but also to most other translators of this period. For this reason, different translations of the same book varied from each other. This freedom of the translators to alter the original text and to follow their personal tastes has resulted in much confusion between the books that they have written and those

[28] Inostranzev, pp. 75-86. For more information about the translators of this period, and the works that they translated from Persian into Arabic, refer to the article by the Mohammad Mohammadi-Malayeri, titled 'Translators and Transcribers from *Farsi* in the First Islamic Centuries', in *Al-Derasat-al-Adabyah*, year VII, vols. 3 and 4, Beirut, 1966.

[29] Refer to the Foreword by Noeldke in the Introduction of *Kalileh va Demneh*.

that they have translated, such that Ibni Mughaffa', for example, has sometimes been referred to as the author of the *Al-Yatimah*, the *Adab-al-Saghir* and the *Adab-al-Kabir*, and at other times as their translator.

2. The following chapters examine the various books in each of the different branches of literature and science that were translated from Pahlavi into Arabic in the first centuries of Islam, and thus became part of Arabic literature. However, this is not a representative sample of all the books that have been passed by the Sassanid Iranians to Islam and were translated into Arabic. Only those books have been mentioned here which find mention in historical sources, and without doubt there would have been numerous books that were translated in the first period of Islam from Pahlavi into Arabic of which there is no knowledge. Historical evidence confirms this fact; sources often mention the names of persons to whom have been attributed the translation of several Pahlavi books, although there are no traces of these books nor their titles. As mentioned earlier Yaqhout has written that Abul Abbas Domiri, one of the scholars and historians of the third century of the Hijra, was one of the translators of Persian books into Arabic and he had translated more than 50 books. However, there is no mention of even one of the books that he translated in historical sources.[30]

---

[30] Accoding to Brockelman, the book of Alexander which is attributed to Ibni Abbas, was one of the books that he translated from Persian into Arabic. *History of Arab Literature*, Arabic translation, vol. II, p. 239; vol. III, p. 104.

# Several History Books Translated from Pahlavi to Arabic

**Recording of Historical Events in Iran before Islam**

The recording of history in the sense of recording of significant events was practised in Iran from ancient times, and at the court of the shahs special secretaries were appointed for this function. There is a reference in the Torah of special offices in the Achaemenian court to the recording of events. In the letter written by the leaders of the Jews to Ardeshir the second, the Achaemenian shah, there is a reference to *Sefr Tawarikh*, or history archives; and the shah's reply confirmed the existence of the register. There is a reference to another letter that the leaders of the Jews wrote to Daryush the Great and requested that the *farman* of Koorosh the Great on the construction of Jerusalem be retrieved from the imperial archives, as well as a reference to the actual retrieval of the *farman*. Greek history books like those of Herodotus and Ketesias, contain references in support of this. Plutarch who lived in the first century (AD 41 or 45-120), has commented on the history of Themistocles, while describing the naval battle between Iran and Greece at Salamis: 'Khashayar Shah was sitting on a throne of gold and a number of *dabirs* were at his presence to record the details of that battle.'[1] From such historical references as also from manuscripts that have survived from the Achaemenian shahs, in which they have recorded important events during their reign, it is clear that the recording of events and archiving of official documents were very important for the Achaemenians, and that special places existed at their court for such records.

---

[1] Langhorne, English translation of Plutarch's *Lives*, p. 1332.

More information is available on the history books of the Sassanid period. In fact, all references from such books that have reached the Moslems and have been translated into Arabic belong to this period. As in the Achaemenian period, so also in the Sassanid period there were special secretaries at the court to write the official journals and to record important events in the empire. It may be assumed that the art of recording events was more developed in this period than in the Achaemenian period. One of the important positions at the Sassanid court was that of the keeper of the Imperial Calendars who enjoyed high standing with the shah.[2] One of the sources used by the Roman historian Agathias (died AD 582) was the collection of Sassanid official journals which were kept in the government archives of Teeshphoon; Sergius, a prominent translator of that period, sought the permission of the keepers of the archives to, copy the names of the shahs of Iran and their great deeds, and after translating them into Greek, provided the information to Agathias.[3]

Thus, the Sassanid shahs were keenly interested in the recording of events, and in particular those that would enhance in their personal fame and glory. This interest is also reflected in the works of Arab writers. Jahiz has written:

Due to the great interest that Iranians had to keep records on events and news, they recorded their great deeds and also their words of wisdom, and matters that were the source of honour and pride for them, on monuments in the mountain, or in tall buildings, and thus protected them from perish and made them eternal.

Bihaghi has narrated a tale from Khosrow Parviz which clearly reflects the policy of the Sassanid shahs on the recording of important events. He writes:

As the wars of Khosrow Parviz with Bahram Choobin ended and his reign over the country was secured, he ordered his *dabirs* to record those wars from the beginning to the end. The *dabirs* did so, and when, they presented it to Khosrow, its preamble did not appeal to him; thus a young *dabir* wrote

---

[2] Christensen, p. 131.
[3] Ibid., p. 70.

an eloquent preamble to it and presented it to Khosrow; the shah was delighted and ordered that he be promoted.[4]

The obsession of the shahs to keep the memory of momentous historical events alive, particularly those that glorified them, was such that they had the scenes of certain events carved in stone or had them painted in places that were exposed to public view. One of these paintings on the Eyvan of Mada'en which has been described in a poem in Arabic by Bohtori (205-84 of the Hijra), is the painting of Khosrow Anooshiravan in a battle between the Iranians and the Romans, which was painted in great detail on one of the walls of the palace of Mada'en and had remained there for centuries.

Arabic sources mention the titles of a number of history books from the Sassanid period that survived and were used by Moslem historians. Many of these books have either been destroyed and only their titles remain, or their contents have been absorbed into Islamic writings, or they have survived like the *Khoday Nameh* in a transformed format as the *Shah Nameh*. In addition to these books there were other books on the history of Iran that were used by the Moslem writers of the first centuries of Islam, of which no trace has survived. For example, Mas'oodi has referred to books that he found in Fars and Kerman, and he has occasionally narrated events from sources that he describes as 'Books of Ancient Iranians'. It is clear that these sources are in addition to the books that he has mentioned in his writings, like the *Khoday Nameh*, the *Ayeen Nameh*, the *Gah Nameh* and the illustrated book that he found in Fars. It can be seen from these and other similar references found in the works of Islamic writers that, in the first centuries of Islam, apart from those books whose titles have reached us, there were other books on the history of Iran that were translated from Pahlavi into Arabic, and of which we are unaware.

**The *Khoday Nameh*** The most important book that has been trans-
lated from Pahlavi into Arabic is the *Khoday Nameh*. This book has been mentioned in many Arabic historical

---

[4] *Al-Mahasen wal Masawe'*, p. 481.

sources, and like most Persian words in Arabic books, its title has been distorted and appears in different forms.[5] A number of scholars have done research on this book and have provided valuable information about it. Among all these efforts mention must be made of work of the German scholar Noeldke and the Russian scholar Baron Rosen, whose research constitutes the foundation for subsequent studies on this book.

The introduction of one of the manuscript copies of the *Shah Nameh* that dates to the fifteenth century AD mentions that the *Shah Nameh* (or *Khoday Nameh*) was written in the days of Khosrow Anooshiravan and completed in the days of Yazdegerd the third by Dehghan Daneshvar. Acquiescing to this, Noeldke has argued that during the reign of Khosrow Anooshiravan there was an official record of history, that even if it was not the same as the *Khoday Nameh*, was considered to be the primary source for it. The book was later completed during the rule of Yazdegerd. What is clear is that the *Khoday Nameh* was written towards the end of the Sassanid period. But this does not exclude the possibility that different materials contained in it existed prior to this period in various other forms. According to Christensen, the original *Khoday Nameh* covered the period up to Khosrow Parviz and whatever matter deals with the period up to the death of Yazdegerd, the last Sassanid shah, was added later by Zoroastrian *Moobadan*. This explains the discrepancies between some of the Iranian and Arabic accounts of the events pertaining to the period between the days of Khosrow Parviz and the death of Yazdegerd. These differences are due to the fact that historians have used different sources to obtain information about this period while all the information about the earlier periods up to the time of Khosrow Parviz was obtained from a single source, the official historical journal of the Sassanids, or the original *Khoday Nameh*. This Pahlavi history book has been used as a source by all Iranian and Arab historians who have written about Iran before the advent of Islam. The Arabic translation of the *Khoday Nameh* was entitled the *Syar al Molook*, and in Persian it was called the *Shah Nameh*.

<hr/>

[5] *Al-Fehrest*, p. 244.

This book has been translated into Arabic several times and there are variations in these translations. The translations available during the days of Hamzeh Esfahani were four books with the title of *Syar Molook al Fors*, translated by Ibni Mughaffa', Mahmood, son of Jahm Barmaki, Zadouyeh, son of Shahooyeh Esfahani, and Mohammad, son of Matyar Esfahani; *Tarikh Molook Al Fors*, extracted from the archives of Ma'moon; two books entitled *Tarikh Molook Bani Sassan*, one collected or copied by Hesham bin Qassem Esfahani, and the other edited by Bahram, son of Mardanshah, the Moobad of the province of Shahpoor.[6] Abu Reyhan Birooni has also mentioned a translation by Bahram, son of Mehran Esfahani (and a different history book entitled *Bahram Heravi Majoosi*)[7] and has quoted from Abul Faraj Ebrahim bin Ahmad bin Khalaf Zanjani's history book[8] all these were apparently translations of the *Khoday Nameh*. According to Hamzeh, one of the authors of the history of Iran, Bahram, son of Mardanshah Moobad, whose book was among the sources of the *Hamzeh*, possessed twenty different Arabic versions of the *Khoday Nameh*.

Christensen has divided the translators of the *Khoday Nameh* into three groups: the first group comprised those who remained faithful to the original text with slight variations based on individual style and some omissions and abbreviations, such as Ibni Mughaffa', Mohammad bin Jahm Barmaki and Zadouyeh Esfahani. The second group included those who added to the original text, such as Mohammad bin Matyar Esfahani, and Hesham bin Qasem Esfahani. These translators borrowed historical events and tales from other books and added them to their translation of the *Khoday Nameh*. The third group comprised those who did not hesitate to borrow from other books in their translations, and ensure greater coherence between the contents of the *Khoday Nameh* and the additional material, they even fabricated some events and stories. Hence, it would be more appropriate to view them as authors rather than

---

[6]  *Tarikh Hamzah*, p. 98.
[7]  *Al-Akhbar-al-Baghyah*, p. 99.
[8]  Ibid., p. 116.

translators. This group was represented by Musa bin Isa Kasravi and Bahram, son of Mardanshah.[9]

On the issue of whether these translations were done independently of the Pahlavi text or that one was adopted from the other, Noeldke has argued that the first translation of the original text of the *Khoday Nameh* was that of Ibni Mughaffa' and others drew upon his translation. Scholars were unanimous on this until Baron Rosen reviewed this issue again in his paper entitled 'On the Arabic Translations of *Khoday Nameh*' and cast doubts on it. Rosen has concluded that although it is likely that the different translations of the *Khoday Nameh* that Hamzeh Esfahani has referred to were all based on that of Ibni Mughaffa' but this alone does not constitute evidence that they used it as their source. On the contrary, the variations in the different translations are evidence that each of the translators undertook to translate the *Khoday Nameh* independently and his personal taste and style influenced it. According to Hamzeh, although Kasravi, who was one of the translators of the book, had several translations at his disposal, none of them were similar. This argument has been accepted by scholars as revealed by Christensen's classification of translators.

Ferdowsi's chief source for his *Shah Nameh* was the *Khoday Nameh*. Noeldke has argued that the copy of the book that Ferdowsi used was an independent translation in Persian and was not related to the translation of Ibni Mughaffa'. On the contrary, Rosen has concluded that the Persian translation was also done on the basis of the Arabic translation and was not independent of it. In an introduction to the book of Tha'alebi, Zotemberg, has noted that the source of Ferdowsi was a copy of the *Khoday Nameh* that contained drawings of the shahs and heroes (*pahlevans*). According to Inostranzev, this view is based on an error in the translation by Mohl of a verse by Ferdowsi to mean: 'An old man named Azadsar, was with Ahmad Sahl in Marv, and had a book which contained the paintings of *Pahlevans*'. Basing his opinion on this translation, Zotemberg made an erroneous judgement.[10]

[9] Christensen, p. 56.
[10] Inostranzev, p. 72.

Noeldke's research on the *Khoday Nameh* and his analysis of its contents reveal that the *Khoday Nameh* was the general history of Iran and its peoples from its emergence till the end of the Sassanid empire. It occasionally intertwined historical events with legends that were originally ancient, but with time had grown and developed, and in the Sassanid period had acquired great popularity.

In addition to historical tales and narratives, the book also contained the principles of Zoroastrian beliefs and biographies. These could be traced to the period before Alexander. The history of Daryoosh, the last Achaemenian shah, and the story of Alexander which was in Greek were later added to it. It offered little information on the Macedonian and Ashkanid periods, and only some of the names had survived. With the passage of time, the historical contents of this book were expanded and greater accuracy was ensured, and in the Sassanid period it acquired a strong Iranian character. During this period, there were many stories and tales about Ardeshir Babakan, the founder of the Sassanid dynasty, part of which had historical origins, and part was pure legend. All these tales were narrated in the *Khoday Nameh*, and later more information was added about the other Sassanid shahs, and eventually the coverage of the book extended to Yazdegerd the first. The most comprehensive period covered in the book that offered more historical facts than any other period was between the days of Khosrow Anooshiravan and the death of Khosrow Parviz.

According to Noeldke, the book was written in an artistic and literary style, with particular emphasis on literary refinement of the orations of the Sassanid shahs on their coronation, or the *farmans* that they issued. These characteristics were so pronounced in the book that they are apparent even in the translated excerpts from the book recorded in Arabic sources. In support of his views, Noeldke has narrated a tale from Jahiz.

The contents of this book are scattered in different Islamic historic and literary works. Portions of the Arabic translation by Ibni Mughaffa' can also be found in a number of Islamic books, such as the *Oyoon-al-Akhbar* and the *Ketab al Ma'aref* by Ibni Qutaybah, the book by Seyed bin Betriqh (of Alexandria) and the *Tarikh Tabari*. According to Noeldke, it is possible to reconstruct the

Arabic translation of the *Khoday Nameh* by collating portions of the translation of Ibni Mughaffa' that are scattered.[11]

**The *Ayeen Nameh***  There is a reference to this book by Mas'oodi in his *Al-Tanbih wal Eshraf* (pp. 104, 106), Ibni Nadeem in his *Al-Fehrest* (pp. 118, 305), Tha'alebi in the *Ghorar Molook al Fors* (p. 14), and Ibni Qutaybah has quoted extensively from it. According to Christensen, there are references to it in the letter of Tansar and Tarikh Hamzeh Esfahani and in the book *Javame' al Hekayat* of *Awfi*.[12] Ibni Nadeem has listed it among the books of history and tales of Iran under the title *Al Syar wal Asmar al Sahiha*[13] (Correct Biographies and Narratives). Mas'oodi has called it the *Ketab al Rosoom*, in Arabic and has added that the complete text of this voluminous book which runs into thousands of pages was available only with the Moobadan and high ranking officials.[14]

The most important book that provides information about the *Ayeen Nameh* is the *Oyoon-al-Akhbar* by Ibni Qutaybah, an Iranian scholar who has to the credit various books of ethics. Ibni Qutaybah drew extensively on Iranian sources for his *Oyoon-al-Akhbar*, and therefore it is a valuable source for the study of the literary heritage of Iran. Compared to other authors who have only referred to the name of the book and described it, Ibni Qutaybah has also quoted from it and therefore it is very significant and useful in providing information about the content of the *Ayeen Nameh*. An examination of what Ibni Qutaybah has quoted and what is available from other sources reveal that this book was a vast collection of the arts and the fields of knowledge of the Sassanid period, the structure and practices of the Sassanid court, and it encompassed all the information that the nobility, princes and governors were required to know in this period, or the type of knowledge that was considered appropriate for them, such as the rules of archery, horsemanship, polo, the art

---

[11] Refer to the introduction by Noeldke on the history of the Sassanid period, the *Tarikh Tabari*.

[12] Christensen, p. 57.

[13] *Al-Fehrest*, p. 118.

[14] *Al-Tanbih wal Eshraf*, p. 104.

of war, literary knowledge, the art of writing, statesmanship and politics, rules of behaviour in the company of the nobility, and the etiquette of the companionship of the shahs. The *Ayeen Nameh* comprised numerous books and papers, each of which was perceived an autonomous undertaking, and all of them constituted the big *Ayeen Nameh*. Mas'oodi has referred to another book, the *Gah Nameh*, which he considered to be part of the *Ayeen Nameh*, and which provided a detailed description of the internal structure of the Sassanid government and the hierarchy of positions within it, which numbered 600 according to Mas'oodi.[15] In the *Al-Fehrest*, Ibni Nadeem has mentioned two other books with the title of *Ayeen*: one is the *Ayeen Tirandazi* by Bahram Goor or Bahram Choobin, and the other is the *Ayeen Chogan Bazi*.[16] Although Ibni Nadeem has listed these two books separately, but in the light of what Ibni Qutaybah has narrated, it is clear that these two books were also a part of the big *Ayeen Nameh* collection, since, much information has been quoted from them on archery and polo in the *Oyoon-al-Akhbar*.

In the *Oyoon-al-Akhbar*, Ibni Qutaybah had given eleven quotations from the *Ayeen Nameh*. In one quote which is relatively longer than the others and covers almost three pages of the *Oyoon-al-Akhbar* (published by Dar al Ketab, Egypt), there are various instructions on the conduct of war, such as the selection of the battlefield and the alignment of armies, ambushing, raiding and other techniques of war that were known in those days.[17] Another quote gives a description of the items that armies could or could not carry to war, such as food, clothing and carpeting.[18] Two other quotes are dedicated to sports, one to archery and the other to polo and its rules, and both provide learning instructions.[19] There are two quotes on the laws of politics and government, one is on the exercise of justice and the qualifications of judges, and the other relates to the biography of the shahs and their practices in government.[20] Quotes

[15]  Ibid.
[16]  *Al-Fehrest*, p. 314.
[17]  *Oyoon-al-Akhbar*, vol. I, pp. 112-15.
[18]  Ibid., p. 116.
[19]  Ibid., pp. 8 and 133.
[20]  Ibid., p. 62.

on the codes of behaviour include information on the etiquette of eating,[21] the description of foods that women of the court, were not allowed to eat such as garlic, onion and other foods with unpleasant odour,[22] and bad practices that marred the beauty of form and attitude and prevented acceptance into the service of the shah.[23] Perhaps, there was a detailed discussion or a special paper in the *Ayeen Nameh* dedicated to the etiquette of eating. Discussing this subject in his book *Al Taj*, Jahiz says: 'Refraining from speaking while eating has many virtues which are contained in the codes of etiquette of the Iranians.'[24] Apart from this, there is some scattered information about Iranian beliefs on '*Zajr et Tayr*', good and bad fortune, etc., in the quotations.

To comprehend what type of book the *Ayeen Nameh* was from these quotations, it is important to include it among the books that were known as the books of *Adab* during the Islamic period. They usually provided a fair amount of information on each field of knowledge of the time, and the purpose of writing them was not to present extensive information on any particular discipline, but to provide diverse information on various aspects of life. This book which was translated by Ibni Mughaffa' into Arabic,[25] as confirmed by Inostranzev,[26] was a very important source for the study of the internal structure and functions of the Sassanid empire, and was extensively used by many historians of Islam.

---

[21] Ibid., vol. III, p. 221.

[22] Ibid., p. 278.

[23] Ibid., vol. IV, p. 59.

[24] *Al Taj*, p. 19.

[25] *Al-Fehrest*, p. 118. Some erroneously believe that this book was written by Ibni Mughaffa'. See the *Oyoon-al-Akhbar*, Dar-al-Kotob, Egypt, vol. 1, p. 8, fn., and the introduction of Ahmad Zaki Pasha in the *Ketab-al-Taj*, p. 19.

[26] Inostranzev, p. 66. For more information about this book refer to the article by the author titled 'The Books of *Ayeen Nameh*, and Parts Remaining of Them in Arabic Literature', *Derasat Adabyah*, vol. I, nos. 2 and 3, pp. 15-29, and to the book by the author *Translation and Transcription from Farsi in the First Islamic Centuries*, vol. I, The Books of *Taj* and *Ayeen*, Beirut, 1964, pp. 230-72.

**The *Taj Nameh***    In the *Al-Fehrest*, Ibni Nadeem has listed Iranian books and has mentioned in two places a book entitled the *Al Taj*: first, among the books that Ibni Mughaffa' translated into Arabic (p. 19), and second, among the books of history and tales of Iran (p. 305). The first reference is to '*Ketab al Taj fi Sirat Anooshiravan*', and the second to '*Ketab al Taj wa ma Tafa'alat bihi Molookehem*', and this difference in names has led a number of contemporary scholars to conclude that in the Sassanid period there were a number of books entitled the *Taj Nameh*.[27] Passages from the *Taj Nameh* are quoted in Arabic books, but none of them are related to Anooshiravan and his life, and this fact substantiates the above conclusion. However, according to a number of scholars, the phrase *Fi Sirat Anooshiravan* is superfluous and the *Taj Nameh* is one book.[28]

Portions of the *Taj Nameh* that have survived are found in the *Oyoon al Akhbar*. The first person who noted this fact and drew the attention of scholars to it was Baron Rosen. He published for the first time the portions that Ibni Qutaybah had transcribed from the *Taj Nameh* in the periodical *Melange Asiatique* (1880), after which researchers began to study and debate the Pahlavi *Taj Nameh*. These excerpts totalling eight in number are advice and *pand* as well as instructions on the practices of government, and conduct at the court in Sassanid Iran. Five of them are quotes from Khosrow Parviz, in the first two he gives his son Shirouyeh advice on the affairs of the army and government,[29] and the other three cover his instructions to his Secretariat, treasurer and chamberlain.[30] Of the remaining three, the first is attributed to one of the shahs and contains a description of the nature and gravity of the shah's responsibilities as compared to those of other people,[31] the second contains a *wazir's* comments

---

[27] Christensen, p. 58.

[28] This opinion was expressed by M. Gabrieli, quoted from Christensen, p. 58. The issue of the multiplicity of Sassanid *Taj Namehs* is covered in detail in *Translations and Transcriptions from Farsi*, pp. 18-52, and the pieces that have survived from four Sassanid *Taj Namehs* in vol. I of the book with clarifications, pp. 53-228.

[29] *Oyoon-al-Akhbar*, vol. I, pp. 11, 15.

[30] Ibid., pp. 45, 59, 84.

[31] Ibid., p. 5, also refer to '*Al-Aadab-al-Soltanyah*', p. 46.

on the virtues of consultation,[32] and the last is a speech by one of the *dabirs* of the shah.[33]

It may be deduced from these excerpts, that in addition to historical issues, the *Taj Nameh* contained other material on applied wisdom and teachings of ethics, such that, if Ibni Nadeem had not listed the *Taj Nameh* under history books, it would have been more appropriate to include it among works of ethics and literature.

Christensen has asserted that the detailed information provided in the *Al Taj fi Akhlaq al Molook* (attributed to Jahiz) concerning the complex and rigid protocol of the Sassanid court, is an adaptation from the *Gah Nameh* or the *Ayeen Nameh*.[34] Although it is not improbable that Jahiz had adapted some material from these two books, the similarity between the contents of the *Al Taj* and the *Taj Nameh* supports a different probability, i.e. the Pahlavi *Taj Nameh* was a significant source for Jahiz, and this probability is further reinforced if one takes into consideration Jahiz's title for his book.

The *Taj Nameh* was also translated by Ibni Mughaffa'. Apparently, the translation of this book enjoyed much fame in the Islamic world and was of great value for scholars and the learned. We can deduce this not only from the different material adapted from this book in Arabic literature, but also from the numerous works written in Arabic with this title. In the introduction to the *Al Taj fi Akhlaq al Molook*, researched and published by Ahmad Zaki Pasha, he has mentioned a number of such books with similar titles including the *Al Taj* by Abu Obaydah (died early third century of *Hijra*), and other books by Ibni Ravandi, Saabi, Ibni Fares and other scholars.[35]

---

[32] *Oyoon-al-Akhbar*, vol. I, p. 27.

[33] Ibid., p. 96.

[34] Christensen, p. 397.

[35] *Al Taj*, the Introduction of Ahmad Zaki Pasha, pp. 35-6. For additional reading on the Sassanid *Taj Namehs* and their Arabic translations, refer to the following: *Ketab-al-Taj* of Jahiz and its relation to the books of *Taj Nameh* in Sassanid Persian literature, *Derasat Adabyah*, vol. I, no. 1, Beirut, 1959, pp. 29-67, *Ketab-al-Taj fi Sirat Anooshiravan*, *Derasat Adabyah*, vol. III, no. 3, pp. 237-64, and vol. III, no. 4, pp. 345-78, Beirut, 1961; *Translations and Transcriptions from Farsi*, vol. I, Beirut, 1964, pp. 18-228.

**Two Historic Books**
**Described by Mas'oodi**
In his coverage of the history of Iran Mas'oodi has referred to two books which, according to him, were among the important Sassanid books. One of them Mas'oodi found in the house of a noble famiy of Estakhr in Fars province, which he has described in his book *Al-Tanbih wal Eshraf.* This book, according to Mas'oodi, not only provided the history of the Sassanid shahs, but also contained a painting of each shah with his biography below it. Since there is no other information about this book, it would be appropriate to provide a translation of what Mas'oodi has to say about it.

In the year 303 in the city of Estakhr in the land of Fars, I saw in the house of one of the Iranian noble families a voluminous book containing much information, and narratives about the justice and the wisdom of the Iranians, which I had not seen in any of their other books such as *Khoday Nameh* and *Ayeen Nameh* and *Gah Nameh*. In this book twenty-seven of the Sassanid shahs were painted, of whom twenty-five were men and two were women. These paintings showed the Sassanid shahs in the last days of their lives, whether old or young, with all the details of their decorations, Crown, features and face. Also written in this book was that they ruled the world for four hundred and thirty three years and one month and seven days, and their custom was that whenever one of their shahs died, they made a statue of him in his official attire and stored it in the treasury so that the particulars of the dead would not be hidden to the living. In that book the picture of each shah who had been to war was drawn standing, and that of a shah who administered the state was drawn sitting, and the biography of each, with the general and specific description of their personal characteristics or the significant events that had occurred in the country during their reign was included. It was mentioned in the history of the book that it had been prepared from what had been found in the treasuries of the shahs of Iran in the middle of *Jamadi Akhar* of the year 113 of the *Hijra*, and was translated from Persian to Arabic for Abdul Malek bin Marvan.

*Mas'oodi* goes on to describe the paintings of Ardeshir and Yazdegerd and praises the beauty of the decorations and the quality of the paper used.[36] As discussed earlier, there was a place called Hosn al Jass where numerous works were found and there were carvings in

---

[36] *Al-Tanbih wal Eshraf,* p. 106.

stone on the mountain of Shahpoor. Inostranzev has argued that the authors of this book probably found the material that they needed among the works in Hosn al Jass.[37]

Christensen has concluded on the basis of his studies that the drawing of the figures of the shahs was a common practice in the middle of the Sassanid period and, therefore, he has doubts about the authenticity of the paintings of the earlier Sassanid shahs in this book, but not about those of the later shahs, because their particulars match those that are found on stone carvings, silver and other objects that have survived from that period. He is convinced that these drawings were made in the days of the Sassanid shahs.[38]

According to Gutchmid, an orientalist, it is likely that this book is the same as the *Taj Nameh*. Based on this view, the wise sayings and also the *Wasaya* and *Ohood* which in the *Taj Nameh* is attributed to the Sassanid shahs, and are evident in Arabic books, were the same descriptions written under the painting of each of the shahs containing their words of wisdom.[39] Until more evidence comes to light, this view will remain only an assumption.

Another historic book that Mas'oodi has mentioned is the one referred to in the *Morooj-al-Zahab*. However, there are no references to this book in any other historic source, and even in the *Morooj-al-Zahab* its name has been distorted. To date, of Mas'oodi's is the only available reference to this book, it is worthwhile to reproduce a translation of his observations here. In his discussion of a strong castle between the land of Aalan and the mountain of Qafqaz, Mas'oodi says: 'What we wrote in this regard has been written in a book known as the Book of *Bankash*, which Ibni Mughaffa' has translated into Arabic.'[40] After a reference to Afrasyab and the wars between the Iranians and the Turks, he says: 'All this is described in a book called *Al Sakisaran*', and adds: 'Ibni Mughaffa' has translated this book from Persian to Arabic and it contains the tales of Esfandyar the son of Bastasf the son of Bahrasf, and the story of his slaying at the

---

[37] Inostranzev, p. 70.
[38] Christensen, p. 62.
[39] Ibid.
[40] *Morooj-al-Zahab*, vol. II, p. 44.

hand of Rostam, and also the story of the slaying of Rostam at the hand of Bahman the son of Esfandyar, as well as the amazing tales of ancient Iranians and the stories of the past and the biographies of their shahs.'[41] It cannot be ascertained what was the title of this book in Pahlavi and what was the title of its Arabic translation. Apparently, the two words—*Al Bankash* and *Al Sakisaran*—are distortions of the same word, however, there are indications that these two words are not the titles of two books, but rather one book. What confirms this is that the Arabic script of the second name (or *Al Sakisaran*) is not certain, and the French publishers of the *Morooj-al-Zahab*[42] have made a guess and have printed it as such. This name has appeared in different forms in different copies, and in one copy it has appeared as *Al Naskin*, which in the Arabic script seems similar to *Al Bankash*, and indicates that the Arabic script of the original word appeared to be similar to these two words, and had later appeared as two separate words due to distortions in transcription. The publishers of the *Morooj-al-Zahab* have no knowledge about the origin of this word.[43] A possibility would be to consider the origin of the word as *Al Sakeeyeen*, and its meaning related to the history of the Secs, which in Arabic has appeared as such. This does not seem too improbable, and a part of what Mas'oodi has quoted from that book supports it.

**Iranian Stories and Tales**    Tales refer to those books that cover the biography of one of the great men of history or one of the renowned commanders or heroes of the Sassanid or other periods preceding it. Numerous such tales that are available today or have been translated into Arabic reveal, that in Sassanid literature, epic and heroic stories and the biographies of past heroes were of great importance. Ibni Nadeem has described such books as historic books, and has termed them 'True Biographies'.

---

[41]  Ibid., p. 318.
[42]  Barbier de Meynard et Pavet de Courteill.
[43]  Refer to the *Morooj-al-Zahab*, vol. II, p. 247.

**The Tale of Bahram Choobin**     This book deals with one of the renowned personalities of the Sassanid period and presents a narrative of an important event of that era. Bahram Choobin was the son of Bahram Goshtasb of the great clan of Mehran, and one of the commanders of the Iranian army. He became famous during the reigns of Hormoz and his son Khosrow Parviz, and he commanded great respect and influence among his soldiers. After his victory in a battle with the Turks, Bahram dispatched the spoils from the war to Hormoz. Hormoz, who had been led to believe by his *wazir* Yazdan Goshasb, that Bahram had not sent him the entire booty, summarily dismissed Bahram from his command. Deeply angered by the shah's attitude, Bahram rose in revolt and his men supported him. At the same time, Vistahm and his brother Bandouyeh, who belonged to the great clan of Espahbodan, and whose sister was the wife of Hormoz and the mother of Khosrow Parviz, dethroned Hormoz and imprisoned him. Following the dethronement of Hormoz, Khosrow the Second (Khosrow Parviz) who was in Azarbaijan, returned to Tisphoon and crowned himself as shah (AD 590). Bahram, however, refused to obey the new shah and with his mighty army headed for the capital. Unable to confront him Khosrow fled and Bahram reached Tisphoon and crowned himself as shah, and minted coins in his own name. Following this, Khosrow pleaded to the Roman Emperor Manris for help, who agreed to help him conditionally. Khosrow returned to Iran and defeated Bahram at Ganzak in Azarbaijan. Bahram fled to Balkh and took refuge with the Turks, he remained there until he was killed at the instigation of Khosrow Parviz. This event was extraordinary on all counts. A commander of the army revolted against the shah and his men supported him, and then he went to battle against the shah and forced him to flee the country; he then entered the capital, with no resistance by any of the dignitaries of the state who could not imagine the monarchy except in the Sassanid dynasty, and crowned himself with manifestations of heroism. Because of the extraordinary nature of this event it was the subject of a beautiful tale that was well known in Sassanid literature. Although Bahram belonged to the clan of Mehran who considered themselves part of the Ashkanid dynasty, and Bahram had used this relationship to usurp the throne, his action was considered extraordinary and his story acquired legendary dimensions.

The story of Bahram Choobin was translated into Arabic by Jabla, the son of Salem. This story, which later appeared in Islamic books and the *Shah Nameh* of Ferdowsi, narrates the biography of Bahram and his heroism in eloquent prose. Among Arabic historians, Dinevari has covered the biography of Bahram in great detail because he relied more than others on Iranian stories, and it is likely that he relied on this story in what he has written.[44] After narrating the tale of Bahram, Mas'oodi says: 'Iranians have a book exclusively on the story of Bahram Choobin and his deeds when he was in Torkestan, such as saving the daughter of the Shah of Torkestan from a wild beast that they called *Sam'*, and which he had captured while on a stroll, as well as on his ancestry and his life.'[45]

It appears from some of the accounts in Arabic books that although Bahram Choobin was portrayed in the official records of the Sassanids as an outlaw and worthy of punishment, to the contrary, among the people and also in this story, he was considered a hero and a courageous commander. Jahiz has narrated a tale that undoubtedly has been taken from Pahlavi books. The tale goes as follows. One day one of the elephants of Khosrow Parviz broke loose in the field and headed towards Khosrow. The shah's party fled except for one man who confronted the elephant courageously and killed it with an ax. Khosrow lauded him and praised his courage, then asked him: whether he had seen a more courageous man. The man replied that he had and if the shah gave him *aman*, he would describe him. Khosrow gave him *aman*, and the man narrated a tale about the courage and gallantry of Bahram, whom Khosrow considered his enemy.[46] It goes without saying that the sources of these tales in Islamic books are different from the official records of the Sassanid court or *Khoday Nameh*, and it is likely that the source of all these is the same story.

[44] Refer to the *Al-Akhbar-al-Tewal*, pp. 82-104; Tabari, part one, pp. 992-1001.

[45] *Morooj-al-Zahab*, vol. I, p. 235, Egypt.

[46] *Al-Hayawan*, vol. VII, p. 53.

**The Tale of Shahrbaraz and Parviz** Another incident involving Khosrow Parviz and one of his commanders, has been recorded as a famous tale in Sassanid literature. Farkhan who held the title of Shahrvaraz was considered one of the greatest commanders and closest confidants of Khosrow and had proved his powers in the wars between Iran and the Romans; he conquered Palestine and Syria and besieged Constantinople. These victories were short-lived and the victorious Iranians army was compelled to retreat in the face of the forces of Heraclius. Khosrow was not only a selfish and proud shah, but also a self-serving and deceitful dictator, Farkhan became concerned about his vengeful attitude and joined hands with Caesar, or so Khosrow believed, or pretended to do so. What followed between him and Khosrow has been properly documented in history. These events and the biography of Shahrbaraz and the accounts of his battles and conquests were the subject of another tale that was famous in Pahlavi literature. This book is referred to as Shahrizad and Abrawiz in the *Al-Fehrest* (Flugel edition).[47] The word Shahrizad is a distortion of Shahrbaraz.[48] Choosing to ignore this issue Inostranzev has assumed the title to be authentic and has described this book as one of the Iranian legends, and believes that there was a relation between this and the legends of the *One Thousand and One Nights*.[49] This assumption is based on the similarity between Shahrizad and Shahrzad, the heroine of the *One Thousand and One Nights*. The fact that Ibni Nadeem has referred to this book in his index of Iranian books of history proves that it was not a book of stories and legends and had no relationship with the book *One Thousand and One Nights*, otherwise it would have been listed among legendary books such as the *Hezar Afsaneh* and the *Kalileh va Demeneh*.

The fact that this event is described as the narrative of Shahrbaraz and Parviz is not an exaggeration, as it was an important event of the Sassanid period and was worthy of becoming the subject of a narrative. The various details about this event presented in the form

---

[47] *Al-Fehrest*, Leipzig edn., pp. 1871-2.
[48] Refer to 'Correction of the Phrases of *Fehrest*', p. 31.
[49] Inostranzev, p. 67.

of stories in the *Shah Nameh* and other Islamic historic and literary books confirm the existence of such a narrative. The change of the name Shahrbaraz to Shahrizad in the *Al-Fehrest* is a distortion, the kind of which is repeatedly seen in Arabic books. As Persian words and phrases were unfamiliar to transcribers of Arabic books, many of these words have been distorted to such an extent that tracing their origins is a difficult task. Even well-known names were distorted, such that in the *Al-Fehrest*, the *Khoday Nameh* appears as the *Bakhtiar Nameh* and the *Ekhtiar Nameh*, the *Ayeen Nameh* has been changed to the *Ethnain Nameh*, and Bahram Choobin has appeared as Bahram Shoos, it is thus possible that the name Shahrbaraz became Shahrizad, especially since such distortions of this name have appeared in other Arabic books as well. In the *Tarikh Hamzeh*, this name appears as Shahrizad[50] in the *Tarikh Ibni Athir* as Shahriyar,[51] and in the *Tarikh Abul Feda* as Shariran. Ibni Nadeem who has referred to this book has not mentioned the name of the person who translated it into Arabic, but as most Iranian tales were translated by Jabala, the son of Salem, it is likely that he translated this book into Arabic.[52]

**The Tale of Rostam va Esfandiar**    This book narrates a famous Iranian tale that enjoyed much fame and significance in Arabic and Islamic literature. As mentioned earlier, in a book the title of which is unknown and Mas'oodi has also referred to it, the tale of Rostam was covered from beginning to end, and it is probable that the contents of these two books were related. The tale of Rostam and Esfandiar was also translated into Arabic by Jabala bin Salem. Although like other writings of that period, the original copy has been destroyed, its contents can be inferred from what has been written about it in Islamic histories, particularly the *Shah Nameh* of Ferdowsi.

**Other Books**    Ibni Nadeem has listed in his index four other books: the book of Karnameh in the Biography of Anooshiravan; the book of Anooshiravan, the book of Bahram and

---

[50]  *Tarikh Hamzah*, p. 54.
[51]  *Tarikh Ibni Athir*, vol. II, p. 347.
[52]  For further reading, refer to *Translation and Transcription*, pp. 132-7.

Narsi, and the book of Dara and Bot Zarrin. Apparently, the first book is the same as the *Karnameh Ardeshir*, and due to the carelessness of the transcribers the name of Anooshiravan has been mistakenly substituted for Ardeshir. This is because the Karnameh of Ardeshir was also famous in Arabic literature and Ibni Nadeem has referred to it in several places in his index.[53] There is no other information about these two books.

It should be borne in mind that Iranian tales are not confined to those mentioned in this index alone, because a study of Arabic literature and particularly the *Al-Fehrest* reveals that there were numerous Iranian tales other than the ones that have been listed, these were generally heroic epics translated into Arabic and popular in Islamic society. The Moslems were aware of these tales either through the *Khoday Nameh* or through another book that was translated into Arabic. Some tales have not been listed in Ibni Nadeem's index. Narrating the biography of Hormoz, the son of Shapoor, *Hamzah Esfahani* says, 'His mother was born Kurdish and a famous tale was written about her.'[54] It appears that Hamzeh had access to the tale or knew about it.

**Writing of History in Islam**     Before the advent of Islam there was nothing in the Arabic language that could be termed as history. What developed as history along with other fields of science and literature was seen after the emergence of Islam. In a listing of Islamic historians, Wustenfeld has enumerated 590 persons, the first died in the year 60 of the Hijra and the last was born in 1061 of the Hijra. Researchers hold diverse views on the emergence of the art of history writing in the Arabic language. Some of them like Margoliouth have asserted that this art emerged in response to the needs of Islamic society independently from previous works or any foreign influence, and its emergence and development followed a normal course.[55] Others like Nicholson have argued that

---

[53] *Al-Fehrest*, pp. 119-26.
[54] *Tarikh Hamzah Esfahani*, p. 43.
[55] Margoliouth, *Lecture on Arabic Historians*, pp. 12-13.

the concept and style of history writing entered Islam following the translation of the *Khoday Nameh.*[56]

What researchers mean by the art of history writing is the structured recording of important events in the context of their causality, or the biographies of individuals who have impacted these events. This is distinct from the oral narrations of events and biographies of true or imaginary personalities in the form of stories or legends, which has been a common practice in all nations even primitive and nomadic ones. Whether the translation of Iranian history books did or did not impact the emergence of the art of history writing in Islam, there is no doubt that these histories and tales greatly influenced the direction of thought and style of Islamic historic writing, because renowned historians in the Arabic language in the first centuries of Islam, most of whom were Iranians, relied heavily on Iranian tales and narratives, particularly for writing the history of the pre-Islamic period. It is for this reason that whatever they have written about the history of Iran and the nations affiliated to Iran is far more realistic and accurate than what they have written about other nations such as Greece and the Roman empire. This is clearly evident from a comparison between the histories of the state of Hirah that was a Sassanid satellite state and the state of Ghassanids on the borders of Syria which was a satellite state of the Roman empire.

The most comprehensive history book in Arabic is the *Tarikh Tabari*. Based on Noeldke's scholarly research on this book and in particular the part that deals with the Sassanid period, the main source that Tabari has used for that section of his book was the *Tarikh Khoday Nameh*. Tabari was not the only one who used the *Khoday Nameh* as a source. All Islamic historians who wrote on the history of Iran in those periods depended on this book. The

---

[56] P. Nicholson, *A Literary History of the Arabs*, p. 348. It must be noted that the first book of this type was written in the Islamic period, and is still available is Ibni Hesham's *Al-Sirah* on the life of the Prophet. It is based on two books by Ibni Eshagh who lived in the first Abbasid period and died in 151 or 152 H, and that *Khoday Nameh* had been translated into Arabic prior to that date; and as quoted from Mas'oodi, the illustrated Sassanid history that he saw in Estakhr, and according to the introduction of that book, was translated into Arabic in 113 H.

discrepancies between the various accounts of the history of Iran in Islamic histories are due to the variations in the different translations of the *Khoday Nameh*. According to Noeldke, Tabari's advantage is that he has presented all the narratives in the order that he found them; whenever there are two different accounts of the same issue the *Tarikh Tabari*, one of them matches the account given by Ibni Batrigh and Ibni Qutaybah and the other matches the account given by Ya'ghoobi and often Ferdowsi. The *Khoday Nameh*, however, was not the only source that was used by Islamic historians, rather all the books of history and tales that were translated from Pahlavi into Arabic were available to and were used by them.

One history book in Arabic that was written prior to the *Tarikh Tabari* is the *Akhbar Tewal* of Dinevari. This book deals with Iranian history, and makes references to Arab and Islamic history only to the extent that was necessary to enhance understanding of Iranian history. Abu Hanifah was from Dinevar and his ancestors till his grandfather Vandad's generation had remained Zoroastrian; he was considered among the great scholars of Islam. According to Abu Hayyan, he was one of the rare personalities who had both the wisdom of philosophers and the eloquence of expression of the Arabs. One characteristic of the *Akhbar Tewal* is that in addition to historical events, it also provides an account of Pahlavi tales or legends. Based on his research on Dinevari, Noeldke has argued that he had access to many Iranian tales which he included in his book with some modifications. This explains why there are references to a number of works that cannot be found in other sources, such as narratives from the translation of the Pahlavi *Sendbad Nameh*.[57]

The book containing the drawings of the Sassanid shahs, which Mas'oodi had seen in Estakhr in Fars, was one of the sources used by Islamic historians. Mas'oodi referred to it in the seventh volume of the *Morooj-al-Zahab*. It was extensively used by Hamzeh Esfahani who not only provided the biographies of the shahs and their deeds, but also described the drawing of each shah in such detail that one gets the impression that he was in possession of that book. If one

---

[57] For example, see the *Al-Akhbar-al-Tewal*, pp. 45ff. for additional reading, see Kratchovsky's introduction to it.

accepts the view of Gouchmand, the wise words of advice that have
been quoted from the shahs of Iran in Arabic literary sources were
the same as those below the drawing of each shahs in that book.

Whatever Islamic histories say about the internal structure of the
Sassanid government and the codes of conduct at the court has been
deduced from books such as the *Ayeen Nameh* and the *Taj Nameh*.
The book of *Gah Nameh* that, according to Mas'oodi, contained the
official titles and positions of the Sassanid government, was another
valuable source available to Islamic historians. The *Pand Namehs,* the
*Andarz Namehs* and Pahlavi literary and ethical books in general had
an impact on Islamic histories.

Although Islamic historians have by and large not mentioned the
sources of all the material that they have used in their writings, they
have occasionally referred to their Iranian sources. Mas'oodi has not
only mentioned the Iranian narratives and ancient Iranian books
that he used, but has also described the historical sources that he
discovered in Fars and Kerman.[58] As previously discussed, he has
even described a number of them at the beginning of his account on
the history of Iran, Birooni says: 'I write here what Iranian scholars
and Zoroastrian *Hirbadan* and *Moobadan* and those whose sayings
are reliable are all in agreement upon'.[59] Ibni Qutaybah has referred
to his sources, particularly in the *Oyoon-al-Akhbar*, and cases has also
named them.[60] Islamic historians not only referred to Iranian works
and drew upon them, but they also viewed them with respect, trust
and preferred them to other narrations. Mas'oodi says:

About the duration of the Ashkanid dynasty, there are also other narratives,
but what we have said we have taken from Iranian scholars, because Iranians
scrutinize details about the history of their ancestors that others do not.
They have faith in what we have narrated, both in words and in deeds, but
others are content with words alone but do not put them into practice.[61]

---

[58] *Morooj-al-Zahab*, vol. I, pp. 192-3, 203.

[59] *Al-Akhbar-al-Baghyah*, p. 100.

[60] Refer in particular to part one of this book.

[61] *Morooj-al-Zahab*, corrections by Charles Pella, Beirut, 1966, vol. I,
p. 277.

# SIX

# Iranian Stories and Fables in Arabic Literature

**Stories and Fables in Sassanid Literature** One area in which numerous books were translated from Pahlavi into Arabic and had a great impact on Arabic literature was stories and fables. These books, like other books, were translated in the first centuries of Islam. As historical evidence shows, the spread of Iranian stories and fables among the Arabs preceded Islam, and apparently the translation of Iranian stories and fables into Arabic in the Islamic era also preceded other types of books. The reason for this is that stories and fables are simpler to translate and are also more comprehensible for the common people.

The historical links between Iranians and Arabs did not begin with the expansion of Islam, but go back to earlier times. Before the advent of Islam, a large part of the territories under the Iranian empire consisted of Arab settled territories. In order to prevent attacks by, or the migration of Arab nomads into Iraq, the Sassanid shahs had created a satellite Arab state in the land of Hirah, which was located beyond the Euphrates in the south-western parts of modern Iraq, and they had entrusted its government to the clan of Al Munzer.

During the reign of Anooshiravan, Yemen also came under the rule of Iran. The story is that during the rule of Zu Nawas in Yemen, the Ethiopians attacked Yemen and conquered it. Zu Nawas, was killed and for seventy years Yemen remained under the rule of the Ethiopians particularly four Ethiopians—Aryat, Abraha, Yaksoom and Masrooq the sons of Abraha. During the reign of Khosrow Anooshiravan, Saif ibni Zi Yazn of the dynasty of Yemeni kings came to the court of Khosrow and appealed for help to oust the Ethiopians. The shah dispatched one of his commanders with an army to Yemen and ousted the Ethiopians and that territory came under his protection.

The Arabs of Hijaz had trade relations with Iran before Islam and sometimes their caravans travelled to Iran. According to a tale, Nawfal and Mottaleb, two nobles of Quraish, concluded an agreement with the Sassanids on the basis of which the shah of Iran permitted the caravans of Hijaz to travel within the territories of Iran. It has in the year AD 606 or a little before that, Abu Sufyan arrived in Tisphoon, the capital of Iran, with a group of the merchants of Quraish and was given audience by the Sassanid shah. At the time when the Prophet was spreading the teachings of Islam in the Arab peninsula and Islam was going through its initial phases, the armies of Khosrow Parviz had penetrated into the territories of the eastern Roman empire and had captured Syria, Palestine and a part of Asia Minor. As a result long before the advent of Islam the Arabs had became acquainted with Iran and Iranian works, and since stories and fables were simpler than other intellectual works and were better suited to Arab tastes, they spread among the Arabs sooner than other literary works. According to Ibni Eshaqh, Nazr bin al Hareth was opposed to the Prophet and when he saw that the Prophet gathered the people around him and preached to them, he called on the people to come and listen to better and interesting tales. He would narrate to the people stories of the shahs of Iran and of Rostam and Esfandiar and other such stories.[1] Nazr bin Hareth had heard these stories in Hirah. Hirah was an important factor in acquainting the Arabs with Iranian literary works; and it not only had a tremendous impact on the literature of the Arab Jahili period, but it also gave birth to many famous Arab legends, such as those of *Juzaima al Abrash wal Zabba'a,* The Castle of *Khovarnagh, Sadir* and *Senemmar* the mason.

In general, two groups of tales and stories can be distinguished in the literature of the Sassanid period. One covers stories about historical personalities or those who were considered as such, and the other includes stories that had no historical basis and were told only for recreational purposes and at times for their moral value. The first group is labelled *dastan,* or narratives, and as these pertain to historical personalities, they have been included under historical

[1]   Ibni Eshaqh, *Ketab al Sirah,* pp. 191-235.

books. The second group that has no historical basis is defined as stories and tales.

With few exceptions, the fables of the Sassanid period were translated from an Indian language and thus represented a character other than the Iranian character, while Iranian stories, which were generally epics, had their roots in an Iranian mentality and environment. Indian fables became popular in Iran during the reign of Khosrow Anooshiravan and, as a result, the influence of Indian thinking was increasingly felt in Iran. Borzooyeh and his companions travelled to India to secure medical and perhaps other books. One of the books that Borzooyeh brought back from India and which is available even today in its Iranian version is the *Kalileh va Demneh*. A perusal of Borzooyeh's introduction to this book as well as his conclusions on religion and other matters of life, and their comparison with the basic Zoroastrian and Iranian teachings, reveals the extent to which Indian thinking and neo-Platonic philosophy, which was of great importance at that time, had infiltrated into Iran and had overshadowed Zoroastrian teachings. In his introduction, after contemplating on the differences between religions and sects, and the hesitation of Salek to select one of them, Borzooyeh's conclusion approximates to a position of withdrawal and isolationism. It may be added that this kind of thinking was new to Iran in those days. According to Christensen, such thinking was the result of Indian and neo-Platonic teachings, because Zoroastrian religion that was based on hard work and production, considered withdrawal and isolation from the world as a sin. The same discrepancy between Borzooyeh's thoughts and the basic teachings of Zoroastrianism can be seen with slight variation between the fables of Indian origin and Iranian stories.

Iranian stories, as mentioned earlier, focused on the biographies of heroes who had excelled in religious or national wars. Therefore, these stories were more in the form of epics. Such stories were the creation of lively and vibrant minds and the product of a vibrant and exciting environment, which was in complete contradiction to the spirit of contentment and submission which characterized Indian fables. Prior to the spread of Indian thinking and neo-Platonic philosophy in Iran, these heroic stories constituted the main body of Iranian stories and tales. After this period, although there is no evidence of a decline in the popularity of such stories, the positive popular response to Indian thinking and neo-Platonic philosophy ensured that Indian fables paralleled Iranian stories and found a place in Pahlavi literature.

**The Emergence of Storytelling in Arabic Literature**    Stories and fables are considered among the oldest manifestations of literary thought of peoples throughout the world, as man has engaged in creating fables from ancient times. The emergence of the art of writing long and complex fables in a structured manner calls for the development of the literary capacities of a people beyond the simple and primitive stage. For this reason, the art of writing stories and fables in Arabic literature began after the advent of Islam. The Arabs, like all other peoples, had their own stories and fables which they had narrated since ancient times. Scholars who have done research on this issue have argued that the Arabs, because of the dictates of their simple and nomadic lifestyle, were not capable of developing complex and substantive fables. Further, due to their limited imagination they borrowed the themes of their fables from other peoples, such as Iranians and Indians. Therefore, the art of storytelling in Arab literature is viewed as a borrowed art.[2]

The emergence of storytelling and the writing of fables in Arabic literature, like most other areas of Arab culture, passed through two main stages: first was the stage of translation and copying, and the second stage was of writing and composition. In the first and second centuries of Islam, when many literary works were translated into Arabic, fables and stories were also translated. These books were well received in Arab society, and they laid the ground for the emergence of the art of writing of fables in Arabic literature. It was not long before that Islamic writers, in both Iraq and Egypt, composed fables on the lines of those that had been translated.

---

[2] Refer to the introduction of Oestrup's articles on 'The Thousand and One Nights', in *Islamic Encyclopaedia*.

The *Al-Fehrest* as well as other writings in this area in Arabic literature, reveal that most books of fables or stories that were translated into Arabic were in Pahlavi. These books contained both Iranian stories and Indian stories that had been earlier translated into Pahlavi. This explains why Iranian stories have been the main source for Arab stories. At the beginning of the chapter in which Ibni Nadeem, had listed the books of fables, he writes,

The first people who wrote fables and recorded them in specific books, and kept them in their archives, and narrated some of them through the tongues of animals, were the ancient Iranians. After them, the Ashkanids, who were the third generation of Iranian shahs accelerated their development, and in the period of the Sassanid shahs, it was further expanded, until the Arabs translated them to Arabic, and refined those fables, and developed others in their meaning.[3]

For Ibni Nadeem, this clarifies the views of the Arabs and their contemporaries on Iranian and Arab stories. In their view, the Iranians were the first people to produce storybooks. This is because when the Arabs began to write stories, they only had access to Iranian books or Pahlavi translations obtained through the Iranians. Therefore, they did not venture in their stories beyond the scope of the Iranian stories that had inspired them. Ibni Nadeem has described the efforts of Arab writers as the refinement of Iranian fables. This is as accurate assessment as the stories in Arabic were more refined, better structured and more suited to the new environment than the older fables. A number of books mentioned by Ibni Nadeem which were translated from Persian into Arabic in the first periods of Islam will be discussed in the following:

**The *Hezar Afsan*** The *Hezar Afsan* (A Thousand Fables) was the source for the first book of stories that later became known as *The Thousand and One Nights* in both Arabic and Persian. The first historical reference in which this book has been mentioned as *Thousand and One Nights* is Mas'oodi's *Morooj-al-Zahab*. In his discussion of *Eram Zatul Emad* and the story related to it, Mas'oodi says:

[3] *Al-Fehrest*, p. 304.

This tale is also of the type of books that have been translated from Persian or Hindi or Greek,[4] such as the book *Hezar Afsan*, the Arabic translation of which is *Alf Khorafa* (A Thousand Fables), and which people today call *Alf Layla wa Layla* (The Thousand and One Nights), and its subject is the story of a shah and his *wazir* and the daughter of the *wazir* and her maid, Shahrzad and Dinarzad.[5]

After a discussion of the practice of writing of legends and its history, Ibni Khaldoon has also covered this topic. He says: 'The first book on this topic that was written was the book *Hezar Afsan* which means in Arabic *Alf Khorafa*.' According to Ibni Nadeem, this book was written for 1,000 nights and contained less than 200 fables. It can be safely asserted that the Pahlavi book *Hezar Afsan*, which was translated into Arabic in the first or second century of Islam, was the same book that in the third and fourth centuries was known as *The Thousand and One Nights*. To what extent are the original tales of the *Hezar Afsan* related to the tales of *The Thousand and One Nights*, which has become famous all over the world, is a question that remains worthy of study and reflection. There are diverse and contradictory views on the sources of the tales of *The Thousand and One Nights* and it is difficult to reach any conclusion.

Silvester de Sassy was commented on *The Thousand and One Nights*. In a number of essays published in the *Journal des Savants*[6] and other literary periodicals, he has ignored the writings of Mas'oodi and Ibni Nadeem, and has described *The Thousand and One Nights* as a completely Arab undertaking. But this view was rejected by a number of scholars who examined the issue and concluded that the source of *The Thousand and One Nights* was the Pahlavi *Hezar Afsan*. This group included German scholar von Humer, who stated his views in a paper published in a German periodical in 1819, and in another paper that appeared in the *Journal Asiatique* in 1823.[7] These two scholars were followed by others who produced similar papers in support of one or the other viewpoint.

---

[4] In a number of copies, it is written Hindi rather than Pahlavi. Refer to *Morooj-al-Zahab*, vol. IV, p. 463, fn.

[5] *Morooj-al-Zahab*, vol. IV, p. 90.

[6] *Journal des Savants*, 1817.

[7] *Journal Asiatique*, 1823.

At the end of this period, which may be described as the first phase in the debate on this book, another viewpoint was expressed which gave the debate a more realistic thrust and facilitated further research on the issue. This viewpoint was first expressed by De Goege, who held that *The Thousand and One Nights* was not a single work written by one author, but contained several groups of stories and fables which differed from each other in terms of their sources and times of writing and over the course of time they were compiled into a single book. De Goege has divided the fables of this book into three groups: first, the ancient fables of Iran which constituted the basis for the book and which were drawn from the Pahlavi *Hezar Afsan*; second, the fables that were added in Baghdad in the Islamic period; and third, the fables that were later added in Egypt.[8] This view was accepted by scholars and prominent orientalists, particularly Muller, Noeldke and Oestrup who based their further studies on it. Noeldke made an extensive study of the tales that were added to the book in Egypt, and Oestrup further developed this view in a study that was published in the *Islamic Encyclopedia*.

Based on the similarities between the original fables of *The Thousand and One Nights* and some of the Sanskrit fables, Couskan has argued that the origin of the *Hezar Afsan* was the ancient Indian fables which were translated into Pahlavi by the Iranians. Such a view based on similarities, with no historical support, is difficult to accept particularly because no historical source that has mentioned the *Hezar Afsan* or *The Thousand and One Nights* contains any reference to this possibility. This is significant in view of the fact that in the case of similar books which were brought to Iran from India, this issue has not been overlooked in that or similar sources. The similarities between some of the fables of the *Hezar Afsan* and Sanskrit fables can be attributed to the general similarities that exist between the ancient Iranian and Indian cultures which have originated from the same source.

Keeping in mind the views expressed by various scholars, it can be said that when the *Hezar Afsan* was translated into Arabic, it was read by Moslems and they gradually added to it stories and fables

---

[8] Refer to his article on the subject in the *Encyclopaedia Britannica*, 11th edn.

of a similar genre because addition to and deletions from such books, which were neither religious nor scientific, but merely for entertainment purposes, could be done easily and without raising any controversy. At the same time the essence of the ancient fables was modified to adapt to the changing environment. Thus, on the one hand, the new additions overshadowed the original fables, and on the other hand, most of the original fables changed in form and content, making it difficult to identify the original Iranian fables in *The Thousand and One Nights.*

**The *Kalileh va Demneh*** The introduction to the *Kalileh va Demneh* mentions that it was brought from India to Iran during the reign of Anooshiravan and Bouzar-jomehr translated it into Pahlavi, Ibni Mughaffa' translated this Pahlavi version into Arabic in the Islamic era. This has been substantiated by research which has provided more details about it. Based on this research, the book that is known today as the *Kalileh va Demneh* was originally translated from an Indian book, the *Panchatantra,* after it was translated into Pahlavi, some modifications were made in the book and a number of chapters were added to it. The *Kalileh va Demneh* met the same fate in Iran as the *Hezar Afsan* after it was translated into Arabic. In other words, after translation from the original and the addition of new material, both these books varied markedly from the original, with the distinction that this difference was less pronounced in the *Kalileh va Demneh* and more in the *Hezar Afsan.* In the *Kalileh va Demneh,* it is easy to distinguish the parts that were added to it in Iran, but in *The Thousand and One Nights* it is difficult and perhaps even impossible.

Silvester de Sassi has concluded on the basis of his research that out of the eighteen chapters of the *Kalileh va Demneh,* two were added in the Islamic period after translation into Arabic, and six were added in the Sassanid period following its translation into Pahlavi, and only ten chapters are from the original *Panchatantra.* The two chapters added in the Islamic period are the first chapter by Ali bin Shah Farsi and the third chapter by Abdullah bin Mughaffa', and the chapters added in the Sassanid period are the fourth, and from the fourteenth to the eighteenth. In his introduction to the book, de

Sassi has noted that in a number of manuscripts the last four chapters were attributed to Iranians during the period of Anooshiravan, but in a manuscript found in Berlin, these four chapters were attributed to Bouzarjomehr Bakhtagan. de Sassi was the first scholar to publish the Arabic translation of the book in Paris in 1816, and included the conclusions of his research in the introduction in French. In his opinion, the chapters translated by Borzouyeh from the *Panchatantra* were not exact translations, rather Borzouyeh borrowed the basic materials, stories and fables from the Indian book, and then modified and reoriented them according to his taste and style of expression, to suit the Zoroastrian environment of Iran, and restructured them into their present form. According to de Sassi, Borzouyeh omitted the portions that did not conform to the Zoroastrian religion or beliefs, and only translated the wise sayings and moral advice. Based on the contents of its introduction, de Sassi has argued that the *Kalileh va Demneh* in its present form is not an exact translation of the original work. Rather it is an amalgam of Indian and Iranian elements: a part of which was added before the advent of Islam, and a part after Islam; from the part that was translated from Hindi, only the main topics and the essence of the fables were adapted from the *Panchatantra*; on the whole, the structure of the book and the rewriting of its stories was the work of Borzouyeh, a purely Iranian exercise.[9]

In his coverage of the writing style of Ibni Mughaffa', Noeldke has argued that the chapter 'The Hermit and the Guest' was probably added by him while translating the *Kalileh va Demneh*, since it seems to have been written by a Moslem. Moreover, he has alleged that the section on the issue of religions in the introduction by Borzouyeh expresses the view of Ibni Mughaffa' himself. Christensen, however, has no doubts about attributing the entire introduction of the book to Borzouyeh, and has viewed it as an example of the intellectual confusion of the Sassanid period and the result of the impact of Greek philosophy, Christian, agnostic, Manavid and Mazdaki thinking on the Zoroastrian religion.[10] This may explain the different views of the

---

[9] See de Sassi's introduction to the Arabic edition of the *Kalileh va Demneh*, Paris, 1816.
[10] Christensen, p. 426.

earlier scholars on the origin of the *Kalileh va Demneh*, to which Ibni Nadeem has also referred. According to Ibni Nadeem, some scholars were of the view that this book, on the basis of its introduction, was written by Indians, while others believed that it was originally compiled by the Ashkanid shahs and Indians borrowed it from them, yet others believed that it was written by Iranians and was brought to India from Iran; some scholars were convinced that its author was Bozorgmehr Hakeem.[11]

The Pahlavi translation of the *Kalileh va Demneh* was well read in Sassanid Iran, and it enjoyed immense importance. Christensen has asserted that the reason for the widespread acceptability of this book among Iranians was the fact that its ethical teachings approximated to the ethical material contained in Pahlavi books which were easily available at that time. The narrative quoted by Dinevari and Ferdowsi, clearly reveals the significance of this book in the Sassanid period. According to Dinevari, when Khosrow rose against his father Hormoz and imprisoned him, Bahram Choobin, a renowned commander of *Hormoz,* rebelled against him, and was planning to wage a war against him. When Khosrow learnt of this, he dispatched one of his confidants to infiltrate the camp of Bahram and discover his intents and plans. Subsequently that man left for Hamedan and stayed in the camp of Bahram for a while. Upon his return, he narrated many stories about Bahram, including one when Bahram entered a house and asked for the *Kalileh va Demneh*, he spent the whole day reading the book. When Khosrow heard this, he turned to his uncles Bandouyeh and Bastam and said:

At no time was I as concerned about *Bahram* as I am now that I heard he persistently reads *Kalileh va Demneh*; because this book, with its contents of wisdom and foresightedness, gives one a view more sound than his own, and caution and determination greater than his own.[12]

In the Sassanid period, apart from Indian fables, there was an interest in Greek stories and many of them were translated into Pahlavi. The story of Alexander, which is narrated in the *Shah Nameh*

---

[11]   *Al-Fehrest*, p. 305.
[12]   *Al-Akhbar-al-Tewal*, p. 98.

of Ferdowsi and other Islamic histories, is one such Greek story which Islamic authors borrowed from the Pahlavi *Khoday Nameh*. Based on the study by Noeldke, the story of Alexander, as narrated in the *Khoday Nameh*, was adopted from a Greek story that was a blend of fact and fiction.

**The *Mazdak Nameh***     Mazdak claimed prophethood in the days of Qobad the First, and a group of people embraced his religion. As his religion did not conform to the institutions of the Sassanid empire, he was killed during the reign of Khosrow Anooshiravan and his followers were severely punished. The *Mazdak Nameh* was not a biography of this man, as the available information does not support this possibility. From the account given in the *Tarikh Tabari* of the trial of Afsheen, it appears that the *Mazdak Nameh* was a book of literature and dealt with ethical issues.

Afsheen was a prominent military commander of the Abbasid period who was envied by many, including the Caliph, for his ability and authority. The Caliph was waiting for a pretext to kill him and he eventually captured, tried and killed him. One of the charges against him was that, a book had been found in his house that was decorated with gold and gems, and contained blasphemous material. Responding to this accusation he said that the book was an Iranian book that he inherited from his ancestors, and he saw no need to remove its embellishment. He added that if the book contained blasphemous material, it also contained material on Iranian literature and culture, and he had benefited from such material and had ignored its blasphemous contents. Like the *Kalileh va Demneh* and the *Mazdak Nameh*, this book could be found even in the houses of judges and no one had any objections to that.[13]

In an account that was quoted earlier from Jahiz, the *Mazdak Nameh* was grouped with the *Kalileh va Demneh* and other literary and ethical books, which leads to the assumption that although the *Mazdak Nameh* was written in the form of stories and fables, it contained literary and ethical material and therefore was popular among Islamic scholars and *dabirs*. It was also translated into Arabic

---

[13] For more details on this trial, see Tabari, part two, pp. 1307-11.

by Ibni Mughaffa', and Aban bin Abdol Hamid Laheghi rendered it inverse.

The *Mazdak Nameh* has been referred to in the *Tarikh Hamzeh Esfahani* and the *Nehayat ul Erab*. According to Christensen,

In order to know all the contents of this book, we must combine what has been quoted in the *Syasat Nameh* of *Nezam ul Molk* with the contents of a *Parsi* tale. *Tha'alebi* and *Ferdowsi* and *Birooni* and the author of *Fares Nameh* and the author of *Mojmal ul Tawarikh*, have all relied on this book in what they have written.[14]

**Other Fables**    Ibni Nadeem has listed a number of other Iranian stories and fables that were translated into Arabic, but there is no trace of these works and most of the words and names in their titles are distorted. This makes the taste of deducing their correct titles difficult and, therefore the readers are referred to Ibni Nadeem's book.[15] A discussion of the distortions of the titles is in order. For example, one of these fables was listed as the *Moshk Zamaneh* of Shah Zaman by Ibni Nadeem. According to Inostranzev, this fable was originally called the *Moshk Daneh* and *Moobadan*, or *Sheykh al Moobadan*, and its contents were based on a famous fable in Pahlavi literature and its characters were *Moobadan* and a maid named Moshk Daneh. Inostranzev has offered this correction on the basis of what has been mentioned about it in the *Al-Mahasen wal Addad*, where the name of the maid girl was correctly mentioned.[16] The distortions in other nouns are of a similar nature.

The books that Ibni Nadeem has listed in the *Al-Fehrest* under the heading of Books of the kings of Babel (Babylon) and *Molook al Tawa'ef*, which are seven in number, should also be added to this list. Often Iranian books which, either on the basis of their subject or time of writing, can be traced to the ancient periods of Iran, are attributed in Arabic sources to the kings of Babel, and the ancient shahs of Iran are also referred to as such. For example, in this list Ibni Nadeem has described Ardeshir as the king of Babel, and he has

---

[14] Christensen, p. 63.
[15] *Al-Fehrest*, p. 305.
[16] Inostranzev, p. 50.

included Ardeshir's book in this list. This is because after the collapse of the state of Babel at the hands of Koorosh the Achaemenian, this region continued to be called Babel within and as part of the Iranian empire; in the Sassanid period, this region was the southern province of Soorestan (Iraq) and was known as Babel. Therefore, in Islamic writings Babel does not always refer to the state of Babel. Also, the Ashkanid shahs are referred to as *Molook al Tawa'ef* in Islamic histories, and as can be deduced from the writing of Hamzeh Esfahani, in the first centuries of Islam, many books and essays attributed to them were common among the Moslems. According to Hamzeh Esfahani, there were many such books.[17]

Another book of fables that was translated from Sanskrit into Pahlavi in the Sassanid period and after Islam was translated into Arabic, and Aban bin Abdul Hamid Laheghi has rendered it in verse was the *Bloohar va Bouzasf*. This book was also translated into Greek and was known as *Barlam* and *Yavasef*; a number of stories of medieval Europe contain traces of this fable. Ibni Nadeem's list of such books does not mention this book, but in the listing of books that Aban had rendered in verse the *Bloohar va Bardanyeh*, has been mentioned which one can assume was the same book, with the word *Boozasf* distorted as *Bardanyeh*.

**Iranian Stories in Arabic Literature** The translation of Iranian and Indian tales and fables rapidly spread in Islamic society. The Arabs' interest in listening to stories, particularly heroic stories, prepared the ground for the rapid spread of such writings. Following the translation of such books, Arabic-speaking writers who were often Iranians, refined them and used them as a model to write other stories. Thus, there appeared in Arabic books containing stories and fables, and a new art developed in Arabic literature, i.e. the art of storytelling.

In the earlier periods of Islam, it was a tradition that when an army went to war, a person would be in-charge of narrating stories to strengthen the morale of the soldiers. The first person who transformed this function into a profession and assigned it to a

[17] *Tarikh Hamzah*, p. 36.

particular person was Mu'awiah. The task of these storytellers was initially to narrate the deeds of martyrs and the great rewards promised to them in Islam, later, however, they did not confine themselves to such accounts and narrated heroic and legendary stories, and over time further enlarged the scope of their narratives. The first person in such a position was Sulayman bin Antar Tahbibi, who in the year 83 of the Hijra was appointed to this task in Egypt. In his coverage of the events of the year 77 and the description of one of the wars, Ibni Athir says that shortly before each battle, Etab bin Wargha would meet his soldiers and narrate epic stories. He would enquire if any of the soldiers could tell stories. When he got no response, he would ask whether anyone could recite the poem of Antarah. Antarah was an Arab poet whose poems were heroic and legendary.

Storytelling flourished in the days of the Abbasids in Baghdad and the Fatemids in Egypt. Although the Egyptians were not innovative enough to produce new material and merely reproduced the fables of Baghdad, there is a clear distinction between the fables of Iraq and those of Egypt in terms of style. In Iraq, the writing of fables was more the work of *dabirs* and men of literature, and therefore, they expressed the higher human emotions and the positive aspects of life, these fables were beautiful, absorbing, balanced and short. The fables of Egypt were often drawn from books or narratives by one person or another, and were compiled by storytellers, and were lengthy with superfluous and unnecessary material.

Among the stories and fables that were translated into Arabic, the *Hezar Afsan* and the *Kalileh va Demneh* were the most widely read, and in their writings Islamic writers relied heavily on these two books more than any other. Among those who wrote on the model of the Hezar Afsan was Abu Abdullah Mohammad bin Abdoos Jahshyari, the author of the *Al-Wuzara' wal Kottab*. Ibni Nadeem writes:

He wrote a book containing a collection of one thousand of the legends of the Arabs, the Iranians and the Greeks, and divided it into a number of separate sections. He wrote this book by bringing together the storytellers and learning from each his best stories, and by selecting from each of the books written in this field any story or tale that appeared interesting and pleasant. In this way he collected four hundred and eighty stories for four hundred and eighty nights, with each story of more or less fifty pages; but before he could complete the task and prepare one thousand stories, death took him away.[18]

The translation of the *Kalileh va Demneh* had a greater impact on Arabic literature. According to Mas'oodi, this book was translated in the days of Mansoor by Ibni Mughaffa'[19] and became a prominent piece of Arabic prose. Public interest in it was rendered several times in verse, and this translation of Ibni Mughaffa' is still considered one of the best literary and ethical works in Arabic. The books of ethics and applied wisdom, whether in the Sassanid or Islamic periods, were of great interest and importance among the class of *dabirs*. Since the *Kalileh va Demneh* was also one such book, it was of great interest to the people in both periods. The Barmakis, who were among the scholarly *wazirs* of the Abbasid period, evinced such a profound interest in the book, that they exhorted Aban bin Abdul Hamid Laheghi to render it in verse so as to make it easier to learn by heart. Aban accomplished the task and received 10,000 *dinars* from Yahya and 5,000 *dinars* from his son Fazl as reward. Ja'far, another son of Yahya, agreed to have him as his *rawiah* in appreciation of his efforts.[20] Besides the *Kalileh va Demneh*, Aban rendered a number of other Iranian works into verse in Arabic, among which were the *Bloohar va Bouzasf,* the *Rasa'el* and the *Elmul Hend.* Ibni Nadeem says that, among his contemporaries, he specialized in transforming books of prose into verse.[21]

The translation of Iranian stories and fables and their rendition in verse by Aban opened a new field for Arabic poetry. Arabic poetry before Aban's time and for a long period after the emergence of Islam was confined to a few areas such as *Ghazal* (romantic), *Wasf* (descriptive), *Madh* (praise), *Hija'* (satire) and *Retha'* (mourning), but Aban used poetry in a different field introduced new types of poetry which have been termed as epic poetry and educational poetry. In

[18] *Al-Fehrest*, p. 304.

[19] *Morooj-al-Zahab*, vol. IV, p. 241.

[20] Besides Aban bin Abdul Hamid, those who rendered this book in verse were Fazl bin Nowbakht, Ali bin Davood, Beshr bin Mo'tamed, Ibni Habaryah, and Ibni Mamati al Masri.

[21] *Al-Fehrest*, p. 119.

epic poetry, the poet composes a story or a historic event or a legend in verse, and in educational poetry, the poet composes a scientific or ethical subject with instructional purposes in verse. These types of poetry were not known in this form in Arabic literature before Aban's time but became common largely due to his efforts. Abul Faraj has attributed a poem of this type to Aban which he has titled the *Zatul Halal*, in this poem Aban had described the beginning of creation, the state of the world and issues of logic. According to Sooli as Aban rendered the *Kalileh va Demneh* in verse, he was told to pen a poem on faith and piety. Subsequently he composed a poem on fasting and *Zakat*. Sooli has quoted in his book *Al Awraq*[22] a short piece from this poem, and also a relatively longer one in verse.

The style followed in the *Kalileh va Demneh* to use animals for the narration of tales with ethical themes was copied by many Islamic writers including Sahl bin Haroon. Sahl was in-charge of the Beytul Hekma of Baghdad and was known for his interest in the heritage of Iran. In addition to Sahl bin Haroon and Abdullah bin Mughaffa'. Ibni Nadeem has listed among those who 'developed legends from the mouths of people and animals' Ali bin Dawood, the *dabir* of Zobaydah. Sahl produced a number of books of fables in Arabic, which have been listed by Ibni Nadeem.[23] One of them written in the style of the *Kalileh va Demneh* was the *Tha'la wa Afra'* and another was the *Al Nemr wal Tha'lab*. According to Mas'oodi, Sahl wrote the first book for Ma'moon, and in its various chapters and its maxims he competed with the *Kalileh va Demneh*, and surpassed it in its composition. Mas'oodi, has added that the *Tha'la wa Afra'* was greatly superior to the *Kalileh va Demneh*.[24] Abu Abdullah Mohammad bin Sharaf Qyravani, has referred to the *Kalileh va Demneh* in his paper and has noted that Sahl bin Haroon also followed the same style for his *Al Nemr wal Tha'lab* which contains famous tales, refined letters and writings.[25] Among Iranian fables, Ibni Nadeem has also

---

[22] The manuscript of this book is available at the Dar-al-Kotob-al-Masryah, Egypt.

[23] *Al-Fehrest*, p. 304.

[24] *Morooj-al-Zahab*, vol. I, p. 159.

[25] This paper by the Syrian scholar Mohammad Kurd Ali is published in *Rasa'el al Baghaa'*.

mentioned a book entitled the *Al Debb wal Tha'lab*. It is likely that Sahl bin Haroon's *Al Nemr wal Tha'lab* was either a translation of this Iranian fable or was modelled on it.

Margoliouth has argued that the art of story writing was transferred from the Indians to the Arabs through the Iranians and their books.[26] This view is pertinent to those Arab stories that were originally adapted from Indian fables or were written under their influence, as they also found their way into the Arabic language through Iran and Iranian literature. However, generalizing of this view to all areas of the art of Arabic story writing is an exaggeration, because, on the one hand, Iranian stories and particularly heroic stories were more widespread among the Arabs than Indian fables, and on the other hand, Iranian stories have impacted Arab stories more than Indian fables have.

A careful scrutiny of Arabic heroic stories and literature reveals that just as Iranian books of history have impacted the writing of Islamic history, so have Iranian heroic stories had a significant influence on this branch of Arabic literature. In fact, these Iranian books were so famous and popular in Islamic society that even several centuries after the collapse of the Sassanid empire, stories and epics continued to be written about ancient Iranian heroes such as the *Qhahreman Nameh*, the *Darab Nameh* and another book by Abu Taher Tartoosi. Although one cannot consider these works as belonging entirely to pre-Islamic Iran, they clearly reveal the influence of ancient Iranian stories.[27]

Gauthier, who has conducted significant research on the character and customs of the Arabs and has written a book with the same title,[28] has asserted that the epic stories of the Arabs were obviously influenced by the heroic stories of Iran. One of the most significant and famous Arab stories is the story of Antar. In Arab literature, Antar personifies courage and gallantry, and the stories written about him are generally heroic and thrilling in nature. As such, the book of Antar is very similar to the *Hasan Kord*, or the *Rostam Nameh*, or

---

[26] Margoliouth, *Lecture on Arabic Historians*, p. 12.

[27] Inostranzev, p. 32, *Encyclopaedia of Islam*, vol. I, p. 108.

[28] Gauthier, *Moeurs et Coutumes des Musulmans*.

the *Amir Arsalan* in Persian. In a book entitled *The Significance of the Arabic Story of Antar for Comparative Literature*, the German scholar Bernard Heller has concluded that the story of Antar emerged in the twelfth century under the influence of Iranian heroic stories, legends and the crusades;[29] a finding that is substantiated by a careful study of other Arabic stories.

**Religious Beliefs and Fables**    Religious fables refer to those fables that from ancient times have gradually found their way into religion, have survived with them, and have been passed on from one religion to another, and remain the basis and foundation of the common beliefs of the people. Some of these beliefs and fables are so ancient that it is quite difficult to trace their sources and to review them with hindsight. Nevertheless, by comparing existing religions and those beliefs that consistently appear with slight variations in all of them, many scholars have attempted to trace and clarify their historical evolution. It must be borne in mind that although these scholars have at times erred or gone astray, they have covered valuable ground with their study and evaluation of such beliefs and have paved the way for further research on this subject. Based on their research, one of the religions that has had a great impact on the religions of the east, i.e. on their beliefs, as well as related fables and legends is that of Mazda worship and Zoroastrianism of Iran. Mazda worship which dates back to an earlier period than Zoroastrianism, and perhaps is the oldest religion based on monotheism, has impacted not only many of the religions of the east, but also a number of European religious sects.

Christensen has presented a valuable discussion on the beliefs and religions of ancient Iran, their moulding with and impact upon the religions of the east. According to him,

The mixing of peoples and races in Asia was suitable grounds for the interaction of different civilizations and beliefs. As we have said, as a result of the mixing of Greek philosophy with the religious spirit of the east, new and interlinked paths emerged. Iranian and Semite thoughts had interacted since long in the Aramite environment of Baynul Nahrayn. The mysterious

[29] Bernard Heller, p. 3.

worships of the people of Asia Minor added a new element to it, and Greek philosophical thinking also found its way into this amalgam, to which the views of alchemists had also been added. Natural forces and morals which were worshipped by these peoples were referred to by their Greek names. Greek and Babylonian and Iranian legends intermixed and the legendary heroes of the east were disguised in the form of Greek gods. The complete separation between the worlds of good and evil, or the worlds of light and darkness, a specific duty that mankind is to fulfil, heaven and hell, the day of judgement and the revival of the world, and the belief in the joining of the self and the other in the relation to divine powers, all these beliefs were the elements of the Mazda religion of Iran, which entered into the common beliefs.[30]

He has identified two reasons for the influence of Mazda on other religions: the first is that in this religion, contrary to other contemporary religions, Mazda was not the god of a tribe or of a particular people, but the god of the world and of man; the second is that in this religion, the link between man and divine powers was on a more solid basis than in other religions.[31]

As can be deduced from the writings of historians, the Zoroastrian religion had spread before the rise of Islam to parts of Yamamah, as also to the southern territories of Arabia that were under the rule of Iran. It is evident from some references of the Jahili period, that the Arabs had been exposed to this religion. Ibni Qutaybah has listed Zoroastrianism among the religions that had spread among the Arabs before Islam; according to him, this religion was common in the tribe of Tamim. He has named a number of Zoroastrian Arabs such as Zarara bin Adas and his son Saheb, Agra' bin Habes and Abu Sud, the grandfather of Wakii' bin Hassan, and has added that *zandaghah* spread to Quraysh from the people of Hirah.[32] Arab writers sometimes referred to the Zoroastrian religion as *zandaghah*.

From the account quoted by Tabari it can be deduced that apart from the exposure of the Arabs to the Zoroastrian religion, many people of Mecca during the time of the Prophet supported this religion and the Iranians and expressed an interest in it. According to

[30] Christensen, pp. 35-6.
[31] Ibid., pp. 22-36.
[32] *Al-Ma'aref*, Wustenfeld edn., p. 399, *Tabaghat-al-Omam*, p. 67.

Tabari, during the wars between Iran and Byzantium, the Moslems were in favour of the victory of the Romans, and as the army of Khosrow Parviz defeated and dispersed the Romans, their foes in Mecca, who on the contrary supported the Iranians, and whenever they met one of the companions of the Prophet, they said: Did you see how our brothers the Iranians defeated your brothers the Romans, and if you rise against us in war or in hostilities, we will also defeat you; and these debates led to the revelation of the *Ayah 'Alam gholebat al Room'*.[33]

According to Goldziher, the abolition in Islam of Saturday as a day of rest was due to the influence of Zoroastrian beliefs. Jews believe that Saturday is a day of rest, because according to a legend of the Israelites, God created the world in six days and rested on the seventh day, which was Saturday. In Islam not only the observance of Saturday was discontinued, but also the belief that God rested on the seventh day of creation. Although Friday replaced Saturday as a day of rest, working on Friday in Islam is not forbidden as working on Saturday is for the Jews.[34] In a book entitled *The Sources of the Koran* the author has identified the beliefs and stories that were common in some of the eastern religions before the Koran. He has dedicated a part of his book to Zoroastrian beliefs and legends, and has written in detail about many of them such as *Ardaviraf* and *Me'raj* (the ascendance of the Zoroastrian *Moobad* to seek guidance from Zoroaster), the Tree of *Toobi* (a tree in heaven), *Jenn, Pari* and *Zarrat ul Ka'enat*.[35]

[33]  *Tarikh Tabari*, part one, p. 1006.
[34]  Goldziher, *Le Dogme et la Lois de l'Islame*, p. 13.
[35]  Thisdall, *The Sources of the Koran*, p. 218.

# SEVEN

# Philosophic and Scientific Thinking in Iran from the Time of Anooshiravan to the First Centuries of Islam

**Cultural Renaissance of Iran during the Time of Anooshiravan**
The scientific movement of the Abbasid era was mentioned earlier, that movement which led to the 'advancement of culture and civilization in the east was the culmination of a process which had begun two centuries earlier in Iran, and which was aborted and remained incomplete due to the Arab invasion. As noted earlier, the expansion and advancement of Islamic culture took place as a result of interaction and integration of different peoples and different cultures. Those who have studied the causes of this process have conceded that the proper environment conducive to this interaction had emerged partially in the Sassanid period and had expanded during the reign of Anooshiravan. Cultural interaction among different peoples of the world has always been a significant factor in the promotion and development of science and civilization, because through interaction, people not only have access to what they have produced but also to other peoples' thoughts and experiences. During the Sassanid period, in addition to the Iranians there were other peoples who had made progress in science and culture and had made strides in certain areas of the fields of knowledge of the time. Among these were the peoples of Greece and India who were renowned the world over. Flanked by these two countries, Iran was the ideal centre for this cultural interaction and it was for this reason that when a shah who was a perpetrator of knowledge ascended the throne in Iran, an era of scientific and cultural renaissance was ushered in. This movement was stalled when the Sassanid empire collapsed in the face of Islamic

expansion, and the centre of government was shifted from Iran. The movement was revived when Baghdad which was situated adjacent to Tisphoon, the capital of the Sassanids, became the centre of Islamic rule under the Abbasids and most functions of the Caliphate were entrusted to Iranians.

Christensen has described the reign of Khosrow Anooshiravan as the beginning of the most significant period of literary and philosophical renaissance of Iran.[1] This is confirmed by historical documents as well. During the period, the foundations for a revival had already been laid, and the commitment of Khosrow Anooshiravan to the advancement of science and knowledge triggered the movement. A perusal of the history of that period reveals that significant work was done to promote and expand science, which was quite outstanding for that period.

This period also witnessed the expansion and development of the institution and hospital of Jondishapoor. Jondishapoor enjoys a prominent position in the history of medicine and in the history of the culture of Iran and Islam in general. The reason is that in this unique centre, physicians from different nations including Iran, India, Greece and Assyria interacted with each other and created a fertile environment for the advancement of medicine. For centuries it was in the vanguard of medical sciences and as such rendered great service to the advancement of culture and civilization. It has been recorded that Borzouyeh did not travel to India only to obtain a copy of the *Kalileh va Demneh*,[2] but also to procure Indian books of science, or to study Indian medicine. However, there remains no evidence of that trip other than the copy of the *Kalileh va Demneh*, but one can assume that Borzouyeh and other Iranian scientists travelled to India for obtaining something more than this book and it led to significant results specifically in the field of medicine.

During this period not only did Greek philosophy spread and develop in Iran, but also a number of Greek philosophers, following

---

[1] Christensen, p. 410.

[2] According to Christensen, the physician Borzouyeh and the renowned Iranian scholar Bouzarjomehr are one and the same person. See his paper 'Bouzarjomehr Hakim'.

their persecution by the Romans, left their country and sought refuse in Iran and were at the court of Khosrow Anooshiravan. Probably, their presence had an impact on the spread of philosophical thinking in Iran. At the court the ones who evinced a greater interest in Greek works or translated them were Assyrian Christians. They were instrumental in the transfer of western thought to the east, whether in the cultural renaissance of Iran or the scientific movement of Islam. In Jondishapoor, too, there were learned physicians from this group. Poulos Persa who translated a part of Aristotle's philosophy for Anooshiravan, and Uranius, the special tutor of the shah who taught him philosophy, were also Assyrian Christians.

Khosrow Anooshiravan often had debates with scientists and philosophers and was greatly interested in these discussions. According to Agathias, the Greek historian, Anooshiravan called the *Moobadan* regularly to discuss with them the issue of the creation of the world and other philosophical topics. He had decreed that every year examinations be held to test physicians and he enthusiastically participated in these proceedings and had a special instructor for the study of philosophy. His passion for the sciences was so deep that when seven philosophers fled the Roman empire and sought asylum at his court, he extended protection to them and, in the pact that he concluded with the emperor of Rome, ensured that they would not be prevented from returning and would not be harmed. According to De Boer, this was despite the fact that their attitude towards the court of Iran was no better than the attitude of French freedom activists towards the court of Russia in the eighteenth century.[3] Anooshiravan's passion for knowledge and learning is documented in Iranian and Islamic history, and has served as a model for Islamic authors. Dinevari says: 'Among the shahs of Iran no one was more concerned with knowledge and more thorough than Anooshiravan. He brought the masters of wisdom and *adab* to him and he honoured them.'[4] According to Braun, Anooshiravan's interest in religious discussions and philosophical debates brings to

---

[3] The English translation is by E.R. Jones, quoted from De Boer, *The History of Philosophy of Islam*, p. 5.

[4] *Al-Akhbar-al-Tewal.*

mind the period of Ma'moon, the Abbasid Caliph, and the debates held during his days.

During this period Greek thought interacted with the thought of other nations including Iranian, Indian and Semite, to lay the foundation for great developments in science and thought. But the Sassanid empire soon collapsed due to internal and external pressures. As time is a crucial factor in the process of scientific and cultural development, the cultural renaissance in Iran did not yield outstanding results as were seen in the Islamic period. Nevertheless, in the history of culture this period should be viewed as one of the pillars upon which Islamic science and culture were built. The integration of these two cultures is so extensive that in order to study the history of Islamic sciences and literature one should before their roots in the Sassanid period.[5]

The era of Anooshiravan's reign is considered one of the significant periods of Iranian history *vis-à-vis* enhancement of Iranian national culture. Efforts were made to translate the fruits of the thoughts of other nations into Persian, thus enriching the scientific treasures of this language. The significance of the Sassanid era lies in the fact that all political and cultural affairs of Iran at that time and in particularly during the reign of Anooshiravan had an Iranian identity and character, and every product of this period was a manifestation of Iranian thinking. The Persian language also underwent a process of development, and had that process continued, Persian would have acquired the status of the language of science in the orient, a position that was later bestowed upon the Arabic language following the rise of Islam and the interest of the scholars of the orient in it.

**Neo-Platonic Philosophy**    Neo-Platonic philosophy more than any other had an impact in the orient and Greek thinking mainly reached the orient through the context of this philosophy. Plato, a prominent Greek philosopher who lived after Socrates and before Aristotle, and founded on the basis of his teachings a new school of Greek philosophy. After Socrates, Plato and Aristotle the period of innovation in Greek philosophy came to

[5] Inostranzev, p. 7.

an end and a new period was ushered in during which philosophers did not propose new ideas or concepts but were engaged in reviving older philosophical theories and critiquing older philosophies, and each group selected one renowned philosopher of the past as its source of inspiration. One such group devoted its energies to reviving the philosophy of Plato and his teachings, and re-interpreted it in an attempt to bridge the widening gulf between the philosophies of Plato and Aristotle and to bring them close together. This group developed its own philosophy and its teachings acquired a distinct character and was identified as neo-Platonic philosophy, which rapidly spread in all the philosophical circles of the east and west.

Since neo-Platonic philosophy emerged and developed gradually, the initial phases of its development are not clear. According to historians, it was founded by Saccas (AD 175-242) and the first person who structured its principles was his student Aflootin (AD 205-70). There is no information about Saccas. The works of Aflootin are available through his student Farfourius, who headed this school of thought after him. These works constitute six volumes and are known as *Tasso'at*(?) in Arabic. After the principles of this philosophy were well entrenched, its reach became increasingly wider and within a short time its followers established several schools in Athens and Alexandria and their teachings infiltrated the scientific and religious circles of that period. As Christianity was also spreading at that time, neo-Platonic philosophy became a powerful weapon in the hands of those who opposed Christianity. In AD 529 the Roman emperor Justinian decreed that the followers of this philosophy should be persecuted and their schools closed down, following which many of them left their native lands and seven of them sought asylum in the court of Iran. Thus, neo-Platonic philosophy found its way to Iran as well, and during the reign of Anooshiravan an environment conducive to its growth developed. Since ancient times Iranians had benefited from the knowledge of Greece and Rome, and during this period as well, they were aware of the scientific and philosophical developments in Greece. Before Greek books were translated into Arabic in the first Abbasid period, the Moslems in Iran were exposed to Greek philosophy and had translated a number of Greek works into Arabic that had previously been translated into

Pahlavi.[6] Apparently in the Sassanid period there were numerous books on philosophy in Iran, and the task of some people was to study and debate these books.

The quote from *Mo'jam-ul-Buldan* revealed that during this period there lived a group of Iranian writers in the region of Arrajan whom Yaqoot referred to as the *Gashteh Daftaran*, and their task was to copy scientific books on medicine, astronomy and philosophy in a special script known Gashteh or Gashtak. The beliefs of Iranians during the Sassanid period, and particularly during the latter part of it, contain numerous examples of Greek philosophy. There are references to the evolution of philosophy in Iran in the writings of Islamic authors. According to Ibni Khaldoon, 'The nations that were concerned before Islam more than others with philosophical sciences were the two great nations of Iran and Rome, and because of their growth and prosperity, science and knowledge was common among them.' He writes on Iran: 'The importance of this science for them was such that some have said that the philosophical sciences originally emerged in Iran and Alexander took them to Greece.'[7] Before Ibni Khaldoon, Ibni Nadeem had also referred to this issue in an extensive discussion,[8] and the *Tarikh Abul Fida* mentions that Shahpoor the son of Ardeshir, made great effort to build-up a collection of philosophy books and to translate them into a Persian.[9]

**Greek Philosophy and Zoroastrian Religion**  Greek philosophy developed in an environment far from the birthplace of religions of the orient and it did not conform to the principles of these religions, and in many cases was even in contradiction to them. For this reason, whenever Greek philosophy found its way into any of these religions, it came into conflict with

---

[6] Ibni Mughaffa' translated into Arabic a number of Greek books on logic and medicine that had earlier been translated into Pahlavi. *Al-Fehrest*, p. 242.

[7] The Introduction of Ibni Khaldoon, p. 479.

[8] *Al-Fehrest*, p. 239.

[9] *Tarikh Abul Fida*, p. 50.

them for a period of time, until eventually, various new trends of thought emerged out of their interaction.

The interaction of philosophy and religion is one of the most significant issues in the history of thought which needs to be studied in detail. The complex beliefs and mind boggling debates that have emerged out of this interaction were the most important intellectual preoccupation of people for many centuries, and the various differences that have arisen in each of the religions have posed the greatest challenges to mankind. The first of such conflicts recorded in the history of this region is related to the teachings of Philo, the Jewish philosopher. Philo, a nomad from Alexandria, lived from 30 BC to AD 50. At that time, Greek philosophy had found a fertile ground for growth in Alexandria. Many Jewish nomads lived around the city and the Torah had been translated into Greek, the scientific language of the times during the reign of Ptolemy the second. Influenced by Greek philosophy, Philo strove to bring his philosophic and religious beliefs to terms, and expressed many of the principles of the Jewish faith within the framework of Greek philosophy. What has been quoted from him is a clear example of the meeting of the two.

When Christianity began to spread in a region where Greek philosophy had already spread and established itself, the followers of Greek philosophy resisted the new religion and Christian churches, particularly the church of Alexandria began to fight them fiercely. This antagonism between Christianity and Greek philosophy continued for a long time, and whenever the balance tilted in favour of religion, the Christians did not hesitate to belittle the philosophers, as seen in the treatment of Roman philosophers by Emperor Justinian. This was one side of the issue. The other side was that as philosophic beliefs infiltrated Christian minds and Christians gradually accepted them, many of the philosophic concepts found their way into this religion and many Christian scholars tried to interpret their religious beliefs within the framework of Greek philosophy. Thus, a new path developed in Christianity, as a result of which different Christian sects began to emerge, leading to numerous conflicts that have been were documented in the history of the church. The first conflict in the fifth century resulted in the emergence of two sects—the Nestorians and the Jacobites, and was about the nature of Christ. The study of this conflict clearly demonstrates the extent to which Greek philosophy had infiltrated Christianity and impacted it.

A similar situation, but in a different context, arose in Iran as a result of the clash between neo-Platonic philosophy and Zoroastrian religion. Not much information is available on the antagonism of Iran's Zoroastrian society towards this philosophy; however, it can be presumed that the Moobadan were not too receptive to this new intruder, and they viewed Anooshiravan's interest in it critically. Historic sources do not clarify the context of the conceptual clash between the followers of Zoroastrianism and the supporters of neo-Platonic philosophy, perhaps because this clash was rarely openly expressed. Or, perhaps it was because of Anooshiravan's interest in philosophy and his support of philosophers, which suppressed the ability of the Moobadan to openly oppose it. It is true that Anooshiravan had supported the Moobadan in uprooting the Mazdakis, nevertheless, the Moobadan were not able to regain the control and authority that they had previously enjoyed during the reign of this shah. Anooshiravan was relatively impartial towards religious beliefs, and obviously, this was contrary to the expectations of the Moobadan. They had expected that he would take stern action against the Christians, their main enemies, but instead he treated them and others with tolerance, and it has even been suggested that the Pahlavi translation of the Old Testament, sections of which are housed in the Volker Kund Museum, was undertaken during this period.[10] This issue definitely had an impact on the evolution of philosophy. Justinian, the Roman emperor, used torture to disperse philosophers under the pressure of the church. If Anooshiravan had also been influenced by the Moobadan, philosophy would have had an entirely different fate in Iran. In a book that Polos the Persian wrote for the shah, and included in it material on the views of the philosophers, he accorded philosophy a higher position than religion. Christensen has pointed out the significance Anooshiravan's tolerance of issues that the Moobadan were not in agreement with, and according to him, the torture of the followers of other religions

---

[10] Christensen, p. 422.

including Christianity in Rome in those days makes the religious tolerance of the court of Iran even more conspicuous.[11]

Another issue that must be taken into consideration in this regard is that Greek philosophy did not spread in the Zoroastrian environment of Iran to the same extent as it did in the Christian environment of Rome in Asia Minor. As far as is known, most of those who were engaged in the study and debate of philosophy were Assyrian Christians, and the venues for such studies were more their own schools. Also, the infiltration of philosophy into Zoroastrian Iran did not last long enough for it to interact critically with Zoroastrian beliefs and to lead to an obvious clash. Perhaps, Zoroastrian religion, as a result of the large volume of myths and superstitions that had engulfed it, did not have the capability at that time to struggle with such a strong foe; in any case, the spread of neo-Platonic philosophy in Iran, which coincided with the spread of Indian thought, gradually found its way into the minds of Zoroastrian Iranians and left an impact in Iran. An example of this impact appeared after Islam in religious schools and debate circles of this period.

### A Look at the Spiritual Conditions in Iran before Islam

Scholars of Zoroastrianism are of the opinion that this religion had a clear message and outlook for life before it lost its way and deviated from its original path, and its emergence represented a great leap forward for civilization and culture at that time. This religion was based on the principle of the eternal struggle between good and evil, and perceived the world as a vast arena for work and for productivity, in which mankind was prompted to continuously fight evil, with the ultimate victory of the good. Thus, the Zoroastrian spirit created an environment of vitality, optimism and hope, and enhanced the capacity of mankind to face the hardships of life. It is obvious that such an ideology could be influential in the progress and happiness of peoples who believed in it and who adhered to its teachings. However, it cannot be said definitely this when Zoroastrians succeeded in keeping their religion free of embellishments, but it is clear that

[11] Ibid., p. 423.

towards the end of the Sassanid period, the principles of Zoroastrians were engulfed in myth and superstition. During this period, its basic principles were overshadowed by superficial and fruitless rituals that the Moobadan continuously expanded in order to strengthen their own hold over society. Simplistic tales as well as superstitions beyond belief had infiltrated this religion to such an extent that the clerics themselves, who are usually the last to recognize the superficiality of these superstitions, had also expressed concern.

Within the Zoroastrian community, there were people who had understood the futility of those rituals much earlier and who struggled to free themselves from that burden. The various movements that emerged in the name of new religions were partially due to this. During the time of Anooshiravan and later, when the environment was more conducive to thought and contemplation, a greater number of people reflected on these issues. The influence of Greek and Indian cultures, as well as the clash of Zoroastrian ideas with opposing ones further enhanced this openness. Neo-Platonic philosophy that had found a suitable environment for expansion in Iran, had to some extent infiltrated religious and non-religious circles, and had become an effective intellectual weapon in the hands of opponents. Christensen has summarized the intellectual environment during the reign of Anooshiravan, 'We can imagine that in the period of Anooshiravan, general public hardships were less than previous periods; however, people felt it more because in this period people thought more.'[12] This is an accurate assessment because the cultural advancement during this period had passed new issues for the people, or at least the intellectuals, and had compelled them to think about many aspects of their lives. Among these issues was religion, and the more they sought to understand its essence, the more they confronted ancient legends and unreasonable customs and rituals. Had this awakening of intellect been focused on a clear and productive path it would have produced valuable results; but that did not happen. Rather, it led to differences in beliefs and scatterization of opinions and ideas which gave rise to adverse outcomes.

[12] Ibid., p. 434.

Although Greek philosophic ideas were effective in opposing the superstitions that had engulfed religion, however, on their own, they did not have a clear spiritual message to be able to replace religion. On the contrary, complex philosophical discussions and arguments only led to confusion. Although the teachings of Indian and Iranian philosophers applied wisdom, which were popular in the form of advice and admonishment, and in terms of ethical content complemented the teachings of religion, nevertheless, they could not fulfil the role of religion. Thus, the unity of thought and word which had earlier characterized the followers of Zoroaster, gradually gave way to conflict and deceit; with the emergence of various religions, the spirit of doubt and uncertainty not only spread among the intellectual class of Iran, but also among the general population. There was lack of trust in religious teachings, which is the precondition for belief, as the enlightened class viewed religious teachings with suspicion and even preferred applied wisdom to religious teachings.[13]

One of the consequences of this was a pessimistic view of the world, a movement towards isolationism and withdrawal and a life-style of hermitry. As we have said earlier, the Zoroastrian religion was originally based on activity and effort and optimism in the world, but much of the heritage of Iran in this period flows with the spirit of pessimism. In the extract quoted from Borzouyeh's introduction to the *Kalileh va Demneh*, his conclusion is dominated by an air of piety and withdrawal from the world. The *Oushanar Dana* reveals: 'Life exists, but it is the body that deceives.' Such views did not conform to the principles of Zoroastrianism. With the spirit of piety and hermitry, another belief found its way into Zoroastrianism which, according to Christensen, was for the ancient essence of the religion of Mazda, the equivalent of a fatal poison[14] and that was the belief in fate. Christensen has quoted from the *Minavi Kherad* from the sayings of heavenly wisdom or *Ravan Kherad*:

Even with the power of wisdom and knowledge, one cannot fight with fate, because, as good or bad is written, the wise become incapable and

---

[13] Ibid., Also refer to the passage from the introduction to the Persian *Kalileh va Demneh*.

[14] Christensen, p. 430.

the ill wishers become capable and clever; the weak become strong, and the mighty become cowards; the lazy become industrious, and the striving become lax.

The *Minavi Kherad* is considered one of the books of the Zarvanis. The belief in fate found its way into Zoroastrianism through the Zarvani sect, and as this sect had much influence on Islam and many of the Iranian thoughts and beliefs found their way into Islam through this sect, it is in order to briefly discuss Zarvani sect.

**The Zarvanis and Their Impact on the Islamic Community**   A phrase in *The Gatts* (a Zoroastrian book) says, 'Those two twin essences that at the beginning appeared in the realm of the intellect, one is the good in thought, in speech, and in deed, and the other is the evil (in thought, in speech and in deed); between these two, the knowledgeable man must select the good and not the bad.'[15] From the meaning of this phrase it has been understood that Zoroaster believed in an essence that preceded these two and was their source, but it is not clear what he named it. Apparently, this issue was the topic of much debate and discussion in the doctrine of Zoroastrianism from ancient times; some believed that this essence was place whereas others believed it was time. The second group was known as the Zarvanis, because time is referred to as *zarvan* in the Pahlavi language. The influence of this group gradually expanded and overshadowed the first group, and with time their views even penetrated mainstream Zoroastrianism, such that when Mani proclaimed prophecy, he called his great god Zarvan, as he wished to conform his sayings to the beliefs of the Zoroastrians.

The Zarvanis had various legends and beliefs, and god worshippers in the Sassanid period followed their beliefs.[16] Another name for Zarvan was Ghaza, and therefore, the belief in fate was one of the main ideological beliefs of this group, and through them found its way into the core of the Zoroastrian religion. The beliefs of the Zarvanis, which had gradually acquired a materialistic context, infiltrated Islamic society through the Zoroastrians, and had a signifi-

---

[15] Refer to *The Gatts*, by Poordavood, Bombay, 1927, p. 17.
[16] For more information see Christensen, pp. 135-44.

cant influence on the religious discussions and debates of that period. *Zarvan* was translated into Arabic as *dahr*, and this group in Islam was called the *Dahryeh*. A paper entitled *Shekand Goomanik Vijar* or 'Clarifications that Eliminate Uncertainties' which was written after the Sassanid period refutes the beliefs of this group:

And the misconception of those who claim that God does not exist, and are known as *Dahryeh*, is that they think they are thus relieved from religious duties, and performing good deeds; and among their baseless sayings which they repeatedly utter, one is that this world with its various transformations, and the order that exists in it with regard to earthly bodies and ideas, is the result of the contradiction of things, and their interaction is the result of the initial emergence of time through eternity; and also, they say that there is neither reward for good deeds nor punishment for evil deeds, and there is no heaven nor hell, and nothing to prompt man towards good or evil, and they also say that the world of being is nothing but material, and that the spirit does not exist.

Tavadia has argued that the object of this passage was not a reference to a religious sect in the Sassanid period, but rather the object was a group called Dahrieh in the Islamic period. He has based his argument on the use of the word *dahr* which he considered completely Arabic in both form and meaning, with no relation whatsoever with the word *zarvan*. Christensen has endorsed Tavadia's view and has cast no doubt either on the phrase being a description of the beliefs of the Zarvanis. He has presumed that in this context the word *dahri* is the translation of the word *zarvanik*, and the objective of the author here was to negate a materialistic philosophy which was the latest evolution in the views of contemporary Zarvanis, although he has conceded ignorance about whether the views of the Zarvanis had developed to such a level in the Sassanid period.[17] The fact that the word *dahri* is, as Christensen has asserted, a translation of the word *zarvanik*, is consistent with the meaning of the word in Arabic dictionaries. The *Qamoos*, has also given the meaning of this word: '*Dahr* sometimes is considered among the titles of god, and means a long period of time, or even a thousand years'; these are the meanings of the word *zarvan* in different periods. In describing the impact of

[17] Christensen, p. 421.

Iranian philosophic thinking on the Islamic environment and the significance of the beliefs of the Zarvanis, De Boer has considered the word *zarvan* as a synonym of the Arabic word *dahr*, and he has interpreted it as fate and the movements of heavenly bodies. According to him,

As this belief conformed with the inclinations of the philosophers and thinkers of that period, therefore it grew widely in the Islamic environment, and its followers in Islam were known as *Dahryeh*, or *Maddyoon*, or *Ahl Zandaghah* and *Elhad*, and they kept jurists preoccupied for centuries.[18]

Another influence of neo-Platonic and Indian thought that survived in Iran and later in Islam was Sufism. For centuries, Sufism in Islam had preoccupied Moslem thinkers, it has been researched and studied in its different aspects by past and present scholars. These researchers believe that to understand the basis and context of such thinking, it is important to first refer to the history of Iranian thought, and then consider the historical development of neo-Platonism in Zoroastrian and later Islamic environments of Iran. In reality, what is known today as Islamic Sufism, of which much remains in the civilization and culture of the orient, is the integration and interaction of various beliefs, thoughts and elements, which have lost their original character during different phases of transformation and has acquired a new one. It has been argued that the emergence of the spirit of Sufism in the orient was originally the product of the interaction of Greek philosophy and Iranian thought in the Zoroastrian environment of Iran, initially, it had a simple and unstructured form and it gradually developed and matured later in the Islamic period, it was during this period when the new thinking conformed to Islamic teachings that the foundations of Islamic Sufism were laid.

*Hey'at* (**Structure of the Universe**), *Nojoom* (**Astronomy**), *Handasah* (**Measurements**)

In the fields of *Hey'at* and *Nojoom* also a number of books were translated from Pahlavi into Arabic, and thus Iranian

---

[18] De Boer, *The History of Philosophy of Islam*, p. 8.

views on these subjects found their way into the Islamic environment. During the period under study, the focus in the field of astronomy in Iran was on clarifying the movement of stars in their variations and diversity, and charting them in geometric figures, on the basis of which laws pertaining to their movements could be deduced. The scope of this science in Iran was similar to that in Greece in the days of Ptolemy. Apparently, at that time the essence of these movements and their causes were not part of this field of science, rather they were discussed under natural philosophy. In fact, astronomy covered in those days—*Hey'ate Koravi va Amali* (?) and *Hey'ate Nazari*—to the extent that it related to solar or lunar eclipse, or the movement of any of the planets, as well as some mathematics, geographic longitudes and latitudes, the particulars of regions and countries, and natural geography. This explains why Iranian books in this field were greatly used by Islamic geographers.

The dependence of this science on *Gah Shomari* and its laws led to the development and expansion of this science in Iran. Maintaining precise calculations of the year and month as well as determining the date for the leap year was the duty of astronomers. During the Sassanid period, observing the leap year was considered among the important religious ceremonies, it was a significant function of the state and the *divan* and was performed with full protocol and ceremony. Birooni has described the manner in which it was performed in the Sassanid period,

This was performed by the shahs in the presence of statisticians and the *dabirs* of the *divans*, and those in charge of official calendars, and the *Hirbadan* and the Judges, who were all summoned to the Court, and after consultations and consensus on the authenticity of the calculations; much money was spent for this ceremony, and even he who estimated the minimum, put the expenditure figure at one million *dinars*.

He adds, 'This day was one of the greatest feasts in popularity and fame, and they called it the Leap Feast.'[19]

The science of the movements of stars was also used to measure cultivated lands and for digging canals and *qanats* in order to tap

---

[19] *Al-Akhbar-al-Baghyah*, p. 44.

underground water. Area measurement at that time in Iran was considered a very important skill, and there were competent masters in the field. Apparently, landscapers constituted a special class among the accountants of the Sassanid period. During the reigns of Qobad and Anooshiravan, the modification of the method of determining agricultural taxes necessitated that all farm lands and orchards in all towns and villages, by type of crops in each, be identified, a task which took several years to accomplish. This clearly demonstrates the significance and the complexity of the work of this class. Perhaps, Birooni's reference to 'statisticians' was to this same class of state functionaries.

The writing of Kharazmi, reveals that the information that was required for this function was part of the field known in Islam as *Handasah*. According to Kharazmi, the word *Handasah* is the Arabized version of the Persian *Andazeh*, and in support of his statement, he has quoted a Persian saying; '*Andazeh ba Akhtar Mari Bayad*', which was a common phrase signifying the interrelationship between the two fields of *Handasah* and *Nojoom* in Iran.[20] Before the advent of Islam, the science of astronomy in Iran was known as *Akhtar Mari*, or accounting the stars. Not much information is available on the issues that were debated in this field in Iran in those days or the skill of landscaping and other measurements, but a careful study of a number of Iranian and Islamic books such as the *Al-Fehrest* and other related books clearly reveals the continuity of the science of measurements into the Islamic science of *Handasah,* and it is apparent that the Arabs first learnt of this science through Iranian books, and for that reason they adopted its Persian designation in an Arabic form. Later, as Greek books in this field were translated into Arabic, they were also integrated into this field and they were all termed the science of *Handasah*. What confirms this is that in ancient Arab books, often the word *Muhandeseen* is synonymously used with *Ashab al A'adad*, which is the same as for statisticians.

The belief in lucky and unlucky days as well as the impact of heavenly bodies on the fate of people were common in Iran since ancient times. Today, it is an established fact that there is no

---

[20]  *Mafatih-al-Oloom*, p. 117.

scientific basis for these beliefs, nevertheless, it in those days they were considered to have a scientific context and, therefore, they were studied in great detail. At the court of the Sassanid shahs, a group of astronomers and astrologers was always in attendance and they were consulted by the shah in all significant matters; they relied on the position of the planets and their movements to predict events which are described in Iranian stories and history. The *Jadvale Ekhtiyarat*, traces of which can be found in various calendars, is an example of such predictions.[21] In any case, since astronomers relied on astrology in reaching their conclusions, this field had an impact on the progress of the science of astronomy.

**Books Translated in these Fields from Pahlavi** A careful persual of the Islamic sciences of astronomy and astrology reveals that numerous books in these fields were translated from Persian into Arabic, but neither the titles nor the details of most of these books can be found from the available historical sources. One of these books that remained for centuries the most reliable source for Islamic astronomers, on the basis of which they made their rulings, was the *Zij Shahryar*, which was translated from Persian into Arabic by Abul Hasan Ali, the son of Zyad Tamimi.[22] This was one of the significant and ancient books of Iran, and like most other great works of the time, there is a legendary story about this book. Quoting this story from *Abu Ma'shar Falaki*, Ibni Rastah has said that the book served as a reference for all the Iranians and the peoples of the world and was the pride of Esfahan, because, according to Abu Ma'shar, this book was kept and cared for in that city.

Another book that was translated from Persian into Arabic is the *Al Zabraj*, that is listed in the printed edition of the *Al-Fehrest*. This is probably a distortion of a name that has not been found.[23] According to Ibni Nadeem, this book was a critique written by the Iranian

---

[21] *Al-Akhbar-al-Baghyah*, p. 230.

[22] *Al-Fehrest*, p. 242.

[23] This is a distorted word originating from the word *al-bazidaj*, which is the Arabic for the Persian word *vazideh* or *gozideh*, meaning selections.

scholar, Bouzarjomehr for the book of Falis the Roman.[24] Three other Iranian books on astronomy have also been mentioned in the *Tabaqhat-al-Omam*. Of these three books, one deals with subject of '*Sowar Maratib Falaki*', which he has attributed to '*Azdrasht*' (?). He has referred to a second book by its Arabic title *Al Tafseer*, and based on what has been discussed about Ibni Nadeem in relation to *Al Zabraj*, it is likely that these two titles are of the same book, Ibni Nadeem has referred to its Pahlavi name while Ibni Sa'ed has referred to its Arabic meaning. The third book he has referred to as the book of *Jamasf*, he has extolled its importance and greatness.[25]

The Italian scholar Nelino who has done valuable research on Islamic astronomy and astrology and has written on Pahlavi books and their influence on Islamic astrology, has stated in his famous book *The Science of Astronomy and Its History Among the Arabs* that the influence of Indian and Iranian scholars in kindling the interest of the Arabs in astrology preceded Greek influence, the Arabs became acquainted with astrology through Indian and Iranian works and learnt significant ways to solve questions in astronomy which were unknown to the Greeks. However, had they remained content with Indian and Iranian works and had not translated Greek works, they would not have attained such heights in this field.

The influence of Iranian books of astronomy on Islamic works is an important issue that merits independent study, but will be referred to here to the extent that it relates to the scope of this book. A significant influence of these books on Islamic astronomy is the use of numerous technical Persian words in Arabic books of astronomy. As technical words and expressions are the best manifestation of the process of historical development of the sciences, it may be concluded that during the period in which this field was developing in Islam, Iranian books of astronomy were widely used by Islamic scholars and constituted a principal source of information for them. Kharazmi has mentioned a large number of Persian expressions in the *Mafatih-al-Oloom*.[26] It should be borne in mind that these words

[24] *Al-Fehrest*, p. 257.
[25] *Tabaqhat-al-Omam*, pp. 24-5.
[26] Refer to *Mafatih-al-Oloom*, pp. 134-7.

and expressions in this as well as other books are only a sample of the words and expressions that have found their way from Persian into Arabic books. The reason is that in addition to these words, many others have entered Arabic through a literal translation of their meaning, and further due to the capability of the Arabic language to accept foreign words, many more words were absorbed into Arabic and completely lost their Persian forms, so that it is extremely difficult, if not impossible, to recognize them without careful scrutiny.[27] The study of books in which Persian words appear intact or with slight modification is very significant, not only for historical reasons, but also for linguistic reasons. This exercise will enable one to identify the original Persian forms of geographic and astronomic expressions that appear in their transformed Arabic forms in modern Persian.

Apart from these scientific Persian expressions, some of the principles of Iranian astronomy and astrology acquired near global recognition. In classic geography and astrology, the inhabited quarter (of the earth) was divided into seven parts, each of which was referred to as *eqhleem* in Arabic. This type of structure was adopted in Islamic books from Iranian astrology and was widely accepted by scholars of other nations as well. Iranian scholars viewed Iran or Iranshahr, known as Khonireth in the *Avesta*, as the centre of the inhabited quarter and depicted the rest of the world by six circles or *keshvar* surrounding the central circle, and considered the inhabited quarter as comprising seven *keshvars*. The Arabs and Moslems later used the word *eqhleem* in place of *keshvar* which they borrowed from the Assyrians, but accepted this hypothesis and its structure.[28]

Another important element of Iranian astronomy which was adapted in Islamic books from Pahlavi books was the solar calendar, which in the Islamic period was named after the Yazdgerdi calendar

---

[27] For details about the evolution of Persian words in the Arabic language, see following articles by Mohammad Mohammadi-Malayeri, 'A Number of Issues on the Evolution of *Persian* Words in the Arabic Language', *Al-Derasat-al-Adabyah*, vol. VI, nos. 1 and 2, Beirut, 1966; 'On the Search for *Persian* Words in the Arabic Language', *Al-Derasat-al-Adabyah*, vol. VIII, nos. 1 and 2, Beirut, 1966.

[28] Hamzeh Esfahani and Abu Reyhan Birooni, quoted from Yaghoot in *Mo'jam-ul-Buldan*, vol. I, pp. 26-7.

of the last Sassanid shah, and became the basis of all Islamic calendars. This calendar was used in Iranian astronomic tables because of its simplicity and ease of use, and was adopted by all other tables and became the official calendar.[29]

**Islamic Authors in Iranian Books of Astronomy**    Following the exposure of Moslems to Arabic translations of Iranian Greek and other scientific works, Islamic scholars began to produce books in these fields. Scholars who wrote on astronomy and astrology fell into two groups: those whose source of knowledge was Iranian books and those who based their study on Greek works.

Arab knowledge of astronomy during the Jahili period, like their knowledge in other fields, had not yet reached a level that it could develop a scientific base or be termed as science. In refuting Ibni Qutaybah's views in his book *Precedence of Arabs Over Ajam* that 'the Arabs are the most knowledgeable of all peoples in astronomy and its laws', Birooni says:

I do not know whether Ibni Qutaybah was ignorant of the knowledge of the farmers of other nations or that he chose to ignore that, because anyone who reviews Arab books of astronomy will understand that their awareness of this subject was not more than the awareness of the farmers of other regions in the understanding of the proper season for each activity, and the periods for, and the types of calamities.[30]

Generally speaking, once the Arabs and Moslems became acquainted with the scientific heritage of Iran, they began to admire it. This is reflected in the works of many Arabic authors. According to Ibni Sa'ed's *Tabaqhat-al-Omam*,

Among the characteristics of the Iranians is their attention to medical science and thorough knowledge of the laws of astronomy, and the impact that they have had on the world of scholarship. The Iranians had observatories from ancient times, and developed theories and schools of thought, one of which is that on which Abu Ma'shar Balkhi based his '*Zeeje Bozorg*'; because as Abu

---

[29]    *Al-Akhbar-al-Baghyah*, p. 31.
[30]    Ibid., pp. 238-9.

Ma'shar has written, that -*zeej*- followed the example of the prominent (?) among the scholars of Iran, and many other scholars.

Ibni Sa'ed has quoted a detailed description given by Abu Ma'shar of Iranian laws of astronomy and their precision.[31] Haj Khalifah has also written on this subject, and has probably drawn on this same book.[32] Abu Ma'shar Balkhi, a prominent astronomer of Islam, acquired his knowledge and fame through Iranian books. Birooni has praised his theory of astronomy, and has added that he deduced his theory from Iranian observations, which are different from what can be obtained from Indian observations.[33] In praise of him and his writings, Ibni Sa'ed said: 'and in addition, Abu Ma'shar was the most knowledgeable in the history of Iran and other nations, apart from the Arabs.'[34] Ibni Nadeem has listed thirty-five books written by him and has said: 'In his field he followed Abdullah bin Yahya Barmaki and Mohammad bin Jahm Barmaki, and he considered them superior to others in knowledge and wisdom.'[35]

Abu Sahl Fazl bin Nowbakht is among the well-known astronomers of Islam. Ibni Nadeem has listed a number of his books on astronomy but the title of the first book appears distorted in the printed edition of the *Al-Fehrest*. These books have been mentioned in the following order: *Kitab al Nahmatan fil Mawalid*; *Kitab al Fa'l an Nojoomi* (?); *Kitab al Mawaleed Mofrad*; *Kitab Tahweel Sena-l-Mawaleed*; *Kitab al Madkhal*; *Kitab al Tashbih wal Tamtheel* and *Kitab al Montahal min Aghawil al Munajjemeen fil Akhbar wal Masa'el wal Mawaleed*. He admitted that he relied on Iranian works.[36] As noted earlier, Fazl, the son of Nowbakht, was one of the translators of Iranian books into Arabic, and the Nowbakhti family was known for its interest in Iran's cultural heritage. It can be asserted that Fazl's books were outstanding examples of Iranian works in astronomy.[37] Omar bin Farkhan had

---

[31] *Tabaghat-al-Omam*, pp. 25-5.
[32] *Kashf-ul-Zonoon*, pp. 68-9.
[33] *Al-Akhbar-al-Baghyah*, p. 40.
[34] *Tabaghat-al-Omam*, p. 89.
[35] *Al-Fehrest*, p. 277.
[36] Ibid., p. 274.
[37] For more information on this topic, see, 'Translators and Transcribers

also translated books on astronomy, and as mentioned earlier he was one of the translators from Persian and had a deep interest in Iranian writings. His works are excellent examples of Iranian writings in astronomy. Birooni occasionally quoted a number of Iranian astronomers in his books, and he possessed several of their books including *Abul Hasan Azarkhor Mohandes*[38] and *Zadouyeh*,[39] and he often relied on their opinions, which indicates their prominent position in this field.

Among Islamic Caliphs, Ma'moon evinced great interest in astronomic works and ancient books of Iran, and engaged in their study and discussion. According to Mas'oodi,

When Fazl bin Sahl had influence over him, Ma'moon paid much attention to debates in astronomy, and followed its rules. In this, he followed the example of past Sassanid shahs such as Ardeshir Babakan, and put much effort in the reading and study and debate of ancient books, and thus he acquired great understanding of them.[40]

---

from Persian in the First Islamic Centuries', *Al-Derasat-al-Adabyah*, vol. VII, nos. 3 and 4, Beirut, 1965.

[38]  *Al-Akhbar-al-Baghyah*, pp. 99, 219.

[39]  Ibid., pp. 217, 221.

[40]  *Morooj-al-Zahab*, vol. IV, p. 245.

# EIGHT

# The Centre of Medicine in Iran before Islam and in the First Centuries of Islam

**Jondishapoor**     In the north-west of Khouzestan and between the city of Shooshtar and the ruins of Shoush, stood a big and prosperous city during and after the Sassanid period, with lush farm lands and running streams and green gardens,[1] and was considered one of the important centres of science and culture during the period under study. This city was Jondishapoor, renowned for its famous medical institute and hospital, which attracted students and scientists from all corners.[2] Jondishapoor acquired significance during the reign of Shapoor the first, the second Sassanid shah, who ordered that Roman prisoners be settled there and consequently set-off its expansion and development. It was an old practice in Iran to settle prisoners of war in under-populated areas where they would cultivate and work, and introduce crafts that were not known in Iran. There are references attributing this practice to Dariush the Great the Achaemenian, and to Orod the Ashkanid and other shahs in Iran.[3] Shapoor the first engaged Roman prisoners in Jondishapoor to construct the famous Cesar dam.[4] With this the process of development and prosperity of Jondishapoor began.

There are a number of tales about the root of the name of Jondishapoor,[5] which are closer to myth. However, according to

[1] *Mo'jam-ul-Buldan*, vol. III, p. 149.

[2] For more information on the location of this historic city, see Rawlinson, 'Journey in *Lorestan*', *Journal of the Royal Geographic Society*, vol. IX, p. 42.

[3] *The Letter of Tansar*, Minavi edn., Tehran, 1311, p. 41.

[4] Christensen, p. 121.

[5] Refer to the narrative that Yaghoot has quoted from Ibni Faghih on this topic.

reliable Islamic sources, the name has been identified as the Arabic abbreviation of the original name of the city Vah Andiou Shapoor. Hamzeh Esfahani,[6] Tabari[7] and others have given the reasons for this nomenclature: when Shapoor defeated the Romans in war and captured Antioch, he was so impressed by that city, that upon his return to Iran he decreed that a city like Antioch be built in Iran, and it was called Vah Andiou Shapoor which means 'Better than Antioch of Shapoor'. Antioch was pronounced *Andiou* in Persian. A similar city and terminology is the city of Vandiou Khosrow or Jondi Khosrow which was built by decree of Khosrow Anooshiravan and was called 'Better than Antioch of Khosrow'. According to Yaghout, Vandiou Khosrow was one of the seven cities of Tisphoon, which was known as the Roman city of Mada'en, and it was here that the Abbasid Caliph Mansoor murdered Abu Moslem Khorasani.[8] Jondishapoor was called 'Betlapat' in Assyrian and was referred to in brief as Bilabad,[9] and according to Tabari, the people of Ahvaz called it Bil.[10] About half a century later, during the reign of Shapoor the second, Jondishapoor became the capital of the Sassanid empire and consequently its importance and prosperity increased. Mani, the founder of the new religion, was also murdered in this city. Even during the Islamic period, one of the gates of this city was known as Bab Mani because after his death, Mani's head was hung from this gate.[11]

**Medical Institute and Hospital**    As mentioned earlier, Jondishapoor was famous for its medical institute and hospital which were one of the biggest scientific centres of the east for several centuries. It cannot be ascertained when it acquired its prominent position, but it is clear that the process began before

---

[6] Quoted by him from Yaghoot in *Mo'jam-ul-Buldan*, under Jondisabur.

[7] *Tarikh Tabari*, vol. II, p. 830.

[8] *Mo'jam-ul-Buldan*, under Jondi Khosrow.

[9] Refer to the article by Colmann Howar in the *Islamic Encyclopedia* under *Djundaishabur*.

[10] *Tarikh Tabari*, vol. II, p. 830.

[11] Browne, *Arab Medicine*, p. 20.

the reign of Anooshiravan, although during his time its development and significance peaked. It can be deduced from Ghafti's tale about the construction of this city that even during the reign of Shapoor the first there were famous physicians active in the city. Ghafti writes:

After conquering Syria and capturing Antioc, Shapoor made peace with the Emperor of Rome, and he asked for the hand of the Emperor's daughter in marriage, and before the marriage he built for her the city of Jondishapoor on the model of Constantinople, and when he brought her to Iran he brought with her several masters of the skills that she was in need of, and among them were knowledgeable physicians who, after arriving in this city, began teaching others, and they continued until they became examples for future generations.[12]

It can be concluded from such narratives that the medical institute and the clout of its physicians were well known before Anooshiravan's time and these tales evolved from that historical background.

According to Sarson, it is possible that this institution was established before the fifth century, and even earlier than the fourth century AD.[13] If Braun's premise is true that Teodosins, the physician of Shapoor the second lived in Jondishapoor,[14] it can be deduced that the city was a centre for physicians early in the fourth century.

In the first half of the fifth century AD a group of Nestorian Christians including scientists and physicians migrated to Jondishapoor from Asia Minor which increased scientific importance of this city. The Nestorians brought with them numerous books on medicine and philosophy which they taught at the institute of Jondishapoor. The reasons for migrating to Iran was the conflict between the followers of the school of Antioch and the school of Alexandria, due to the influence of Greek philosophy on Christian religion. The bone of contention was whether Christ was a single natural entity with two distinct dimensions, an earthly one and a divine one, or he was two distinct natural entities, one human and one divine. As the master of the school of Antioch was a priest named Nestor, the followers of this school were called Nestorians. This conflict gradually escalated

[12] *Tarikh-al-Hokama'*, pp. 132-3.
[13] Sarton, *Introduction to the History of Science*, p. 435.
[14] *Arab Medicine*, p. 20.

and finally in AD 431 a large conference was organized to examine and resolve this issue. The conference endorsed the position of the Alexandria school, and as the Nestorians did not accept this verdict, the Roman Emperor Zeno shut down their school in the city of Raha and compelled them to migrate. The Nestorians sought refuge in Iran, and the Sassanid shah permitted them to establish their school in Nasibein.

**Jondishapoor in the Days of Anooshiravan**    Undoubtedly, the golden era in Jondishapoor coincided with the period of Iran's cultural renaissance during the reign of Anooshiravan, who evinced a keen interest in science and knowledge and strove to enhance the glory of his court and the significance of his country by inciting competent scientists and physicians, he introduced important measures to develop the academy and hospital of Jondishapoor. The classification of physicians and structuring of the internal organization of the institute goes back to the time of Anooshiravan. During this period, physicians in Iranian society were considered a distinguished class, and had their own structure and codes of conduct. The leader of the class of physicians was given the title of Dorost Bad (or Dorost Bod?), and as the most knowledgeable among them was selected for this position, the Dorost Bad was at the same time the special physician of the shah, and the director of the hospital of Jondishapoor.

Before being granted the right to practise medicine, physicians had to obtain special permits. Although no information is available about this practise, it can be assumed that the issuing of such permits and the organization of the professional affairs of this class was among the responsibilities of the Dorost Bad. Christensen has opined that as it was very difficult to obtain such permits, only distinguished physicians were able to secure them. Several historical books contain references to examination sessions for physicians during the reign of Khosrow Anooshiravan. At times there were debates among physicians from different parts of the country in order to exchange knowledge and benefit from each other's experiences. Ghafti has given an account of one of these sessions in his book the *Tarikh-al-Hokama'*. According to him, in the twentieth regnal year of Khosrow

Anooshiravan, the physicians of Jondishapoor met at the *farman* (decree) of the shah, and debated on issues in the medical sciences. The minutes of their discussions were recorded. He adds that various issues were carefully scrutinized reflecting their level of knowledge and wisdom. It can be deduced from the writings of Ghafti that these records were available during his time and he himself had seen them. This session was chaired by Jibra'il, the leader of the physicians, who held the title of Dorost Bad.[15]

The journey of Borzouyeh, leading a delegation of physicians to India, should be seen as a significant step towards the advancement of the medical sciences in Jondishapoor. Borzouyeh, Iran Dorost Bad[16] travelled to India with a group of Iranian physicians to bring books of medicine back to Iran. This journey had valuable consequences for the institute and hospital of Jondishapoor and also increased its significance and scientific wealth.

Reference has been made earlier to the seven followers of neo-Platonism who travelled to Iran. During their sojourn, they lived in Jondishapoor. Some scholars believe that the presence of these philosophers in Jondishapoor had an impact on the city's scientific position. As far as philosophic ideas and the dissemination of neo-Platonism is concerned, this is possible but in the case of the medical sciences it is not clear to what extent these philosophers had knowledge of medicine and whether their knowledge had any impact on this scientific centre.

Although historical sources do not provide much information on the periods following Khosrow Anooshiravan, but the fact that this institution survived in the Islamic period reveals that it enjoyed much support and patronage throughout the Sassanid period, and its foundations were so solid that it remained active for more than two or three centuries after the collapse of the Sassanid empire and continued to render valuable services.

---

[15] *Tarikh-al-Hokama'*, pp. 132-3.

[16] Ibni Mughaffa' has translated this as 'Head of the Physicians of *Fars*'. See the Introduction by Borzouyeh to the Arabic *Kalileh va Demneh*.

**Iranian Medicine and**        Little information on Iranian medicine
**a Number of its Vestiges**   in the Sassanid period is found in Zoroastrian books that are available today
such as *Vandidad, Deenkard* and *Houspaem*. Drawing upon the
available sources, Christensen has provided substantive information
on the subject in his book.[17] It has been presumed that the basis
of Iranian medicine was Zoroastrian, and although physicians were
handed by a chief who held the title of Iran Dorost Bad, they were
under the supreme supervision of the Zoratostrotema or Moobadan
Moobad, and were considered to be a part of the class of priests and
holy men.

As mentioned earlier, Zoroastrian religious books provide information on the medical sciences in the Sassanid period. This indicates
that Iranian religious books contained information on the medical
sciences, but it does not mean that the medical sciences in the Sassanid period were exclusively discussed in books of religion, or that
Iranian physicians were in the same class as the Moobadan. Other
evidence indicates that Iranian medicine was also recorded in books
other than religious ones, and apart from the Moobadan, there were
other scholars who were engaged in the medical sciences. Scattered
accounts by Islamic authors confirm this. According to Ibni Sa'ed,
the Iranians had an advantage in medicine and astronomy. This
means that the Moslems became acquainted with Iranian medicine
and astronomy through books other than Zoroastrian religious
books, because they had no interest in Iran's religious books or in
extracting any information from them.

From the *Tarikh-al-Hokama'* it can be deduced that the physicians
of Jondishapoor had written numerous books on medicine. After
describing the establishment of Jondishapoor, Ghafti says: 'Some
prefer the cures provided by the physicians of Jondishapoor and
their methods to those of Greek and Indian physicians, because these
have taken the wisdom of each nation, and they have added to it,
and have produced clear practices and books that contain all these
advantages.'[18]

---

[17] Christensen, pp. 413-20.
[18] Ghafti, *Tarikh-al-Hokama'*, p. 133.

In the Sassanid period there was a special script for the writing of medical and philosophical books, which was called Gashtaj and Kastaj in Arabic and Gashteh in Persian. Although there is not much information on this script, various accounts reveal that the script used for these books was somewhat different from that used for religious books.[19] Describing Reyshahr, Yaghoot writes that in the Sassanid empire there was a particular group of people who transcribed books in the Gashtaj or Gashteh script, and Yaghoot calls them the Gashteh Daftaran. If one recalls that this script was used to write medical and philosophical books, and that Reyshahr was located in Khouzestan near Jondishapoor, then it can be assumed that there was a link between this group and the institute in Jondishapoor.

Occasionally, Islamic books mention the names of some of the books which were translated from Pahlavi into Arabic. Ibni Mughaffa' translated Oranius' (the physician of Shahpoor the second) book on medicine. The book that is listed by Ibni Nadeem under the title of *Sirak* was translated in the Sassanid period from Sanskrit into Pahlavi, and in the Islamic period Abdullah bin Ali translated it from Pahlavi into Arabic.[20] Neither of these books was religious or spiritual in content. If one evaluates the science of medicine and its significance in Iran before the advent of Islam merely on the basis of the incomplete information available in Zoroastrian religious writings, it would be akin to using the information available in Islamic religious writings to understand the extent of progress made in medical sciences in Islam.

Apart from books on the medical sciences, books on veterinary sciences were also translated from Pahlavi into Arabic. Ibni Nadeem has listed two such books—one of them was the *Kitab Al Baitara*, but he has not given the title of the other book which he says dealt with the treatment of animals such as horses, mules, cows, sheep and camels, and also contained information on their characteristics

---

[19] For details of the seven Persian scripts refer to the clarification quoted by Ibni Nadeem from Ibni Mughaffa' in *Al-Fehrest*, p. 13. For the Kashtaj script, see p. 239 of the same book.
[20] *Al-Fehrest*, p. 303.

and shape. This book was translated into Arabic by Ishaq bin Ali bin Soleyman.[21]

Three other books are mentioned in the *Al-Fehrest*—*Bonian Dokht, Bonian Nafs* and *Bahram Dokht* which, according to Ibni Nadeem dealt with the subject of *bah* or stories and tales that were intended to be erotically arousing. Such books were used to treat sexual impotence. These three books were also translated from Pahlavi into Arabic.[22]

It can be presumed that books on botany and pharmacy were translated from Pahlavi into Arabic, although their names are not available. This is based on the fact that the Iranian influence on Arab and Islamic botany was obvious. The best manifestation of this influence is the numerous Persian words and expressions that appear in Arabic books in these fields. Many plants and medicines mentioned in these books are referred to by their Persian names, and most of the names that appear in Arabic are literal translations of the same Persian names or their meanings, and they must have been adopted from Pahlavi books.

**The Scientific Significance of Jondishapoor in the Sassanid Period**

The institute in Jondishapoor enjoys a prominent position in the history of culture in general and the history of ancient medicine in particular. As discussed earlier, the interaction and integration of different cultures have always the progress of science and civilization. The advantage of the institute and hospital of Jondishapoor was that, in a period in which no adequate opportunities and mechanisms existed for the interaction of scholars of different nations and the development and dissemination of culture, Jondishapoor was able to attract scholars and physicians from various countries, and provided to them the opportunity to benefit from each other's knowledge and experience. This interaction and integration took shape in a manner that was not possible elsewhere.

In order to further clarify the significance of Jondishapoor and the service that it rendered to the scientific world of that time, it

[21] Ibid., p. 314.
[22] Ibid., p. 305.

is worthwhile to discuss similar institutions that were active during the same period elsewhere, and compare them in terms of their achievements. As is well known at the time when the institute in Jondishapoor had developed and progressed in Iran, there were other institutes in the Christian world where sciences were taught. As these institutes, like other Christian institutions, were under the influence of religion and the church, they were not able to promote sciences other than those that were affiliated with religion. This is because in such institutions religious and philosophic issues that had developed as a result of the interaction between Greek philosophy and Christianity, constituted the most important, if not the exclusive, range of topics that were taught and debated. Even if there was some interest in other branches of science such as medicine, the teaching of these sciences and the attention that was given to them remained marginal to religion based topics.

Another significant distinction was that teaching in the institutions of Western Asia and Greece was confined to Greek medicine while in Indian institutions it focused exclusively on Indian medicine. In Jondishapoor there was no room for religious and doctrinal debates, and as its achievements indicate, the institute followed its own scientific path, and hosted Greek and Assyrian Christians, Zoroastrian Iranians, Hindu scholars, Arabs such as Hareth bin Kaldeh Thaghafi and Nazr bin al Hareth and followers of other religions. The achievements of this institute were scientific in nature with no trace of religious influences, and teaching was not confined to Greek, Indian or Iranian medicine, but rather an amalgamation of the conceptual and practical experiences of these three nations as well as other nations. For this reason, the advancement in medical sciences in this institute was vastly superior to that in the Christian institutes of Rome and Western Asia.[23]

It is worth noting that in an age of rampant religious fanaticism, in which religious differences not only obstructed understanding among different nations, but were also the primary cause of conflict and confrontation among them, the institute in Jondishapoor opened its gates to scholars and students of all religions, and led them all towards a true objective, without prejudice.

[23] Oleary, *Arabic Thought and Its Place in History*, p. 42.

Sarton has referred to the institute in Jondishapoor as a 'university'. Although this terminology is a modern one and it may be inappropriate to use this word to describe a teaching institution at a time when such modern institutions did not exist, but considering what this word denotes, it is the best description of the type of activities that took place in that institute. In short, Jondishapoor had the same characteristics as a modern university. In the same way that any university represents the common culture of the world, Jondishapoor also had this advantage that at least in medical sciences, it was unique in its own world. Although this institution was located in Iran, and was in every respect considered an Iranian institution, but it was not exclusively for Iranian physicians and Iranian medicine. Just as there were physicians from other nations who worked and taught at the institute, the scientific works that represented the essence of the efforts and the thinking of other scientists in the world were also taught and used there. The fact that in addition to Zoroastrian Iranians and Christian Assyrians, we find the names of other physicians, and among them a number of Arabs, such as Hareth bin Kaldeh Thaghafi and Nazr bin al Hareth who, in the Jahili period, had come to Jondishapoor and learned medicine, demonstrates that the institute and hospital of Jondishapoor was one of the significant and famous centres for medicine in the world in those days. Jondishapoor maintained its importance during the Arab conquest and the period of languish, and continued to render valuable service to the culture and civilization of this region, because it was here that much of the heritage of Iran and scientific works of the world of that time were preserved and passed on to the scholars of Islam.

**The Teaching of Medicine in Jondishapoor**   A number of orientalists who have written about Jondishapoor have argued that the basis of teaching in the institute was Greek medicine, and others have also presumed that the medium of instruction was Assyrian or Aramite. Expressing a similar view, Braun has written that pharmacy and botany were purely Iranian sciences and free from Greek influence.[24] Sarton has

[24] *Arab Medicine*, p. 22.

argued that apart from Greek physicians, Iranian, Assyrian and Indian physicians in the institute were also influential.[25] According to Colman Howar, Greek sciences were taught in Jondishapoor under the supervision of Assyrian Christians in the Aramite language.[26] Other scholars have offered similar arguments.

If one accepts these viewpoints, one must conclude that in Sassanid Iran two types of medicine were practised which were completely distinct from one another and pursued an independent path. One was Greek medicine that was taught under the supervision of Greek or Assyrian Christians, and the other was Iranian medicine which was taught on the basis of Zoroastrian books under the supervision of Iranian physicians. There is, however, no historical evidence to support this.

It appears that this perception is the result of the distinct and special position of Jondishapoor. As explained earlier, in this institute various medical books were taught and physicians from different nations worked there. Since a great number of Christians lived in Jondishapoor the city had acquired a Christian character; and because most European writers consider Greek culture and civilization as the only source of ancient civilization and Assyrian as the only language of eastern Christians, they have concluded that the institute was a Christian school and representative of Greek culture and civilization which held sway in Iran and that its language was Assyrian.

There is neither any evidence in support of Colman Howar's argument that medical sciences were taught in Jondishapoor in the Aramite language nor any basis for this claim. If Aramite was used in Iran it was during the Achaemenian period and in the administration of the *divan*; but in the Sassanid period, particularly in relation to this institution, there is no reference to the Aramite language in any of the historical sources.

To obtain a clearer picture of the teaching of medicine and the language in which it was taught in Jondishapoor, the pre-Islamic period should be divided into two parts: the first was the period before Anooshiravan, and the second after Anooshiravan. In relation to the first period it can be assumed that the institute and hospital

[25] Sarton, *History of Science*, p. 435.
[26] See his article in the *Islamic Encyclopedia*.

had more of a Christian and Greek character, while majority of the physicians were Nestorian Syrians or Romans, Assyrian or Greek books were also taught there. However, in relation to the second period, such an assumption is erroneous because it is hard to imagine that Jondishapoor had not yet acquired an Iranian character and Iranian was not its official language.

It was mentioned earlier in relation to the cultural renaissance of Iran that one of its prominent characteristics was that it was completely national and Iranian in character and content. In other words, although efforts were made to introduce sciences that were developed in other countries and to expand the glory of the court of Iran by inviting prominent scholars, there was an attempt to translate various books in different fields of science into Pahlavi so that they would be accessible to the Iranians. There are numerous indications and examples to confirm that most or all the foreign books that were translated into Pahlavi, were from the time of Anooshiravan or later.

As already mentioned, the Pahlavi translation of the *Ahde Atiq* was done in this period, as also a part of Greek logic and a number of Greek books on philosophy, besides Indian books on medicine, literature and culture were translated into Pahlavi. One of those masterful pieces, the *Kalileh va Demneh*, is available even today. When the Arabs and Moslems undertook to translate foreign books, they translated many of the Indian books and a number of Greek works from Pahlavi.

Keeping in mind the fact that Anooshiravan dispatched envoys to distant countries to obtain copies of foreign books to be translated into Pahlavi, it would be different to accept that medical books and the official language used in the institution in Jondishapoor would be other than the official language of Iran. Or, to accept that when Borzouyeh brought back a number of books from India during the reign of Anooshiravan, medical books were translated into Assyrian and the *Kalileh va Demneh* into Pahlavi.

The presence of Assyrian or Greek physicians in the institution does not prove that the language used in the institution was also Greek or Assyrian. For example, Oranius, in the court of Shapoor the second, and Polos the Persian and many other Christians in the court of Anooshiravan were Assyrian, but their work was in

Pahlavi. In fact, Polos the Persian himself translated Greek works into Pahlavi. Besides, there were Indian physicians in Jondishapoor where Indian medicine was also taught, Indian books were translated into the Iranian language and at no time was the Indian language used in Iran, hence, there is no reason to assume that the situation was different in the case of Christian physicians and their books.

The large number of Christians in the city should not be taken as evidence that Greek or Assyrian was widely used, as the translation of Ibni Atiq shows that the Christians in Iran also used the Iranian language. In the Islamic period, the majority of physicians and alchemists were Christians, but their works were generally in Arabic, which was the dominant language of that period. Similarly, in the Sassanid period, physicians and other scholars used the dominant language of the period, i.e. Pahlavi for their works and even in Jondishapoor this was the dominant language.

Qhafti writes that when Mansour, the Abbasid Caliph, fell ill in Baghdad, he summoned Georgis, the son of Bakht Yashoo', the chief of the hospital of Jondishapoor. When Georgis met on the Caliph, he praised him in Persian and Arabic, and the latter was impressed by the eloquence of his expression.[27] Georgis, was an Assyrian Christian, and this account reveals that the common languages at that time were Persian and Arabic, whereas before the advent of Islam it must have been Persian, or Pahlavi.

**Jondishapoor in the Islamic Caliphate** The Arabs conquered Jondishapoor in the seventeenth year of Hijra. In the description of Hormozan earlier, we briefly referred to the battles that took place between him and the Arabs during the conquest of Khouzestan, and we said that, as Hormozan proceeded from Ramhormoz to Shushtar to resume his resistance, Omar dispatched a powerful army under the command of Abu Musa Ash'ari to assist the forces that were fighting Hormozan in Khouzestan, and after surrounding Shushtar from all sides they finally conquered the city and captured Hormozan. As mentioned earlier, following the defeat of Hormozan, the Arabs easily conquered other

---

[27] *Tarikh-al-Hokama'*, p. 158.

cities of Khuzestan and after the fall of Shushtar they conquered Jondishapoor which also became a part of the Islamic territories.

After the fall of Jondishapoor, the institute and hospital continued to function for two or three centuries and rendered valuable services to the Arabs and Moslems, and even played a vital role in the scientific movement of Islam, but after the collapse of the Sassanid state, the past vitality and glory of the institute and hospital which they had enjoyed during the reign of Anooshiravan were irretrievably lost.

In the first century of the Hijra, or during the period of conquests, the Arabs, who were the custodians of the Islamic territories, focused their attention on war and paid little attention to institutions such as Jondishapoor, and therefore, the Caliphs made no attempt to administer Jondishapoor and to assist or even encourage its physicians: hence, this institution was totally isolated from the heart of the Caliphate in Damascus, a process which was further aggravated by the geographical distance from the seat of power.

In the Abbasid period as well, despite the fact that the Islamic state had gradually gained stability and the Caliphs had become better acquainted with the manifestations of science and knowledge and had evinced an interest in them, their interest in Jondishapoor remained limited, particularly after another medical institute and a hospital were established in Baghdad. When Haroon Al Rashid wished to build a hospital in Baghdad, he entrusted this task to Jebra'il, the son of Bakht Yashoo', who was one of the physicians in Jondishapoor and stayed at the court of the Caliphate. He summoned Deheshtak, the chief of the hospital at Jondishapoor to compel him to accept this task, but Deheshtak refused on the grounds that he was not duty bound to the Caliph as he did not receive any pay from the Caliphate, and his objective in administering Jondishapoor[28] was to do good and charitable work. Nevertheless, he agreed to send one of his students for this job.

Throughout the period of the Caliphate when it was active, the administration of the hospital of Jondishapoor was in the hands of the physicians of the hospital, who worked independently and without any assistance from the Caliphs. The administration of the

[28] Ibid., p. 338.

hospital was under the charge of the Assyrian Christian family of Bakht Yashoo'. They had lived in Jondishapoor since the Sassanid period and had continued to administer the hospital during the period of languish.

With the drawn of the Abbasid period, this family established itself in Islamic society, it produced a number of famous physicians who assumed responsibilities in the Caliphate and enjoyed much fame. For example, Jebra'il was considered among the nobility of his time and his annual income from his property in Jondishapoor Shush and Basrah alone was 800,000 *derhams.*[29]

The first time that the physicians of Jondishapoor visited to the capital of the Caliphate was during the days of Mansour, the Abbasid Caliph. As mentioned earlier, when he fell ill, he summoned Georgis to Baghdad. He was the most renowned physician of Jondishapoor, which was still the biggest scientific centre of the time. From this time onward, the Abbasid Caliphs had one of the physicians of Jondishapoor, often a member of this family, at their court, and this was one of the reasons for the decline of the scientific significance of the institute in Jondishapoor and the increasing scientific significance of Baghdad, until eventually a hospital was built in Baghdad which assumed the position that Jondishapoor had enjoyed.

The history of the Abbasid Caliphate contains the names of many physicians of Jondishapoor. During the reign of Mansour, three of them successively stayed at the court of the Caliphate. Among them were Georgis, his student Ibrahim who was sent by Georgis, after the latter returned from Baghdad and was unable to go back because of poor health. The third has been mentioned by Ghafti as Ibni Shahlafa, he also went to Baghdad after Georgis.

When Georgis was in Baghdad and even after his death, the leadership and administration of the hospital in Jondishapoor was entrusted to his son Bakht Yashoo', who remained in Jondishapoor till the time of the Abbasid Caliph Mahdi. Around this time the Caliph summoned him to Baghdad to treat his son Hadi, whom he cured. He remained in Baghdad for a while until he was relieved and he retuned to Jondishapoor. Bakht Yashoo' resumed his duties

[29] Ibid., p. 143.

in Jondishapoor until Haroon Al Rashid was taken ill, and he went to Baghdad to treat him. Bakht Yashoo' remained at the court of the Caliph till his death.

Jebra'il succeeded Bakht Yashoo' and enjoyed high standing at the court of Haroon Al Rashid. None of his contemporaries nor any member of his own family surpassed him in stature and wealth. He established the first hospital of the Islamic era in Baghdad based on the model of the hospital at Jondishapoor. He brought together physicians and scientists in this field from every corner and transformed that city into the medical centre of the Islamic world.

Bakht Yashoo', the son of Jebra'il, who should be referred to as Bakht Yashoo' the second, succeeded his father and remained at the court of the Caliph. He was expelled to Jondishapoor during the reign of Al Wathiqh Billah when all his property and wealth were confiscated. However, it was not long before the Caliph forgave him and summoned him to Baghdad.

Besides the members of this family, there were other learned physicians in Jondishapoor who were renowned in the Moslem world. One of them was Issa, the son of Chahar Bakht who was a student of Georgis, he enjoyed a privileged position and wrote several books on medicine.[30] Another was Yuhanna, a student of Chahar Bakht,[31] who was also one of the prominent scientists of the Moslem world and had great influence on the cultural movement of the Abbasid period. Masouyeh whose father was from Jondishapoor, played an important role in the establishment of the hospital in Baghdad. Micha'if (?), the brother of Yuhanna, was also a prominent physician of Jondishapoor in his time.[32]

The last physician of Jondishapoor who has been mentioned in history was Shapour, the son of Sahl, who was the chief of the hospital of Jondishapoor and he died in the year 255 of Hijra. Shapour was a scientist and a famous physician. His book *Aghrabadi* on medicine and alchemy was used by physicians and alchemists for centuries.

[30] Ibid., p. 247.
[31] Ibid., p. 188.
[32] Ibid., p. 328.

**The Impact of Jondishapoor on the Cultural Movement of Islam** When the centre of the Caliphate was established in Baghdad and this new city overshadowed Tisphoon and became the political and economic centre of Islamic society, the physicians of Jondishapoor also moved to Baghdad either in search of wealth and glory or at the behest of the Caliphs and made that city the centre of their activities.

The Amavid period was not conducive to the growth and development of the hospital in Jondishapoor. If this institution was able to continue its activities during that period, it was due to the efforts of the physicians and the solid base that it had built during the Sassanid period.

The Abbasid period is considered the golden period of Islam as far as advancement in science is concerned, but the Caliphs focused their attention on Baghdad, which they wished to promote in every respect, and they invited many masters of the arts and sciences to that city; others were also attracted to Baghdad.

When the first hospital was built in Baghdad, it led to the further decline of Jondishapoor. As the significance of the scientific institutions of Baghdad increased, the position of Jondishapoor diminished, and it was not long before the city's hospital fell in to disuse and the city itself withered, until only ruins stood where there had once been a lively city; ruins that held in their depth the legacy of the past glory of Jondishapoor. With the passage of time even the physical traces of Jondishapoor disappeared, but its substantive impact on the development of medical sciences survived through all subsequent Islamic periods, as the institute and hospital of Jondishapoor were used as models for other similar Islamic institutions, and its significant vestiges were prominent in the cultural movement of Islam.

In addition to the scientific significance of Jondishapoor, it also played a vital role in the impact that Iranian culture had on Arab and Islamic culture and civilization. This is because Jondishapoor was the only Iranian institution that during the period of languish had remained relatively unaffected by the insecurity and uncertainty in the wake of the Arab conquests, and during the subsequent period of tranquillity, all the scientific works housed in this institution became available to the Arabs and scientists who had been trained there made attempts to develop a sound basis for medicine in Islam and left behind a valuable heritage.

It is obvious that medical sciences flourished in Islam and famous Moslem physicians arose who maintained for centuries their position as masters in the field. However, it must be borne in mind that the most significant sources of knowledge acquired in this field and passed on to the Moslems were the valuable works of scholars and physicians in Jondishapoor, as well as the works of Iran, Greece, India and Assyria that had been collected and recorded in Jondishapoor. Moreover, those who laid the foundation of medical sciences in Islam as well as wrote or translated books on medicine in Arabic were the physicians of Jondishapoor.

In order to understand the position of Jondishapoor in the history of medical sciences in general and the history of Islamic culture in particular, it is important to discuss the founding of the first hospital in Baghdad during the days of Haroon Al Rashid. Available information reveals that the hospital was an exact replica of that in Jondishapoor and was administered under the supervision of people who had been trained in Jondishapoor.

Although nothing definite can be said about the technical aspects of the hospital, it would be relevant to mention briefly what Ghafti has written on this subject. Ghafti has quoted from Jebra'il's biography of Masouyeh, one of the physicians of that period. According to the account, when the Caliph entrusted the task of setting up a hospital in Baghdad to Jebra'il, the latter summoned Deheshtak, the chief of the hospital of Jondishapoor, to entrust to him that task. Deheshtak declined, but promised to send someone who was ideal for the job. This person had been mixing medicines for forty years, i.e. since his childhood, and although he was illiterate, he could not only diagnose all illnesses, but also prescribe medication, and therefore, he had an advantage over other physicians in the knowledge of the medicines and their wage. Deheshtak then said to Jibra'il, I will send this person to Baghdad, and you assign him as an assistant to one of your students, then entrust this assistant with the administration of your hospital, and be assured that the affairs of the hospital will proceed according to your expectations. Jebra'il agreed and Deheshtak kept his promise and the work of the hospital began.[33] This person was Masouyeh, the father of Yuhanna and Mikha'il who became masters in medicine and were renowned throughout the Moslem world.

If one considers the hospital of Baghdad as the first institution of its kind that was established in Islam, and its institutional organization as the model for the founding of similar institutions, the extent of the impact of Jondishapoor on Islamic medicine will become clear. At the time when the foundations of Islamic civilization and culture were being laid, and Arabic was building up its scientific wealth through copying and translation of books in various sciences, and books were being produced in Arabic, the physicians of Jondishapoor and their students were the only vanguards of medical sciences in the Moslem world and were considered great scholars in this field for several centuries.

There is a narrative about the life of Hunain bin Eshaq who was a renowned physician and had translated numerous Greek medical books into Arabic. Hunain was from Hirah and had a passion for knowledge and virtue. When he came to Baghdad, he attended the classes of Yuhanna who was a competent professor of medicine. During the classes Hunain repeatedly asked questions which annoyed Yuhanna. One day when Hunain asked a question, Yuhanna lost his temper and castigated him saying that the people of Hirah had no business to study medicine. Intend they should sell herbs in the alleys. Then he expelled him from his class.

Ghafti, writes that the reason for Yuhanna's action was that people from Jondishapoor considered themselves as the only masters of medical sciences, and did not deem any one worthy of it except their own kith and kin and did not accept any outsider.[34] This tale reveals the extent to which the physicians of Jondishapoor enjoyed an unrivalled position in the Moslem world.

The first medical books produced or translated into Arabic were by this group of physicians. As mentioned earlier, many of the medicines were referred to by their Persian names in Arabic books. There is no doubt that the original sources of these names

[33] Ibid., p. 383.
[34] Ibid., p. 174.

were comparative Iranian books that were found in Jondishapoor. As the authors of these books were physicians of Jondishapoor who were fluent in Persian, most of these expressions were used in their original form in these books.

Two of these books became very popular; one was the *Al-Kannash* by Georgis, and the other was the *Aghrabadin* by Shapour, the son of Sahl, the last chief of the hospital in Jondishapoor. These books used in various hospitals and by alchemists for several centuries.[35] Issa the son of Chahar Bakht, also authored several significant works.[36]

One of the significant Islamic academic institutions established in Baghdad in the first Abbasid period was Baitul Hikmah, built by the decree of the Caliph Ma'moon. Ernest Diez who has done research on that institution has argued that it was built on the model of the institute of Jondishapoor, and Ma'moon was influenced by it in his decision.[37] As the Baitul Hikmah was an important product of the scientific movement of Islam and a crucial factor in its continuation and expansion, therefore, while investigating the various factors that led to that movement, Ernest Diez's views should also be taken into account.

---

[35]  Ibid., p. 207.
[36]  Ibid., p. 247.
[37]  *Islamic Encyclopedia*, see under *Masjid*.

# NINE

# Hekmah and Akhlagh (Applied Wisdom and Ethics) in Iran and Islam

One of the fields in which many books were translated from Pahlavi into Arabic and which had a significant impact on Arabic literature was practical wisdom and ethics. Practical wisdom and ethics refers to that category of books which in the Sassanid period were in the form of 'Andarznameh' or 'Pandnameh', and constituted a significant part of Pahlavi literature. When they were translated into Arabic and were adapted to the new environment, they were known by titles such as Adab, Hekam and Wasaya, they enjoyed great importance in Islamic society and led to other works in this field in Arabic literature.

Traces of some of these books in Arabic literature as well as the titles mentioned in historical Islamic sources indicates that numerous such books were translated from Pahlavi into Arabic and narratives on this issue reveal that Iranian works of ethics were also immensely popular particularly among scholars and writers.

**Ethics in Islam**  In various Islamic periods many books were produced on ethics and practical wisdom thus enriching Arab and Islamic literatures. However, all these books did not originate from a single source; rather they had different origins and were influenced by various factors, the study of which is not only important for Arab and Islamic cultures, but is significant and essential for the history of Iranian culture as well.

The contents of these books on ethics are so varied in terms of topics and substance that it is difficult to categorize them and determine the origin of each category. Nevertheless, all ethical works in Arabic can be grouped into four broad areas: (a) Literary ethics, or ethical literature; (b) Religious ethics; (c) Philosophical ethics; and (d) Mystical ethics.

What is known as religious ethics consists of teachings and judgements that are based on religious doctrine; and the biggest sources of it in Arabic and Islamic literature are the Koran and *Hadith*. Religious ethics refer to the category that falls under the principles and teachings of religion. Many books in this field were written in Arabic and Persian, for example, the *Makarem-ul-Akhlagh* by Tabarsi.

Philosophical ethics refers to those topics that were borrowed from Greek philosophic books in Islamic writings, and have produced works that are different from Islamic religious works. Among the scientific and literary works that the Arabs borrowed from the Greeks, were those on the science of ethics which were translated into Arabic. The science of ethics, according to Aristotle, is a component of applied/practical philosophy. Although there were numerous literary works in this field in Greek, the Moslems and Arabs considered the Ethics of Aristotle which was translated into Arabic as the base. The Ethics of Aristotle was also translated into Arabic by Farabi. In any case, for the Moslems, this was the most important and reputed book on philosophical ethics. Other books were also copied such as the *Tafsir* of Farfurius, which was translated by Ishaq bin Honayn, the Republic and Politics of Plato, and the Book of Ethnology containing neo-Platonic debates on ethics. There were numerous works of this genre in Islam authored by Moskouyeh, Ghazali, Akhawan al Safa and Khajeh Naseer ud Din Tousi.

Mystical ethics does not focus on a particular topic to the extent that religious and philosophical ethics do. In essence, mystical ethics refers to a combination of religious and neo-Platonic teachings and mystical concepts of piety that developed and their meaning changed with time. The ethical issues covered in these books are neither new nor different from those discussed in other books; however, they have all been presented under the garb of mysticism and have acquired a mystical context, for example, the Mystical books of Ghazali, particularly his *Ehya' Oloum al Din*.

**Ethical Literature**　　Literary ethics refers to the collection of teachings, maxims, and ethical material that Arabic writers collected from various sources and collated under the general title of *Adab*, for example, *Oyoon-al-Akhbar* by Ibni Qutaybah. In these books that constitute one of the main fields of Arab literature, the ethical tales have not originated from a single source, but have been collected from different sources as self-standing pieces and have been compiled into a book with no specific sequence.

Apart from Islamic teachings which had an impact on these writings, other sources also greatly influenced their evolution and development. Inostranzev has mentioned two of these sources: the ethical works of Iran and the ethical works of Greece. According to him, Greek ethical works, particularly those of Aristotle and Pythagoras, reached Arabic literature through old Persian works.[1] This seems probable if one takes into account the fact that the period in which these references found their way into Arabic writings, Greek books had not yet been translated into Arabic.

The most important factor that had an impact on Arabic ethical literature and gave it its characteristic form was the books of ethics of Iran, a great number of which had been translated into Arabic. Moreover, when Islamic writers first attempted to produce such books of *Adab*, the most important sources that were available to them and which they used as their models were Iranian works of ethics.

One of the characteristics of this genre of Arabic books of ethics is that they normally contain practical teachings and instructions about personal and social life. Unlike philosophic works that discuss general ethical issues, or religious works that contain only religious teachings, or mystical works that focus on the spirit of piety and hermitry, these books focus on practical living and offer advice on the refinement of ethics, purification of the self, and improvement of behaviour and attitude, etc.

Books on education, self-refinement and etiquette in the company of royalty and nobility, codes of the court, and those offering guidance to the shahs and influencing their attitudes such as the *Kalileh va Demneh* fall into this category.

---

[1] Inostranzev, p. 54.

PAHLAVI *ANDARZNAMEHS*   During the Sassanid period, Iranians evinced a keen interest in this genre of literature, as there were numerous works on practical wisdom and ethics in Pahlavi literature under the general title of '*Andarznameh*' and '*Pandnameh*'. Many of these works were translated into Arabic in the early centuries of Islam and several of them are found in Pahlavi literature even today Christensen has explained that Iranian interest and enthusiasm in translating the *Kalileh va Demneh* were due to the fact that its ethical contents were similar to those of the *Andarznamehs* and other books of advice and practical wisdom in Iranian literature; books that were highly popular among Iranians of that period.[2]

Iranians' interest in this genre of writing was noteworthy for Islamic authors and they have referred to it in their writings. Jahiz says, 'The Iranians carved on large rocks the major events of their history and the exhortations of common benefit, and also such matters that manifested their greatness and glory, and they also placed them as monuments in great buildings.'[3] Explorers and geographers of the first centuries of Islam make occasional references in their works to historical sites of the pre-Islamic period that they had seen in Iran thus confirming Jahiz's observation. For example, Ibni Faghih has described a great rock in Hamedan, and it appears from his writing that he himself had seen it. According to his description, on the side of a mountain near Hamedan, two large arcs were dug, each arc had three carved tablets, and on each tablet were written twenty lines of maxims and advice.[4]

Such was the significance attached to this type of ethical writings that phrases of exhortation were often written on the hems of garments, margins of carpets edges of tablecloths or on other objects either alone or in addition to other decorative designs. History books repeatedly mention such phrases that have either been copied from the crown of some shah, or from the wall of a building. Mas'oodi describes a large *khan* belonging to Anooshiravan, which was covered

---

[2] Christensen, p. 426.
[3] *Al-Mahasen wal Addad*, p. 201.
[4] *Al-Buldan*, p. 243.

with wise sayings in various gems and stones.[5] Ibni Qutaybah also copied a number of phrases from the *khan* of Anooshiravan. Contemporary Persian literature contains a collection of this genre of ancient writings known as '*Rahat ul Ensan*' or the *Pandnameh* of Anooshiravan, and it is mentioned in the introduction that it offers words of wisdom that were inscribed on the crown of Anooshiravan.[6]

Books that fell under the category of *Andars* were based on Zoroastrian religious teachings, and were primarily in the possession of the Moobadan and were mostly written by Zoroastrian clerics. Contemporary Pahlavi literature, contains a number of papers entitled *Andars*, which are extracted from ancient Iranian writings and Sassanid papers, such as *Andars Oushnardana* and *Andars Azarbad Marsepandan*. The first of these papers was published by the Parsi scholar Arvad Bahmanji Nosarvanji Dahabar with a valuable introduction in English. In the introduction he has briefly discussed the *Andars Namehs* of the Sassanid period and has listed the names of renowned Zoroastrians who produced *Andars*, such as Azarbad Marsepandan, his son Zardosht and his grandson Azarbad Zardosht, Bakht Afarid, Bozorgmehr, Khosrow Anooshiravan, Behzad Firooz, and Azar Faranbagh Farrokh Zad. He has also provided some information about the important post of *Andarz Bod* in the Sassanid period, and its different levels and grades.[7]

Although books on ethics and *Andars* were written since ancient times in Iran from the reign of Anooshiravan onwards, they received greater attention and in addition to Iranian books, a number of Indian and Greek works were also translated into Pahlavi. It is not clear whether the *Kalileh va Demneh* was the only book that was translated into Persian. Iranian books of ethics contained numerous tales about Greek philosophers like Aristotle and Pythagoras and as mentioned earlier, these tales found their way into Arabic literature through Iranian books, which revealed that during the Sassanid period Iranians were familiar with Greek works of ethics.

---

[5] *Morooj*, vol. II, p. 204.

[6] This collection was published by Scheffer, Paris, 1873, also by Sa'eed Nafisi, *Mehr* periodical, vol. II.

[7] This paper was translated into Persian with a summary of its introduction by Rashid Yasami, *Mehr* periodical, vol. II.

**The Listing that Ibni**          Under the heading of books writ-
**Nadeem has Mentioned**          ten on *Pand*, *Adab* and *Hekmah* in
                                  Persian, Greek, Hindi and Arabic,
Ibni Nadeem has listed books that have been translated from different languages into Arabic.[8] A review of this listing would be useful
for the study of the sources of Arabic literature and ethics. The listing
mentions forty-four books which were translations or adaptations
from Pahlavi sources. Although several titles are not clear because of
distortions of the words, this list is very valuable for obtaining the
titles of some of the Iranian ethical books that were translated into
Arabic and had an impact on Arab literature.

Inostranzev has reviewed this listing and has provided very useful
information about a number of the books listed.[9] He has divided all
the books listed into three groups: the first group contains books that
were translated directly from Pahlavi; the second group covers books
that were written in the first Abbasid period and were influenced
by Pahlavi books; and the third group includes books of unknown
origin, although some of them have their origins in Iranian works.

According to Inostranzev, fourteen of the listed books definitely
fall in the first group, and has argued that several others probably
belong to this group as their titles are distorted and not clear. The
fourteen books in the order that they have appeared in the listing are
as follows:

The first book attributed to Zadan Farrokh covers the education
of his son, of which there is no trace in Pahlavi literature. Zadan
Farrokh was a renowned personality in the Sassanid period and had
produced many wise sayings. Perhaps, he was one of the Moobadan
or an important official of the court. Tabari has mentioned Zadan
Farrokh, the son of Shardaran as one of those who conspired to kill
Shahr Baraz.[10] It is likely that he wrote this book although there is no
evidence to support this.[11] According to Inostranzev, this book was

---

[8]    *Al-Fehrest*, pp. 315-16.
[9]    See *Iranian Influence on Moslem Literature*, Chap. 3.
[10]   *Tarikh Tabari*, part one, p. 1063.
[11]   Zadan Farrokh was a popular name in Iran before and after Islam.
The commander of the Imperial Guards during the time of Khosrow Parviz

of the same genre as many of the *Pandnamehs* and *Andarznamehs* of that period, for example, the *Andars Azarbad Marsepandan* or the *Pandnameh* of Anooshiravan and the *Pand Nameh* of Bouzarjomehr.

Another book listed by Ibni Nadeem is the one that Mehr Azar Jashnas, the Moobadan Moobad addressed to Bouzarjomehr, the son of Bakhtagan.[12] Two other books have been listed one of which, according to Ibni Nadeem was on *adab*, and the other was on housekeeping. Because of their titles being distorted, they cannot be clearly read, but it may be assumed that they were Iranian works and Ibni Nadeem listed their original titles which is why they are distorted.

Ibni Nadeem has listed another book under the title: *Ahd (covenant) of Kasra to his son Hormoz advising him, and the response of Hormoz to him.* Flugel has argued that the word *Kasra* in the title refers to definitely Khosrow Anooshiravan. Based on this view, Inostranzev has alleged that the first part of this book that contains the letter of Khosrow, is the same as the paper *Andars Khosrow* in contemporary Pahlavi literature. The copy that Ferdowsi relied upon also contained the letter of Khosrow, because in the *Shahnameh*, some material has been copied from this letter, but no reference has been made to Hormoz's response.

Two other books entitled *Ahd Kasra* have also been listed. Inostranzev has argued that it is likely that all three books refer to the one mentioned earlier. Considering the fact that Ibni Nadeem was a stationer and book keeper,[13] and the books that he has included

---

was known as Zadan Farrokh (*Tabari*, part one, p. 1043). During the Caliphate of Ali bin abi Taleb in Iraq, one of the Iranian *dehghans* of the lower Euphrates who was killed by Khawarej because of his support for the Emam was named Zadan Farrokh (*Tabari*, part one, p. 3423). The name of the Iranian *dabir* of Hajjaj bin Yousef, the *Wali* of Iraq was also Zadan Farrokh (*Tabari*, part two, pp. 458, 1034).

[12] The name Mehr Azar Jashnas has been distorted in the *Al-Fehrest*, and Flugel, the publisher of this book has not been able to decipher it. Justi who found this word in a different place in the *Al-Fehrest* among the books of Ali bin Obaydah Rihani has read it correctly. Inostranzev has also corrected this name as such. Mehr Azar Jashnas is the Arabic form of Mehr Azar Gashasb.

[13] *Warraq* was one who sold, bound and transcribed books.

in the *Al-Fehrest* were either those that he had seen or had in his possession or had obtained details about them from reliable persons, it is highly improbable that he would list the same book three times under different titles.

Ibni Nadeem has listed the *Ahde Ardeshir* which contained advice and counsel from Ardeshir Babakan to his son Shahpoor. Following its translation into Arabic, it became immensely popular among Moslems. According to Ibni Nadeem, this book was one of the ten books that were unanimously accepted as outstanding.[14] Because of its popularity, Balazori, the renowned Islamic writer, rendered it in verse.[15] The fame and popularity of this book is evident from a review of the literary sources of that period. The description of the book by Abu Hanifeh Dinevari clarifies the significance of this book both in the Sassanid and Islamic periods. Dinevari writes in the biography of Ardeshir: 'Then he wrote his famous *ahd* to the shahs and they accepted and followed it, and they safeguarded it and made it their example.'[16]

The Letter of *Tansar*, one of the historical and significant documents of the Sassanid period, contains several references to this book which included the directives and decrees of Ardeshir. One such reference reads: 'I wrote this directive for future shahs so that if they lack the ability to enforce belief, they may read my book and accomplish'.[17] Another reference reads: 'In compliance with the will and testimony of the shah, they have written that, the ignorance of the shah about the affairs of the people is a manifestation of corruption. . . .'[18] A part of the Arabic translation of this book is available today and is known as the *Ahde Ardeshir*. Excerpts from a manuscript of the book dated 710 of the Hijra have been published by the Egyptian writer and scholar Ahmad Beyk Teymour in a book entitled *Rasa'el al Bolagha*.

References to Ardeshir Babakan appear in Arabic literary books of wisdom, knowledge and *Hekmah*, and many of his makings have

---

[14] *Al-Fehrest*, p. 126.
[15] Ibid., pp. 113-14. Refer to the biography of Balazori.
[16] *Al-Akhbar-al-Tewal*, p. 47.
[17] *The Letter of Tansar*, Minavi edn., p. 20.
[18] Ibid., p. 25. Also refer to the notes by Minavi, pp. 60-1.

been reproduced in these books. Undoubtedly, the main reason for his fame was the *Ahd Nameh* and its rendition into verse. Besides, references to his sayings in Arabic and Islamic books have been borrowed from this book, such that one can understand the original context of the book from the compilation of these references.

According to Inostranzev, the *Ahde Ardeshir* is an example of the type of books that have appeared in Arabic literature, such as the *Rasa'el Omar bin Hamzeh*, the *Al Yateemah* of Ibni Mughaffa'', and *Rasa'el* of Ahmad bin Yousof, the *dabir* of Ma'moon; and he has concluded that a part of the contents of this book can be found in the *Al Tanbeeh* by Ahmad bin abi Taher.

Mas'oodi has referred in the *Morooj-al-Zahab* to a book attributed to Ardeshir that, according to him, was known as the *Karnameh*, and contained his biography and the description of his battles.[19] The *Al-Fehrest* contains a reference to a book entitled *Sirah Ardeshir*, which was one of the books that Aban bin Abdul Hamid Laheghi had rendered into verse.[20] It can be deduced from this that apart from the *Ahde Ardeshir* which covered ethical and literary topics and was rendered into verse by Balazori, there was another book following on the biography and life of *Ardeshir*, which was also translated from Pahlavi into Arabic which Aban rendered into verse. Whether it is the same book as the one referred to as the *Karnameh Ardeshir* in existing old Persian texts, or that based on the description given by Mas'oodi, it was a more substantive book, is a question that requires further study. Another book was written by the Moobadan on maxims and literature, but Ibni Nadeem has neither mentioned its title nor its author.

Another book contained the letters exchanged between Kasra and one of his *Marzbans*. Inostranzev has argued that this book pertained to a historical event during Anooshiravan's reign, i.e. the conquest of Yemen. As discussed earlier, during the reign of Anooshiravan, the Yemenis requested the court of Iran to assist them in repelling the Ethiopians, who had conquered Yemen years earlier. Anooshiravan dispatched a force to their assistance under the command of one

[19] *Morooj-al-Zahab*, vol. II, p. 161.
[20] *Al-Fehrest*, p. 119.

of his *Marzbans* whom Tabari has identified as Vahrazan. Vahrazan expelled the Ethiopians from Yemen and ruled that territory for a period of time. Both Dinevari and Tabari have described his letters to Khosrow and Anooshiravan's response.[21] According to Inostranzev, it is likely that this book contained collection of these letters as well as a description of the conquest of Yemen and Anooshiravan's directives on the administration of that territory.

Two more books have been mentioned in the list, but there is no other information available about them, however, it can be deduced from their titles that they contained philosophic material. Among the books listed by Ibni Nadeem the title of one can be translated as 'Issues that the Emperor of Rome Sent with Boghrat the Roman to Anooshiravan',[22] and another title as 'The Dispatch of Philosophers by the Emperor of Rome to the Shah of Iran to Seek Questions of Wisdom'. Although nothing definite can be said about either of these books, they were probably related to the migration of philosophers to Iran during the reign of Anooshiravan or earlier.

In addition, a number of other Iranian books of ethics have been mentioned in the listing, one of which discussed ethical subjects and sayings of various wise men, and following Ardeshir's decree its contents were sourced from the archives of books that had been written by scholars on *tadbeer* (management).

Another book was written for Hormoz, the son of Anooshiravan, but its author cannot be identified because of distortions. This book contains letters exchanged between Kasra and Jamasb. Jamasb been listed as Jawasb by Ibni Nadeem, apparently it has been distorted. Jamasb was an Iranian scholar but there is no information about when he lived; however, various scientific and ethical works in Zoroastrian literature are attributed to him. Ibni Nadeem mentions him along with Zoroaster, and discussed earlier, one of the Iranian

---

[21] *Al-Akhbar-al-Tewal*, p. 65. *Tarikh Tabari*, part one, pp. 949-50, 985, 1040.

[22] For more information on this subject refer to the article by Mohammad Mohammadi-Malayeri, 'The Book of Questions Attributed to Khosrow Anooshiravan and Translation of a Piece of it', *Derasat Adabyeh*, vol. VII, nos. 1 and 2, 1965, pp. 45-72.

books on astronomy has been recorded in the name of Jamasaf, which apparently is the same as Jamasb.

The titles of other books mentioned in the list, are not clear. One of these books is the *Syreh Nameh* which had been included under the *Ahadith* and *Akhbar*, and its author has been listed as Hadahood bin Farrokhzad, which appears to be a distortion.

In addition to these books, which are considered to be definitively Iranian and which were translated from Pahlavi, Inostranzev has also identified eleven books from the first Abbasid period, or the period of Iranian influence on Arabic literature, such as the book that Ebrahim bin Ziad wrote for Mahdi, the Abbasid Caliph, and the one that Mohammad bin Layth wrote for Haroon Rashid and Yahya bin Khaled Barmaki.

Of the remaining books mentioned in the list, Inostranzev has argued that the majority were based on Iranian sources. Among these are the two books that we have referred to, one in *Adab* and the other in housekeeping. And as we have said, they were translated by *Mehr Azar Jashnas*. He has also raised the possibility that the *Alradd Alal Zanadeghah* was the work of Zoroastrians and was translated into Arabic; there were two other books, one of which he has attributed to Ali bin Raban Nasrani and the other was translated by Ibni Nadeem himself. These books were similar to the *Adab al Arab wal Fors*, and were produced in the Islamic periods along the lines of similar Iranian works. According to Inostranzev, the remaining books listed by Ibni Nadeem were part of numerous works on *Adab* and *Akhlagh* that found their way into Arabic literature through Pahlavi works, from Greek writings.

**A General View of the**　　Ethical literature was one of the most
**Ethical Literature of Iran**　important fields of literature that found
　　　　　　　　　　　　　　　its way into Arabic literature through
Pahlavi writings. Here it suffice to note that literary and ethical writings in Iran existed in Pahlavi literature in various forms, and after translation into Arabic it was also divided into different areas.

In his general review of the history of Iran in the *Morooj-al-Zahab*, Mas'oodi says: 'We have provided their (meaning the *Shahs* of Iran)

*Akhbar, Siyr, Wasaya, Ohood, Mukatebat, Tawghi'at, Khatabahs* of coronation, and *Rasa'el* in our earlier books.'

Without describing Mas'oodi's books on such issues, it is important to examine this phrase in order to study the ethical literature of Iran. This is because this phrase refers to all the various topics that have been translated from Pahlavi into Arabic on history and *Adab*, and each area referred to by Mas'oodi represents a particular category of such works that he and his contemporary Islamic authors and *Adibs* were familiar with.

**AKHBAR AND SIYAR**    The books that Mas'oodi has classified as *Akhbar* and *Siyar* were Pahlavi translation of works on general history and the biographies and lives of the shahs and the nobility. As mentioned earlier, Pahlavi literature contained two categories of works on this; one was the writings that dealt with the general history such as the *Khoday Nameh*, and the other known as *Dastan* included books on the life and biography of a shah, a commander or a distinguished person, and the description of events related to them. Apparently, writers such as Mas'oodi and Ibni Nadeem considered the first type as *Akhbar*, and the second type as *Siyar*.

**WASAYA**    The works that are known as *Wasaya* in Arabic deal with the advice and guidance about each of the Sassanid shahs on their deathbeds. There were many such *Wasaya* in Pahlavi literature, and several of them were translated into Arabic. Examples of such advice can be seen in the *Tarikh Tabari*, Dinevari's *Akhbar Tewal* of and the *Tarikh Hamzeh Esfahani*, particularly the *Shahnameh* of Ferdowsi. Literary books such as the *Oyoon-al-Akhbar* also contain such advice. After narrating the lives of the Sassanid shahs and the circumstances of their death, Ferdowsi has discussed their sage advice to their successors. Hamzeh Esfahani has also narrated the sage advice of each of the shahs that was reproduced from the *Wasaya* that were attributed to them.

This type of material reached the Moslems primarily through the *Khoday Nameh*. However, it can be presumed that independent pieces containing collections of *Wasaya* existed in Pahlavi literature and were translated into Arabic. We referred earlier to the views of Gouchmid on the book of history containing the paintings of the shahs which Mas'oodi had found in *Estakhr* in Fars, and that probably there were also phrases under the painting of each of the shahs containing their words of wisdom, and whatever has been copied in literary books from the *Tajnameh* on such words of guidance were taken from those phrases.

'OHOOD    Ibni Nadeem's list also mentions a number of books of this category, such as the *Ahde Ardeshir* and the *Ahde Anooshiravan.* Apparently, there were more important and numerous books of this type in old Persian literature, and considerable literary material found its way through these books into Arabic literature. The *Ahd* consisted of a collection of decrees and instructions that were issued by the Sassanid shahs on various matters ranging from codes of government to ethical guidance given to their successors or to the nobility in the realm. In Pahlavi literature, many such pieces are attributed to the shahs, particularly those who were well known in history.

In addition to those listed by Ibni Nadeem, there were other books of this category that were translated into Arabic. Mas'oodi has written about the *Ahd* of Shapoor,[23] Ibni Toghtogha has quoted a few phrases from the *Ahd* of Qobad to Khosrow Anooshiravan[24] and Ferdowsi has not only composed verses from these two books, but also from similar books attributed to the other shahs which he has called the *Andarz.*

MUKATEBAT    One category of literary and ethical writings of Iran was in the form of letters exchanged between two persons, normally containing advice from father to son. There were numerous such writings in Pahlavi literature attributed to the shahs of Iran or to scholars and scientists. Ibni Nadeem has listed a number

---

[23] *Morooj-al-Zahab*, vol. I, see the description of the reign of Shapoor, the son of Ardeshir.

[24] *Al-Aadaab-al-Sultaniyah*, p. 89.

of such books, however, there were other books of this category that were available to Islamic authors.

One of these writings is a letter from Khosrow Parviz to his son Shirouyeh. The story goes that when Shirouyeh succeeded in overcoming and imprisoning his father Khosrow Parviz, he sent him an elaborate letter describing the injustices he had committed during his reign which had compelled Shirouyeh to take such an extreme step. In response, Khosrow answered and negated each one of his allegations and offered him advice on sound government.

Dinevari,[25] Tabari[26] and Ferdowsi[27] have referred to this incident and have quoted from this letter in some detail. According to Tabari, the messenger who delivered Shirouyeh's letter was Asfad Joshnas, the chief *dabir* or *Iran Dabeer Bod*. Dinevari has identified him as Yazdan Jashnas or the chief of the *divan* of Rasa'el; and according to Ferdowsi, the messengers were two Iranian scholarly *dabirs* named Asta Goshasb and Kharrad Barzeen. Asta Goshasb and Asfad Jashnas was one and the same name that had been distorted through Arabization. Other names mentioned by Dinevari and Ferdowsi were also distorted.

Of course, nothing definitive can be said about the date of this letter or its style, or its details. However, it is an established fact that in Pahlavi literature there was a letter with such specifications which was an important source for Islamic authors and historians. Ferdowsi has written that Shirouyeh's message to Khosrow Parviz was an oral one, and Khosrow Parviz's response was in several verses.

There is a possibility that these messages were recorded later and found their way into Pahlavi literature and were widely read as letters. Although these letters focused on a political and historical event, in their writing, and particularly in the letter of Khosrow Parviz, their literary and ethical aspects were also taken into consideration, and they were among the literary pieces of Pahlavi language. In his *Oyoon-al-Akhbar*, Ibni Qutaybah has quoted extensively from Khosrow Parviz's letter on advice and guidance on government and

[25] *Al-Akhbar-al-Tewal*, pp. 112-13.
[26] *Tarikh Tabari*, part one, pp. 1054-65.
[27] *Shahnameh*, Khavar edn., vol. V, pp. 247-73.

the codes of monarchy, such as the conditions and qualifications of the collector of *kharaj*, praise for consultation and reproach for imposing one's opinion, the methods of punishment and the costs of neglecting them, and self-restraint.[28] Other books have also drawn upon this letter.[29]

Apart from this letter, there were similar other writings in Pahlavi literature which were translated into Arabic such as the letters that Mas'oodi has attributed to Shapoor in the *Morooj-al-Zahab*, including a letter to Caesar and his response, and another to several functionaries of state.[30] Other letters have been mentioned in historical sources such as the letter of Bahram the fourth to the commanders of the army, and the letter of Khosrow the first to the Padgoospan of Azarbaijan.

According to several researchers, such letters and literary works were recorded in the Pahlavi *Taj Nameh*, from where they found their way into Islamic works.[31] This is not far from the truth, because as discussed earlier, although Ibni Nadeem has listed the *Taj Nameh* among history books, its contents were more of a literary and ethical nature. It would not be far from the truth if we say that letters and writings of this type that had a literary content, were recorded in the *Taj Nameh*, or at least a similar book, and found their way to the Moslems through such books.

*TAWGHI'AT*    One of the categories of Pahlavi writings that became part of Arabic literature and led to similar works in Islamic literature was the *Tawghi'at* attributed to the shahs of Iran. It was customary at the Sassanid court that every petition written to the shah, whether on the affairs of the state, or injustice of the rulers or any other matter, was responded to. One of the *dabirs*, apparently

---

[28]  *Oyoon-al-Akhbar*, vol. I, pp. 17, 30, 59, 288, 328.

[29]  For more information on these letters, refer *'Ketab-al-Taj* that *Ibni Qutaybah* has Copied from . . . ', *Translation and Transcriptions from Farsi* . . . vol. I, pp. 120-47, Beirut, 1964; 'On One of the *Sassanid Taj Namehs*', *Derasat Adabyah*, vol. VI, nos. 3 and 4, 1965.

[30]  *Morooj-al-Zahab*, vol. I, pp. 164-5.

[31]  Refer to Christensen, p. 57; Inostranzev, pp. 66-7.

Iran *Dabir Bod*[32] drafted a concise response to the petition under the instruction of the shah, and once it was signed by the shah, it was sent to the *dabirkhaneh* where it was recorded as an official document or letter. The same procedure applied to *farmans* or letters that were directly issued by the shah to other shahs or to governors. Such instructions which were generally issued in short and precise terms were referred to as *Tawghi'*, in Arabic and the *dabir* who was responsible for them was the *Saheb ul Tawghi'*.

The technical prose of the Sassanid period will be discussed later. The *Tawghi'at* of this period were considered among the literary and artistic writings as mentioned earlier, because, each *Tawghi'* was issued by the shah and was drafted by the principal *dabir* of the court, and all efforts were made to ensure that the expression and phrases used were refined and its meaning was harmonious. Often their contents were highly ethical in nature interspersed with wise sayings. For this reason, although the *Tawghi'at* were merely administrative directives, over time their ethical and literary aspects developed to such a degree that they occupied a distinctive place in Pahlavi literature, and were translated into Arabic and used by Moslem scholars and *dabirs*.

The Sassanid court, according to available evidence, had a special book for recording all the *Tawghi'at* that were issued by the shah, and at the end of each month they collected, sealed and maintained in the imperial archives. In this manner, a number of collections of *Tawghi'at* accumulated in the Pahlavi language, and were available to the *dabirs* and scholars.

Most of the *Tawghi'at* that were available were from the time of Khosrow Anooshiravan. Ibni Qotaybah writes that Anooshiravan had decreed that all letters written to the functionaries of state should have a space of four lines for his own *Tawghi'*.[33] Ferdowsi has described the *Tawghi'at* of Anooshiravan in greater detail. In the *Shah Nameh*, he composed in verse thirty-six *Tawghi'at* with a brief of the contents of the letters and the *Tawghi'at*. There is no doubt that such accounts found their way into Islamic literature from Pahlavi books.

[32] Christensen, p. 389.
[33] *Oyoon-al-Akhbar*, vol. I, p. 8.

These *Tawghi'at* became models for Moslem *dabirs* and scholars to replicate. Bihaghi has quoted the following *Tawghi'* from Abdullah bin Taher, 'who that strives reaps, and who that sleeps dreams', and according to Kasravi, this phrase is an exact translation of a similar *Tawghi'* by Anooshiravan.[34]

**Coronation** It was a custom of the Sassanid shahs to deliver a
**Orations** lengthy and eloquent oration on their coronation. These orations were in an artistic and beautiful style, and were elaborate literary pieces, and generally contained the same type of sophisticated ethical material as the *Pand* and the *Andarz*. Historians have often referred to these orations and have praised their eloquence. Arabic literary sources contain several quotations from these orations, such as the *Oyoon-al-Akhbar*. Ferdowsi has composed in verse the type of material found in the *Pand* and the *Andarz* attributed to each Sassanid shah at the beginning of his reign. No doubt, this material was adapted from their coronation orations from old Persian literature. Dinevari has quoted extensively from Hormoz's oration on the occasion of his coronation.[35]

It is worth noting that in these orations as also in other types of writings the focus was more on the literary and artistic aspects than on others, and the authors of these works adopted the prevalent ostentatious style and used artistic phrases to express profound meanings. This characteristic was so prominent in these writings that it was discernible even in their Arabic translations. In any case, these orations were considered primarily as literary and ethical pieces, and the fact that we see numerous examples of them in Arabic and Islamic sources, leads us to the conclusion that the pieces that were translated of this type to Arabic were also great in number.

*Rasa'el* According to Mas'oodi, there are references to other writings which are known as *Rasa'el*. *Rasa'el* referred to the same letters that were earlier discussed under *Mokatebat*. But, as in

---

[34] *Al-Mahasen wal Masawe'*, p. 310.
[35] For details of this oration, see *Al-Akhbar-al-Tewal*, pp. 77-80.

the phrase there is reference to both *Rasa'el* and *Mokatebat*, it is clear that there were some differences between the two types of letters. However, it is difficult to definitively say what was the difference.

Arabic literary writings in the second and third centuries of Hijra included innumerable Iranian maxims, which maintained their original characteristics for a long time, but like most other Iranian cultural works, were eventually absorbed into Arabic literature and acquired an Arabic character. In his paper 'Distinction between the Eloquence of the Arabs and the Iranians' Abu Helal Askari quoting Abu Bakr bin Dorayd has written that the *divan* of the poet Saleh bin Abdol Qoddoos, contained a collection of 1,000 maxims each of the Arabs and of the Iranians.[36] Ibni Modabber, a scholarly Islamic *dabir* and talented writer, has noted in his paper 'The Letter of the Virgin' that the learning of Persian maxims among other Iranian works was a precondition for the profession of Arabic writing and Arab *dabirs*.[37] It is clear from this reference that a large number of Iranian maxims were available to Islamic writers and *Adeebs*, and were highly rated at that time.

In Moskouyeh's *Javdan Kherad*, which is also known as the *Aadaab al Arab wal Fors*, there are numerous quotes from different genres of Iranian writings attributed to the shahs, the Moobadan and other scholars that were translated into Arabic, Moskouyeh has described them at times as *Wasaya* and at others as *Hel am* and *Aadaab*. Two of these pieces will be discussed here.

**The *Pand Nameh* of Bouzarjomehr** One of these pieces consists of Moskouyeh's excerpts from the Arabic translation of the *Pand Nameh* of Bozorgmehr under the title of 'What I Selected from the *Aadaab* of Bozarjomehr'. The scholarly studies of Christensen on Bozorgmehr and works attributed to him including the *Pand Nameh*, which has also been translated into Persian,[38] relieves one of the need for a lengthy discussion on this.

[36] Quoted from Ahmad Amin, 'Collection of Letters', p. 218. See *Duha-al-Islam*, vol. I, p. 190.

[37] *Rasa'el-al-Bolagha*', p. 187.

[38] This paper was translated into Persian by Abdol Hossein Meykadeh, *Mehr* periodical, vol. I.

According to Haj Khalifeh, the *Pand Nameh* was translated from Pahlavi into Persian in the days of Nooh, the son of Mansoor Samani (366-87 of the Hijra) at the behest of the shah. It was known as the *Zafar Nameh* and it was translated by Ibni Sina, the *wazir* of Nooh. According to Schefer, this is the same paper that he had published under the title of the *Zafar Nameh* in the first volume of his book *Selections of Persian*. Christensen has refuted this and has argued that Schefer's *Zafar Nameh* is a remote replication of the original.

Ferdowsi has quoted a part of the *Pand Nameh* in the *Shah Nameh*. Giving due consideration to the core substance and the structure of topics, Ferdowsi has not deviated too far from the original. However, according to Christensen, the *Pand Nameh* has also undergone considerable modifications and changes here, including the deletion of material on the religion of Mazdak, and the substitution of material on Zoroastrianism with general advice on piety, which has totally altered its distinctive character.

It has been deduced from the large number of words and phrases that Ferdowsi has borrowed from the original *Pand Nameh*, that he used a Persian translation of the original old Persian text rather than an Arabic translation, and therefore it has been proposed that in the preparation of this section of his book, Ferdowsi has referred directly to the same *Zafar Nameh* mentioned by Haj Khalifeh. In any case, it must be kept in mind that the Arabic translation of this book was completed before the Persian translation. This is confirmed by the fact that there are many references to the wise sayings of Bouzarjomehr in books that were produced prior to the Persian translation, such as the *Morooj-al-Zahab*, the *Al-Fehrest* and the *Oyoon-al-Akhbar*, which drew upon this *Pand Nameh*. Moreover, during Mas'oodi's time many works of this Iranian savant were popular among Arabs and Moslems.[39]

Generally speaking, the Arabic translation of the *Pand Nameh* acquired much fame in Arabic literature and had a strong influence on Arabic literary writings. Most of the sayings and advice quoted from Bozorgmehr in these Islamic writings are from this book, and its influence is evident in Moskouyeh's book as well. In addition to this *Pand Nameh*, there was another *Andarz* in Pahlavi literature which, according to Christensen, was also used by Ferdowsi and Mas'oodi.

---

[39] *Morooj-al-Zahab*, vol. II, p. 225.

**The Sassanid *Javdan Kherad*** The *Javdan Kherad* is another book on practical wisdom, which was translated from Pahlavi into Arabic and excerpts from it have been reproduced in the beginning of Moskouyeh's book which is also known as the *Javdan Kherad*. This book is referred to here as the Sassanid *Javdan Kherad* to avoid confusion. Like many other Pahlavi books, no accurate information is available either about its author or the date of its publication. This *Javdan Kherad* was a collection of Zoroastrian practical wisdom, *Andarz* and ethical teachings; it was highly regarded in Pahlavi as well as Arabic literature. There is a legendary tale about its origin and translation. A tale narrated in Moskouyeh's book, which Tartoosi has also quoted in the *Saraj al-Molook* from Fazl bin Sahl, is an example of such works, and reveals the extent to which Iranians valued them, and how they impacted the Islamic environment so that even the Arabs began to appreciate them.

According to Fazl bin Sahl, when Ma'moon ascended the Caliphate in Khorasan, each of the shahs and the princes of neighbouring territories sent presents to express their respect. The shah of Kabolestan dispatched to the court of Ma'moon an old wise man, who is named in *Saraj al-Molook* (the word is Moobadan in Moskouyeh). Zouban remained at the court for a period of time and Ma'moon greatly benefited from his wisdom and advice, particularly in the dispute with his brother Amin. As a token of this appreciation Ma'moon gave him 100,000 *derhams*. But he refused to accept the money, and wanted something that was more valuable. Ma'moon asked him what he wanted. He replied that he wanted a book written by a distinguished Iranian that was a collection of the best writings and sciences of the land. Zouban described the book and spoke highly of it. He said that it was buried in the Eyvan of Mada'en. Ma'moon ordered that the book be brought from the Eyvan where it was buried in a small glass chest. When the book was unearthed, Ma'moon handed it to Zouban. Zouban read a spell in his own language and blew on the lock of the chest. He opened the chest and removed a packet of silk cloth which contained 100 sheets of paper. Zouban collected the scattered papers and returned home.

According to Fazl bin Sahl,

After Zouban departed, I went to his home and asked him about that book. He said, this is the book *Javdan Kherad*, written by Ganjour, the *wazir* of the shah of Iranshahr. I took a few pages of the book and Khazr bin Ali translated them. When Ma'moon learned of the translation he asked for it and when he read it, said, I swear to God that this is the word and not what we have.

The beginning of the manuscript copy of Moskouyeh's book or the *Aadaab al Arab wal Fors*, which is in the Al Sharqyah Library of Beirut, contains a phrase which has been translated as follows:

The book *Javdan Kherad* which Hooshang Shah left as souvenir for his successor, and Ganjour the son of Esfandyar the *wazir* of the shah of Iran translated from the ancient language to Persian, and Hasan bin Sahl, the brother of Zul Ryasatain, translated to Arabic, and Ahmad bin Moskouyeh completed by adding to it the wisdom of Iran and India and Arabia and Rome.

**Other Ethical Works of Iran**    In the discussion of translators of Pahlavi works reference had been made to a book, the Book of *Mahasen*, that Ibni Nadeem attributed to Omar bin Farkhan, as this book, according to researchers, was a translation of a Pahlavi work and for this reason Ibni Nadeem has listed Omar Farkhan among translators of Pahlavi books. As there are numerous books in Arabic literature with this or similar titles such as the *Mahasen al-Aadab* and the *Mahasen al-Akhlagh*, and since the study of this topic is important for understanding the impact of Iranian culture on Arabic literature and review of Iranian ethical works, the following explanations are in order.

On the basis of his study and exposition of this issue,[40] Inostranzev, has noted that Pahlavi ethical literature contained pieces that focused more Zoroastrian religious aspects and were distinct from other similar works. This scholar believes that the book *Al-Mahasen* of Omar Farkhan represents this group of Pahlavi books in Arabic literature. In other words, Omar Farkhan has imitated in the writing of this book the same style that Zoroastrian writers followed in producing such books, and he has translated their exact contents into Arabic, of

----

[40] *Iranian Influence on Moslem Literature*, Chap. 4.

course, with certain modifications dictated by the new environment. As mentioned earlier, numerous books in Arabic have the title of *Al-Mahasen*, and Ibni Nadeem has listed a several of them. Moreover, the authors of these books were Islamic scholars who appreciated Iranian works, or were familiar with them. Ibni Qutaybah also produced a book by this title which was considered the first imitation of Omar Farkhan, since the literary fame of Omar Farkhan preceded that of Ibni Qutaybah.

Of the books produced by Shiites with this title mention can be made of the *Mahasen al-Akhlagh* by Abul Nasr Mohammad bin Mas'ood Ayashi, and Abu Abdallah Mohammad bin Khaled Barmaki's *Al-Mahasen*. This point is noteworthy as far as the relationship between Shi'ism and Iran and Iranian writings is concerned.

A similar book is attributed to Ibni Haroon, an Islamic writer. He authored the *Ketab al Adab*. Books on the subject of *Adab* in Arabic literature, particularly in the second and third centuries of the Hijra, were closely related to Iranian writings because they were clearly influenced by Iran. For this reason Inostranzev has argued that Esfahani's book *Mahasen al Adab* contained material from Iranian literary works.

Arabic literature included books like the *Al-Mahasen wal Addad* and the *Al-Mahasen wal Masawe'*. The authors of these ethical works not only described good deeds and noble qualities, but also discussed the opposites of these deeds and qualities. Although it is difficult to find a book with such a title among the works that have been translated from Pahlavi, Inostranzev has argued that these books were originally translations of Pahlavi books that dealt with ethical topics in the same manner by contrasting good and bad traits under the title of the *Shayad na Shayad* or the *Shayest la Shayest*; these books were very popular and numerous in Pahlavi literature between the sixth and ninth centuries AD.

The first book of this category in Arabic is Jahiz's *Al-Mahasen wal Addad*. As is evident from his works, Jahiz relied heavily on Iranian literary works, and on the basis of his views on a number of Persian words, it can be said he was proficient in the Persian language.[41]

---

[41] *Ketab al-Hayawan*, vol. I, pp. 65, 66, 69; vol. VII, p. 39; and *Al-Mahasen wal Addad*, p. 70.

Several books attributed to Jahiz have been written on the lines of Iranian works for example, the *Al Taj* and the *Estetalat ul Fahm* which is either a translation of the *Javdan Kherad* or a copy of it. His other works also contain Iranian content. Therefore, it is possible that in the *Al-Mahasen wal Addad*, he was influenced by Iranian books of this type. A book by Bihaghi is also entitled the *Al-Mahasen wal Masawe'*.

It is worthwhile to mention what Inostranzev has written about the Pahlavi book *Rowshana'i Nameh*. Ibni Nadeem has mentioned among the books written by Ali bin Obaydah Rihani one that Jousli and Hofman have called the *Rowshana Nik*. According to Inostranzev, this book is a copy of the Pahlavi *Rowshana'i Namak* in its title and content, and falls under the category of writings in which ethical issues are discussed from a religious and spiritual perspective.[42]

---

[42] See *Iranian Influence on Moslem Literature*, Chap. 7.

# Books Written in Arabic
## on the Topic of *Adab*

Moslem scholars' vitality and eagerness in translating and copying books in the various fields of science and literature, and their efforts in transcribing books, and also producing new works, led to the emergence of a valuable body of literature in the sciences and the arts in Arabic which were unprecedented in that language. The books that were written or translated in literature and ethics were known in general as *adab*.

The books on *adab* constitute one of the most important branches of Arabic literature. Prominent researchers and those who have knowledge of, and insight into Iranian and Islamic cultures have generally accepted the view that this branch of Arab literature has been clearly influenced by Iranian works.[1]

One of the reasons for Iranian influence on this area of Arabic literature was that the composition of literary books and letters in Arabic began at a time when the most important sources of literature and ethics that were available to Islamic authors were Iranian works. Of course, it should be reaffirmed that ethics in this context does not refer to religious ethics, the source of which was the Koran and Islamic teachings; rather it means literary ethics or ethical literature which has other sources as well. Besides, those who wrote books in this area were often Iranians or were knowledgeable about Iranian culture and literature, and therefore, they considered Iranian works as models for their own work which was occasionally reflected in their writings. It would be appropriate to quote from Jahiz who has discussed the advantages of poetry over prose:

---

[1] Christensen, p. 68, Inostranzev, pp. 37, 53-62.

The books of India and the maxims of Greece were translated and the *Adab* of the Iranians were copied (to Arabic). Some of them improved (through translation) and there was no deterioration with others. But if the wisdom of the Arabs (poetry) is translated into any other language, this miracle which is rhythm will be destroyed, although even if they copy that, they will not find in terms of meaning, anything which the Iranians have not already covered in their books, which they have written on their codes of life and their maxims, these books have moved from one nation to another, and from one century to another and from one language to another until they have reached us, and we have been the last to inherit them.[2]

In the first centuries of Islam when numerous books were produced in various scientific disciplines, most Iranian writings also developed and were transformed. A review of the *Al-Fehrest* and other books that were written in Arabic in these disciplines reveals the extent to which the translation and writing of books was widespread at that time. This movement provided the developing Islamic culture with such strength and capacity that it was able to absorb foreign elements with ease and provide to them its own distinctive character, as is obvious with regard to the foreign words that were introduced in the Arabic language in abundance.

The borrowing of foreign words, if not as obvious in some areas of science such as medicine and philosophy, was definitely prominent in works of literature, particularly those that were translated from Pahlavi. It is for this reason that there is no significant trace of their original Arabic translations in Arabic literature because with the composition of books in Arabic modelled on their lines, with additional topics that were more complete and more suitable to the new environment, eventually the original translations were over-shadowed and gradually absorbed.

**The Literary Heritage of Iran and Its Transformation in Islam** In the Islamic period, in conformation with the requirements of the new environment, the literary and ethical books of Iran underwent several transformations, as a result of which they moved away from their original character

---

[2] *Ketab al-Hayawan*, vol. I, p. 38.

and closely approximated to the character of the Arab and Islamic environment. The first such transformation was their translation into Arabic. As mentioned earlier, during this period, translators did not hesitate to alter the contents of literary and ethical books, by making additions or deleting certain issues from the original text to make them more suitable to their own tastes and to the tastes of their readers and to adapt them to the Islamic environment, because such alterations did not threaten the basic framework and structure of these books.

As Zoroastrian books could not have survived in the Islamic Caliphate with the form and content which they had in the Sassanid period, some of the translators of these books deleted their contents which were directly related to the Zoroastrian faith, and to ensure that their translations confirmed to the Arabic style and taste, they altered them to the extent that did not distort the essence of their contents. Shrewd and eloquent translators placed these books at par with Arabic books, and thus paved the way for further transformations in the future.

The phase of translation of books of other nations was followed by the phase of writing and composing. During this period, Islamic authors produced writings that were modelled on the same books that had earlier been translated. A noteworthy feature of these writings is that in the earlier ones the Iranian influence is more obvious, whereas in the ones produced later the Iranian influence is weaker and is overwhelmed by the Islamic and Arabic character.

In considering the political and cultural developments of Iran, and comparing them with the history of Iranian and Arab sciences and knowledge before and after the advent of Islam, the influence of Iranian books on Arab literature can clearly be defined, and its historical path identified. However, this task requires an exhaustive and careful study because of the basic transformations that have occurred in them; researchers who either did not have the time for a thorough investigation or neglected such a study, failed to identify this issue and therefore did not focus on it.

To clarify the phases through which Iranian literary heritage passed in Arabic literature, it is important to briefly review a number of Iranian books, each of which is considered a prominent specimen of its genre, to exmine their role in bridging Pahlavi literature and Arabic literature.

**The *Aadaab* of**   In most of the scientific and technical fields of his
**Ibni Mughaffa'**   era like history, literature, ethics, philosophy, logic, legends and stories, Ibni Mughaffa' translated books from Pahlavi into Arabic, and some of his translations like the *Kalileh va Demneh* have survived to this day. He is also credited with books like the *Al-Adab-al-Kabir*, the *Al-Adab-al-Saghir*, and the *Al Yatimah*, which some historians believe are his original works whereas others believe are his translations.

Ibni Mughaffa' lived towards the end of the Amavid period and at the beginning of the Abbasid period, and the books that he translated or wrote are considered among the first books that were written in Arabic and have survived to this day. By examining these books, the phase of initial transformation in such Iranian writings in Islam can be understood.

One of the distinguishing characteristics of these books is that they do not resemble any of the other Arabic writings in their form, style and content. The first literary books in the Arabic language are generally collections of Arab tales, narratives and poems, collected from diverse sources, with no specific common theme; but the books of Ibni Mughaffa' are different. He had no interest in Arab tales, accounts and poems, and unlike other Islamic authors, he did not quote prominent Arabs. Therefore, in his works one rarely finds Arab or Islamic traces, such that if their language was not Arabic, it would not be possible to distinguish merely on the basis of their contents that they had been written by an Islamic or Arabic writer.

A contemporary Arab scholar has described the books of Ibni Mughaffa':

The *Aadaab* of Ibni Mughaffa', though in expression and structure are clearly Arabic, however, in overall form and content are *A'ajami* (Iranian), because he never quotes Arab poetry, or Arab allegories, or Arab wisdom, or Arab authors or their lives. And this is contrary to the ways of all the Arab writers like Jahiz and his peers. He thus is either a translator from Persian, or he has relied on themes common in his days, or he has developed all this material from his own intellect.[3]

This characteristic is due to the fact that these books, both in terms of content as well as structure and form, were a direct imitation of similar Iranian books, the same books which were considered the most important sources of knowledge for Ibni Mughaffa' and many of which he himself had translated.

For this reason some Islamic writers hesitated to attribute the writing of these books to Ibni Mughaffa'. In the *Al-Fehrest*, Ibni Nadeem has argued that the *Al-Adab-al-Kabir*, the *Al-Adab-al-Saghir* and the *Al-Yatimah* were some of the books that Ibni Mughaffa' had translated from Persian,[4] and he has even mentioned the Persian name of the *Al-Adab-al-Kabir* as the *Mah Farajashnas*,[5] but in a different section of the *Al-Fehrest* he has noted that the *Al-Yatimah* was Ibni Mughaffa's original work.[6] As there were books other than the *Adab-al-Kabir* in the Islamic period which were known by their Pahlavi titles, it is necessary to add a clarificatory note.

**Arabic Books that were Known by Pahlavi Titles** A significant point that emerges from the study of the *Al-Fehrest* is that during the Islamic cultural movement numerous books on the subject of *adab* and ethics were written which had Pahlavi titles. Unfortunately, most of these titles have been distorted because Arab transcribers were not familiar with them, it is therefore difficult to decipher them. However, records show that the

---

[3] Khalil Mardom Beig, *Ibni Mughaffa'*, p. 66.

[4] *Al-Fehrest*, p. 118.

[5] According to the reading of Justi and Hoffman.

[6] *Al-Fehrest*, p. 126. Further studies have revealed that the *Al-Adab-al-Kabir* and the *Al-Adab-al-Saghir* were not written by Ibni Mughaffa', but were translated by him. These two books are more representative of the pre-Islamic literature and culture of Iran than Islamic literature. For details see '*Adab* and *Akhlagh* in Iran Before Islam, and a Few Samples of it in Arabic and Islamic Literature', by Mohammad Mohammadi-Malayeri, Tehran, 1352, p. 112.

composition of such books was common and well known in Arab and Islamic society.

Despite the importance of this issue for the study of the civilization and culture of the east, it has not received the attention of researchers it deserves. Undoubtedly, such studies will not only offer fresh and valuable insights into the cultural interaction between Iran and Islam, and according to Goldziher, but will also alter many of the current theories and views about Islamic civilization and culture and its sources.

Books by Ali bin Obaydah Rihani, one of the writers of the second century of Islam, include the *Mehr Azar Jashnas*, the *Kei Lohrasf*, the *Rowshana'i Namak* and *Adab Javanshir*. Ibni Nadeem says about him. 'He was an eloquent scholar, and was considered among the confidants of Ma'moon, and he wrote on ethics. He was accused of *Zandaghah*, and he was a capable writer.'[7] From this description it can be concluded that Rihani was not only influenced by Iranian writings, but he also borrowed from them. By ethics, Ibni Nadeem is referring to the type of maxims for which Pahlavi literature was the main source. At that time *Hekmah* was used basically in this sense, and did not refer to philosophy exclusively, as was the case in the later centuries. The accusation of *Zandaghah* is evidence for the source of Rihani's information and knowledge and the context of his literary interests. This is because, as we said earlier, *Zandaghah* was an accusation generally made of Iranians who were interested in their Iranian heritage, and showed no concern for Arab writings.

Reference has been made to Rihani's *Rowshana'i Namak* which, according to Inostranzev, contained an excerpt from a Pahlavi work of the same title. This title found its way into Islamic Persian literature, and is the title of one of the books of Naser Khosrow Alavi.

In any case, if Rihani's book is not the Pahlavi *Rowshana'i Namak*, at least it is a direct imitation of it. This can be said not only about the *Rowshana'i Namak*, but also about all Arabic books that have Pahlavi titles; a fact that is substantiated by many references. In general, the books that Islamic authors wrote in imitation of Pahlavi books were known by the same titles because of similarities in their

---

[7] *Al-Fehrest*, p. 119.

contents. Rihani's books belonged to this category, also the *Al-Adab Al-Kabir* and the *Al Taj*.

During this period, the replication of earlier works was very common. Generally speaking, the period of replication followed the period of translation and finally the period of intellectual autonomy.

There are numerous such books on *adab* and *akhlaqh*. Rihani's *Mehrazar Jashnas* shared its like with a book which was discussed under the Pahlavi works of ethics. The Sassanid *Javdan Kherad* was replicated by Islamic authors several times. In the *Taraz al Majales*, Khafaji says that this book was seen by Jahiz who praised it highly.[8]

It is highly probable that Moskouyeh had borrowed the contents of the *Javdan Kherad* from the copy that Jahiz had transcribed, because, after quoting from that book, Moskouyeh says:

Abu Othman Jahiz has transcribed from the saying of Hasan bin Sahl, that 'all that we covered is all the material translated from the papers that we obtained'. But much has been eliminated from it due to discontinuation of topics, because the Moobadan Moobad made available the papers of this book to us in a discontinued and unorganized manner. ( ? )[9]

It is likely that the transcribed book was the Arabic *Estetalatul Fahm*. The similarity in the meanings of the two names and in their content supports this probability.

**The *Ketab al Taj fi Akhlagh al Molook***    Jahiz's *Ketab al Taj fi Akhlagh al Molook* represents another phase in Iranian cultural works in their interaction with Arabic literature. In the first phase, Arab and Islamic elements were insignificant in the books of that time and their contents were not too different from their original Iranian sources. However, in the later phases, their Iranian character waned and their Arabic elements increased to such an extent that they were totally Arabic and Islamic in nature.

Reference had been made to a Pahlavi book, the *Taj Nameh* and to its impact on Arabic literature which was due to the fact that it served as a model for Islamic writers and numerous works in

[8] *Taraz al Majales*, p. 104.

[9] *The Javdan Kherad*, manuscript available in the Eastern Library, Beirut, p. 17.

Arabic literature were based on it, including Jahiz's *Al Taj fi Akhlagh al Molook*. This book contains a different genre of Pahlavi writings, of which various books and letters were translated into Arabic. This genre included books on the protocol of the court, general information that was considered essential for princes, the nobility and commanders, information that was new to the court of the Caliphate, and Iranian books were the only sources from which the Arabs could obtain such information.

To clarify this issue, it is necessary to survey the history of Islam, in terms of its social and political developments, which also had a great impact on Arabic culture. We had said earlier that with the spread of Islam and the establishment of the Islamic state, the Arabs, for the first time in their history became a ruling class, and thus, entered the international political arena.

Prior to the rise of Islam, the lifestyle of the Arabs was very simple and they were unaware of the codes of behaviour that existed among the civilized nations of that time. For this reason at the dawn of Islam and the period of *Kholafa' Rashedeen*, the leaders of Islam led a life similar to that of the common people, and nothing in their appearance distinguished them from others. For example, a *Bedwin* Arab talked and interacted with the Caliph in the same manner as he did with a neighbour or a friend or a peer; neither the Caliph expected a different attitude, nor the *Bedwin* had the capacity to express any other attitude.

When the Caliphate passed into the hands of the Amavids, the Islamic community was under the influence of foreign elements and had to some extent shed its original simplistic character. In course of time, the Amavid Caliphs imparted a monarchic character to the Islamic Caliphate, and in their imitation of royalty, they distinguished themselves from common people, appointed gatekeepers, and refrained from accepting anyone in their presence. Thus, the audience of the Caliphs acquired a grandeur of its own, and presence in such an audience and the companionship of the Caliph was transformed from its traditional form. This trend continued to develop until it reached its zenith in the days of the Abbassids in Baghdad.

In that period it was no longer permissible for anyone to sit in the presence of the Caliph and to speak his mind, or to seek his audience, whenever he desired. Certain norms of conduct and behaviour had to be followed whether in sitting or rising, speaking or listening, eating or drinking. Courtesy, pleasant speech and proper conversation were among the preconditions of civilized behaviour. The Caliph perceived himself as the shah, and he expected that the protocol and practices followed in the courts of the shahs be adhered to in his presence. Thus, the Arabs were confronted with unprecedented rules and restrictions pertaining to their conduct, which they saw as an undesirable burden imposed upon them, that could not be avoided.

Under such circumstances it was natural that the behavioural norms, codes and practices of the Iranians would be the best model for the Arabs to follow. For this reason, the Abbasid Caliphs also followed the example of the Sassanid shahs in matters concerning government, protocol of the court, etc. As a result, many Iranian books and letters on *adab* were translated into Arabic; and in replicating those works, other books that were more suitable to the Islamic community and the Caliphate were produced, among which was the *Al Taj fi Akhlagh al Molook*.

In the introduction to his book, Jahiz has given his reason for writing it,

Although many of the commoners and some of the privileged adhere in general to the dictates of conformity and obedience, nevertheless, they are unaware of the protocols that apply to them in the presence of kings, and therefore, we have collected in this book the *adab* of kings so that people learn about them and follow their example.[10]

In various places, Jahiz has mentioned the source from which he borrowed material on *Aadab*. The following quotation is from the beginning of the chapter on the classes of companions and musicians, and the protocols followed in the courts of the shahs and the Caliphs:

We begin with the shahs of Iran, as they were the vanguards in these matters, and we have taken the codes of government and the classification of the commons and the distinguished, and the treatment of, and the assigning of the rights and obligations of the different classes of people from them.[11]

---

[10]   *Al Taj fi Akhlagh al Molook*, p. 2.
[11]   Ibid., p. 23.

At the beginning of each chapter, Jahiz first quotes the narratives and tales about the shahs of Iran on a particular topic, and then discusses whatever has been written about the Arab Caliphs. In this book Iranian and Arabic works are covered in parallel; however, traces of its Iranian origins are still evident. At times Jahiz is so overwhelmed by his Iranian sources, that he deviates from his main task and forgets his own environment, and describes parts of their contents which are exclusive to the Sassanid period, and are in essence in contradiction to the Islamic environment and the court of the Caliphs. For example, he writes about Nowrooz and Mehregan,

Mehregan is the beginning of winter and the cold season, and Nowrooz is the beginning of the warm season; but there are functions that exist for Nowrooz that do not exist for Mehregan. Among these are, that Nowrooz is the beginning of the year, and the time for opening the *Kharaj*; for appointment and termination of state functionaries; the minting of coins of *dirhams* and *dinars*, and the cleaning of Fire Temples, and the pouring of water (a *Nowrooz* custom) and so on.[12]

In another section, he describes the justice of the shahs at Nowrooz and Mehregan,

Then they admit the people, and they receive their letters of complaint, and if among them a letter is found with a complaint against the shah, they give precedence to it, and the shah summons the Grand Moobad and the *Dabir Bod* and the *Hirbadan Hirbad*, and the Announcer calls, that anyone who among the people has a complaint against the shah should step forward. . . .

Jahiz continues and describes the trial of the shah in the presence of these three people.[13] These two narratives show that the Jahiz occasionally deviated from the task of composition and engaged in translation because their content has no relevance to the Islamic period and to the Caliphate.

There are many such references in this book which appear to be Arabic and the product of an Islamic environment, but a close scrutiny reveals that they are writings of the Sassanid period. In a number of cases he has also mentioned his Iranian sources. For example, while describing the qualities of those who are close to the shah, and those

12 Ibid., p. 146.
13 Ibid., p. 160.

whose services the shah required such as judges, physicians, *dabirs*, companions, confidantes and clowns, he says: 'And such we also found in the books of the Iranians and their shahs.'[14] From the title of his book as also from its contents, it can be said that Jahiz used the Pahlavi *Taj Nameh* as one of his sources, but according to the Russian scholar Kratchowski, it was the only source that he used in writing his book.[15]

Apart from the *Al Taj*, there are other books in the Arabic language on this subject, i.e. the codes of kings, which constituted an important field in Arabic literature. These books were initially modelled on Iranian books, although their topics were often Arabic or Islamic, they belonged to the same category as found in similar Pahlavi works. In this category mention must be made of the *Aadab al Molook* and the *Saraj al Molook*. Tartoosi, the author of the *Saraj al Molook*, borrowed material from the *Javdan Kherad* as he himself has pointed out in Chapter 63 of his book.

As already discussed, Pahlavi's works included numerous letters which were in the form of guidance and advice from father to son, or from one shah to his heir. These letters were intended to guide the shahs in their duties and became models for writers and *adeebs* during the Islamic period, and they attracted the attention of the *dabirs* of the Caliphate. For this reason, they continued to be used during the reign of the Caliphs and were fairly common in the history of Islam.

***Oyoon-al-Akhbar***   From the third century of the Hijra, a new category of books emerged in Arabic literature that were used mostly by the class of *dabirs*, functionaries of the *divan*, and for the education and refinement of members of this class.

It was mentioned earlier that one of the main qualifications required for the position of *dabir* was a wide range of knowledge of the different aspects of life, whether functional or social. Therefore, the functionaries of the *divan* made every effort to obtain such information mainly to earn the respect of the public for their wisdom,

---

[14]   Ibid., p. 138.
[15]   Refer to his letter in the introduction to *Al Taj fi Akhlagh al Molook*, with corrections by Ahmad Zaki Pasha.

and to secure their position in the state by winning the appreciation of the Caliphs.

We provided earlier an account of the important Iranian sources that the *dabirs* of that period relied upon for these purposes, when no comparable Arab sources existed, and we do not see the need to repeat that here. From the latter part of the second century of the Hijra onwards, a number of the *dabirs* of the *divan*, or writers who were close to them collected such information and copied it in exclusive books in order to facilitate access to the scattered knowledge. Thus, numerous books appeared that are generally referred to as the *Adab al Kateb* or the *Adab-al-Kuttaab*.

The *Oyoon-al-Akhbar* of Ibni Qutaybah is the best specimen of such books from that period in the Islamic community and particularly scholarly circles. For centuries it was the primary source of knowledge and wisdom, and any Islamic author who wished to write on such topics, used this book as his model and replicated it, as is clear from the *Eqd ul Farid* of Ibni Abd Rabbeh and other books.

One, the characteristics of these books is that they do not have particular subject or theme, as their authors did not intend to focus on any specific topic. The objective of these writers was to sift through the various pieces of information that they obtained from different people, or the issues that they read in one or another book, and to present under a single cover whatever they believed would enhance the knowledge and social standing of whoever read it. The content of these books was general in nature, and the word '*adab*' was used to describe them.

Though Ibni Qutaybah attempted not only to structure his book more than any other author of *adab*, but also to focus and categorize the topics, the ad hoc diversity and scatterization of topics in his book are obvious. Nevertheless, an investigation of these books is extremely important for understanding the history of Islamic culture and its development.

The historical significance of the *Oyoon-al-Akhbar* lies in the fact that it is an encyclopedia of information that was considered important during the author's lifetime and it offers a panoramic insight into the general culture of the authors and scholars of that period. Ibni Qutaybah has covered in his book all the literary knowledge of his time. A review of this book reveals the literary spirit of that time and the various sources that were available in each field to scholars. The *Oyoon-al-Akhbar* presents a picture of one phase in the process of transformation of Iranian heritage in Arabic literature, until it acquired an Arab and Islamic character.

In general, Ibni Qutaybah has relied on two categories of sources in writing this book: one is the information that he acquired orally from his contemporaries and which he wrote in that form, and the other is the information that he obtained from various literary books and papers that were in use in at that time.

The most important books and papers that he had at his disposal were works that had been translated from Pahlavi literature, such as the *Ayeen Nameh*, the *Taj Nameh*, the *Khoday Nameh*, the *Kalileh va Demneh*, the *Aadab* of Ibni Mughaffa', Khosrow Parviz's letter to his son Shirouyeh, and Khosrow's letter to *Bouzarjomehr*. Besides these, he depended on other Iranian works but he did not list them and only mentioned them in passing such as 'and I read in a book of the Iranians'. He has also quoted advice and sayings from Indian books and has made one reference to a Greek phrase, but has not mentioned any title. As mentioned earlier, among the books that were translated from the Pahlavi language into Arabic were also those that in the Sassanid period had been introduced in Pahlavi literature from Sanskrit or Greek. It can be presumed that Ibni Qutaybah had quoted from these books. There is a referei :e to the Torah and the Bible in the *Oyoon-al-Akhbar* and materi·¹ has been quoted from them.[16] The only traces of Arab books in the *Oyoon-al-Akhbar* are

---

[16] The question whether Ibni Qutaybah h ; quoted from an Arabic translation of the Bible or from copies in other languages needs further scrutiny. The first Arabic translation of the Bible was by Abul Faraj Abdollah bin Teeb, and published by Ciasca, therefore, it can be said that during Ibni Qutaybah's time the Bible had not been translated into Arabic as Abul Faraj lived after Ibni Qutaybah. It is also not known whether Ibni Qutaybah was proficient in any other language such as Hebrew or Greek, in which the Bible was written. In a letter to the Orientalists Society of Paris, the Lebanese scholar, Louis Sheikho has referred to manuscripts found near the Maronite church in Louayzah from an ancient Arabic copy of the Bible. As mentioned in this letter, the manuscripts are from the translation by

those of Jahiz, mentioned once, and the Ibni Wahshyah's *Al Falaha* from which he has quoted a few phrases.[17] In view of this and the fact that the *Oyoon-al-Akhbar* is the most complete collection available from Ibni Qutaybah's time, it can be concluded that the most important writings in this field that were in circulation among authors and particularly the class of *dabirs* were the same translations of Iranian books and papers, as no books had been written in Arabic in this field.

The *Oyoon-al-Akhbar* represents another phase in the transformation of Iranian books in Islam. The books that were written prior to this in Arabic such as the writings of Ibni Mughaffa', were in style and content, if not direct translations of, at least direct copies of Iranian writings, but after this period, books appeared which were less influenced by their Iranian sources and conformed more to the Islamic environment. The *Oyoon-al-Akhbar* spearheaded this movement. From this period onwards, the cultural heritage of Iran gradually became part of a wider context that later became known as Islamic civilization and culture.[18]

It should be mentioned here that the *Oyoon-al-Akhbar* has great significance for the study of pre-Islamic literature of Iran, because Ibni Qutaybah has quoted extensively in this book from Pahlavi works, which he obtained from the Arabic translations of those

---

Diadasaron, dated 732 of the Hijra. Its transcriber has acknowledged that he copied it from a manuscript by the monk of Margurins (?) church in the monastery of Shahram, by the name of Yuhanna Mo'tamen known as Ibnu-Shaikh, who copied it from a manuscript by Sam'an, a famous monk, who had copied it from another manuscript by the monk Ibni Muhabrak, who in turn copied it from an old manuscript that he found in Antioch. Thus, the Arabic translation of the Bible goes back to the tenth or ninth century AD, that is, the period of Ibni Qutaybah. Refer to this letter in *Journal Asiatique*, vol. II, 1897, pp. 301-7.

[17] For more information see *Islamic Encyclopedia*, vol. II, p. 427.

[18] For additional reading on the transformation of Iranian writings in Arabic, see article by Mohammad Mohammadi-Malayeri 'One of the Important Sources for Research into Iranian Literature in the Sassanid Period', *Iran Shenasi*, Secretariat of the Union of Iranologists, Tehran, *Bahman* 1346 (February 1968); *Derasat Adabyah*, vol. VIII, nos. 3 and 4, Beirut, 1967.

books. Moreover, this book is the only historical source that mentions these quotations and offers information about them, if the *Oyoon al Akhbar* had been lost there would have been hardly any information about the *Taj Nameh* and the *Ayeen Nameh*.

**The Origin of**      Through the word *adab* has been repeatedly
**the Word *Adab***    used here, its meaning is not clear because of the
                       numerous transformations it has undergone; it
is important to clarify its meaning as it is directly related to the topic under discussion.

Scholars and linguists hold diverse views on the origins and root of the word *adab*. This is because this word began to be commonly used at a time when, as a result of the interaction of the Arabs with other peoples, many words and idioms were introduced into Arabic from other languages. There is no specific reference to this word in the Arabic language prior to this period.

In his book *Shafa' al Ghalil*, Khafaji has described the word *adab* as a *dakhilah,* i.e. words which were used in Arabic, but their roots did not exist in the Arabic language, or their meanings were not known to the Arabs. Contemporary scholars have also commented this subject.

The Italian orientalist Nellino has no doubts about the Arabic character of the word *adab*, but has failed to find its root in Arabic from which this word could have been described. He has argued that *adab* is a simplification of the word *aadab*, which according to him, is the plural form of *da'ab*, like *be'er* is the singular form of *aabar* and *ra'am* is the singular form of *aaram*. Taha Hussein, the contemporary Egyptian scholar, has alleged that the word *adab* found its way into Arabic from another language, and was not used in any of the Semite languages. According to him, it is likely that it was borrowed from one of the ancient Arabic dialects that are now extinct. Anstans Karmali, an eminent Arab linguist, has stated that the word *adab* is a derivative of the Greek word Eduepes (meaning good orator), and has added that the word *adeeb* was used originally in this same sense.

It is not possible to ascertain the date when this word was first used in the Arabic language. Writings from the Jahili period—those that can be authenticated—do not provide any evidence of the use of this word in that period. It is not found in the Koran or what has been narrated since the dawn of Islam. However, towards the end of the Amavid period the word *adab* was commonly used in discussions and debates. It can be concluded that this word came into use some time during the Amavid period.

Today, the word *adab* in Arabic has the same meaning as the word *adabyat* in Persian, and covers the same general meaning that is understood by the word literature in western cultures. However, this sense was not as general during the period under study, but developed in due course as the Arab civilization and culture underwent transformations.

According to Taha Hussein, the word was first used to denote teaching in the manner which was prevalent in the Amavid period; i.e. teaching through the narration of poetry and events, or sayings and tales related to the Jahili period, or accounts of Arab heroes both ancient and contemporary; in short, what was considered essential as general knowledge for the Arab nobility.

It appears that Taha Hussein has taken the initial meaning of the word *adab* to be completely relevant to Arab history and heritage, and has assumed it to be an outcome of the Arab lifestyle and state of mind; in other words, the narration of poetry and events, accounts related to Arab affairs, stories, tales, legends, etc. In general, all other Arab scholars are unanimous in their opinion because they rarely extend their study of the literary developments in the Arabic language beyond the scope of this language, and they do not take into consideration external factors. As a result, they rarely consider the possibility that the sense of the word *adab* and the topics that it covered, particularly in the initial period of its usage, extended beyond the Arab environment and Arab history and knowledge, and incorporated issues that were unprecedented in Arab history and were unknown to the Arabs. This is not only a basic issue in the history of Arab literature, but also in the history of Iranian culture, and thus merits careful consideration.

The narration of poetry and stories related to the Arabs and their history, as seen in the *Oyoon-al-Akhbar*, were incorporated into the general sense of *adab* and constituted one of its significant elements. However, there is no evidence to indicate that the word *adab* was initially used exclusively in this sense, and it had no meaning other than this for the contemporaries of the Amavid period. On the contrary, there is evidence that what Taha Hussein has identified was not the initial meaning of the word *adab*, and that this meaning was subsumed under the general meaning of the word *adab* in later periods. To clarify this issue, it is important to review the meaning in which the word *adab* was used and the sense that was intended by it in the books available from that period around that period.

To understand the meaning of the word *adab* in the Amarid period and get an idea of the varied areas of knowledge that it covered, Ibni Mughaffa's works are the most appropriate sources of information. This is because his contemporaries considered his books as the finest examples of the word *adab*; not only did they classify them under the general title of *adab*, but they also titled them as such—the *Al-Adab-al-Kabir*, the *Al-Adab-al-Saghir*, and the *Aadaab Ibni Mughaffa'* for the collection of his books. The most important characteristic that distinguished him from other Islamic authors was that in his writings there are no references to Arab sources, whether from the Jahili or from the Islamic period, as seen in other Arab literary books; there is no mention of Arab poetry or accounts of Arab events, or incidents related to the Arab Jahili period or tales and stories of ancient and contemporary Arab heroes. In other words, although there is nothing in these books that conveys the meaning of the word *adab* as defined by Taha Hussein, these books are still identified as *adab* and considered among its finest specimens.

Ibni Nadeem has listed under the general category of books on *Pand, Adab* and *Hekmah*, those whose contents do not conform to the definition given by the Taha Hussein, because the majority of them were either translated from Pahlavi or were modelled on them or were influenced by them. It is worth mentioning that among the works that were translated from Pahlavi, there were books on *adab* which had no relation to either the Jahili or the Islamic period.

The book that Moskouyeh wrote on the basis of the Pahlavi *Javdan Kherad* and included in it a diversity of wisdom and maxims, became known as the *Aadaab al Arab wal Fors*. Jahiz, Ibni Mughaffa' and their contemporaries used the word *adab* to convey a meaning approximating to ethics and advice and often used them synonymously.

Hence, it is clear that the word *adab* had a different denotation initially which was unrelated to Arab heritage; later its meaning grew with the expansion of the Islamic environment to incorporate Arab poetry, stories of ancient Arab personalities, etc., all of which imparted to it a general and comprehensive meaning. The focus here is on the initial meaning of the word.

A review of Arab literary works reveals that the word *adab* was first used in the same sense as is understood today in Persian, namely, encompassing characteristics such as good nature, purity of spirit, self-cleansing, refinement in speech and mastery of the art of behaviour, particularly towards elders and distinguished people. Verbal or written materials on such topics were also known as *adab*. In other words, *adab* was the title used to indicate two categories of material: one that contained ethical and spiritual meanings, i.e. the category of books that Ibni Nadeem has listed under the *Al Mawa'ez wal Aadaab wal Hekam,* and also the type of material contained in the *Aadaab Ibni Mughaffa'* and the *Aadaab al Arab wal Fors*; and the other that contained etiquettes of appearance and social ethics such as codes of behaviour and pleasant companionship, i.e. the type of material contained in the *Al Taj fi Akhlaq al Molook* and others, which are sometimes referred to as the *Aadab al Molook*.

The books in Arabic that were modelled on the Pahlavi *Andarz Namehs* and *Pand Namehs* were known as books of *adab*[19] and this indicates that at the time that these books were written, they were the best examples of the meaning of the word *adab* in that period. It should be borne in mind that the authors of the book of *adab* in Islam were mostly Iranians or were familiars with Iranian works.

Although this initial meaning of *adab* became obscure in the later periods as a result of transformations in its context, in the Amavid and the first Abbasid periods, it was clearly understood and because of this, *adab* and *aadaab* were often attributed to Iranians. In the excerpts from Jahiz on the transcription of the ethical books of Iran,

[19] Christensen, p. 68.

he spoke of the books of India, the logic of Greece and the *aadaab* of Iran.

Ibni Teghtegha provides a review of the sciences of each nation and lists among the characteristics of the Sassanids, wisdom and counsel, *aadaab*, history and geometry, and he enumerates the knowledge of the monarchs of Islam as oratory sciences such as *Nahv*, *Lughah*, poetry and history.[20] Addressing Kasa'i, the tutor of his son; Haroon al Rashid says,

Ali bin Hamzah, we have elevated you to a position which you could not have attained with your own efforts; so narrate for us of poetry that which is more pure, and of words those which contain the most good, and tell us of the *Aadaab* of the Iranians and of India.[21]

The fact that Taha Hussein has linked the word *adab* to the education of the nobility is correct and is supported by historical evidence; this point is vital in clarifying the meaning of *adab*.

**The Teacher and the Educator**   In Arabic writings of the late Amavid and early Abbasid periods, two designations were used for teacher which conveyed different meanings: one was *Mu'allem* (teacher) and the other was *Mu'addeb* (educator). The basic instructors who taught children of the common classes in the *Maktabs* were called *Mu'allem* or teacher; and those who taught the children of the nobility, were called *Mu'addeb*. *Mu'allem* and *Mu'addeb* had very different social positions and standings. This difference is evident in Ibni Qutaybah's *Abdul Malek bin Saleh* in which he addresses the *Mu'addeb* of his son: 'I made you a *Mu'addeb* when you were a *Mu'allem*, and I brought you close to myself and into my company when you were distant with the boys, and as long as you do not comprehend your inferiority then you will not understand your superiority now.'[22]

During this period two terms were used for school in Arabic literature, one is *Maktab* and the other is *Kottab*. According to

[20]  *Al Fakhri fil Aadaab al Sultaniyah*, p. 22.
[21]  *Ibni Abil Hadid*, vol. IV, p. 137.
[22]  *Oyoon-al-Akhbar*.

Noeldke, *Maktab* was the general institution for teaching, whereas *Kottab* was the institution for the children of the privileged classes where they learned *adab*.

It is obvious that the distinction between the titles of *Mu'allem* and *Mu'addeb* and between *Maktab* and *Kottab* was due to the difference in the subjects that were taught in each. The *Mu'allem* taught his students basic reading and writing and perhaps briefly the teachings of religion, but the *Mu'addeb* went beyond reading and writing, and prepared his students for the companionship of the Caliphs and the nobility or for the profession of *dabir* and service in the *divan*; in other words, he taught them *adab*.

This meaning of the word *adab* is not alien to Iranian history and Iranian writings. The court of the caliphs borrowed many practices from the Sassanid court, and the great men of the Caliphate, particularly in the Abbasid period, imitated the court of Iran. What the Islamic *Mu'addebs* taught the princes and the children of the nobility in the court of the Caliphate was, with slight modification, the same kind of material that Iranian princes and *Vaspouhran* learnt. Although it is difficult to give the precise word that was used in the Sassanid period to convey this meaning of the word *adab*, there is no doubt that this type of education was borrowed by the Caliphate from the Sassanids, in the same way that two types of teachers, one for the common children and the other for children of the nobility, was a product of the aristocratic society of Iran, and did not emerge from the simple lifestyle of the Arabs or the letter and spirit of Islam.

During the Sassanid period, in addition to the codes and protocol of the court, and the type of information contained in the *Taj Namehs*, the *Ayeen Namehs* or the *Andarz Namehs* and the *Pand Namehs*, the art of riding and horsemanship, archery, polo, chess, etc., were an integral part of the culture of the aristocracy, and it was expected that the nobility be well versed in these arts. It is difficult to specify which Pahlavi word was used by the translators for *Mu'addeb*, but it is clear that the instructors of riding and archery who, in the Sassanid period, taught the children of the aristocracy and were part of the *divan* of *sepah*, were referred to as the *Mu'addeb* in Arabic books.

According to Dinevari, among the reforms that Babak, the son of Nahravan, *dabir* of the *divan* of *sepah* of Anooshiravan, introduced was 'to structure the work of the *Mu'addebs*, so that they would not fail to provide the service for which they charged the people for the teaching of riding and archery.'[23] Tabari has mentioned among those who conspired to kill Shahrbaraz a person by the name of Mahiay or Mahyar and has identified him as *'Mu'addeb al Asawerah'*.[24] The Asvaran were considered among the distinguished classes of the Sassanid Sepah. Ferdowsi has often used the Persian word *Farhangi* in reference to the *Mu'addeb* in Arabic histories, but it is not known whether this word was used in the Sassanid period as a synonym of *Mu'addeb*.

In the Persian translation of the *Letter of Tansar* which is from the Arabic text, *Mu'addeb* has been referred to as *'Mu'allem Asawerah'* in a phrase which clarifies the levels of topics that each taught.[25]

During the Caliphate, the word *adab* denoted this basic meaning, but over time it incorporated other categories of knowledge that were a product of the Islamic and Arabic environment, and this led to a modification in its meaning.

**Transformations in the Meaning of *Adab***    It is evident that the initial meaning of the word *adab* was open to much expansion, and it was this susceptibility that led to its transformation. Initially, because of the limited horizons of Arab culture, the knowledge that was required for personal qualities like good character, good habits and refined speech was confined to a set of books and writings, some of which had been translated and contained material on wisdom, refined character and etiquette. Nevertheless, with the expansion of Islamic culture and the emergence of new fields of knowledge, they were also incorporated into the meaning of *adab*.

As scholars wished to strengthen the foundations of Arabic which is the language of the Koran, they began to collect all information on Arab heritage whether in the Jahili or the Islamic period, and in course of time, they had collections of poems, narratives and epics

[23] *Al-Akhbar-al-Tewal*, vol. I, p. 21.
[24] *Tarikh Tabari*, p. 1063.
[25] *Letter of Tansar*, pp. 15-16.

of Arab life, which were until then orally transmitted from one generation to the other. Gradually, learning this material became an element of refinement and knowledge for the Arabs, Moslems and their privileged classes, particularly since they also included wise words and advice of the type that were translated from Pahlavi. Thus, these areas of knowledge were referred to as *adab*.

During the time of Hasan bin Sahl, the *wazir* Ma'moon, the meaning of *adab* included playing the *Oud*, chess, polo, knowledge of medicine, geometry, riding, poetry, history of Arab wars and battles, diverse tales and narratives and information believed to be essential for dialogue and conversation.[26]

Mention should be made here of the transformation that was seen in the books of *Adab*. This is because the meaning of *adab* was closely related to the contents of these books, and to the extent that the topics covered therein expanded and diversified, the meaning of *adab* was also enlarged. At this time, Arab linguistic sciences (such as *sarf, nahv,* and *lughah*) also emerged because of the efforts of Islamic scholars. It is evident that mastering these sciences and the Arabic language was a prerequisite for pursuing any field of sciences and the arts, and since these sciences were directly relevant to the *aadab* of speech and debate, particularly for the class of *dabirs*, these sciences were also included in the domain of *adab*, and soon other fields of knowledge related to prose and poetry such as *Ma'ani, Bayan,* and *Badi'* became part of the meaning of *adab*, until eventually this word covered virtually all areas of Arabic knowledge.

Two factors led to the rapid evolution and development of the linguistic sciences related to the Arabic language. First, Arabic was the language of the Koran, therefore, Moslem scholars and jurists had to be proficient in it in order to understand the Koran. Second, most of the Moslems who studied *adab* and the sciences were from non-Arab nations, therefore they had to master the Arabic language and understand its linguistic intricacies and structure, and in the process they worked hard to fill in any grammatical gaps that they identified. This is the reason that the foundations of the linguistic

---

[26] *Zahr-al-Aadaab*, vol. I, p. 142.

sciences in Islam were laid down by non-Arab scholars, particularly Iranians.

Within a relatively short period, the range and diversity of the various areas of knowledge, which were initially scattered and ad hoc, became so vast that mastering them was beyond the capacity of any single scholar, thus specific areas of specialization emerged, each demanding years of study. As a result, in addition to the various fields of sciences that emerged and which required specialization, the function of *adeeb* called for general knowledge about all the various fields, without specializing in any. It was said: 'if you wish to become a scholar, then select one of the fields of knowledge; but if you wish to be an *Adeeb*, then pick the best of everything.' '*Adab* is to pick a handful from each field.' In this way, the meaning of the word *adab* evolved over time to incorporate the diversity of knowledge that existed in every period. Thus, the scope of the meaning of *adab* has varied with time, today it conveys the same meaning as the English word literature and contemporary Arab scholars recognize it as such.

**More about the Origin**    A discussed earlier, according to Prof.
**of the Word *Adab***    Nellino, this word is a simple form of
*aadaab* and the plural of *da'ab*, and to demonstrate the possibility of this irregular form of plural, he has cited the examples of similar plural forms of *aabaar* and *aaram*. This view, however, is not based on evidence. The available sources reveal that the two words—*adab* and *aadaab*—have been used together since the beginning, one as the singular and the other as the plural. If *adab* was a simple form of *aadaab*, then the word *aadaab* should have been used exclusively for some time before its simplified form *adab* emerged, following which *Aadaab* would have become obsolete. Moreover, at no time in various phases of its transformation has either *adab* or *aadaab* been used in the sense of *da'ab* and this meaning is totally inauthentic.

Undoubtedly, what led Nellino to this view was that there is no such root in the Arabic language, and he did not consider any other roots outside the Arabic language. Taha Hussein's view that *adab* found its way into literary Arabic from extinct ancient Arab dialects is also problematic. As Taha Hussein himself acknowledged that not only does *adab* not exist as a root in the Arabic language, but also in none of the Semitic languages that have common roots with Arabic.[27] It is improbable that this word was derived from an ancient Arab dialect. Also, the meaning of the word *adab*, does not support such a view, because since its inception the word was used to convey a meaning that was not a product of the Arab environment, and the Arabs were not familiar with the meaning it denoted in the Amavid or Abbasid periods. If it is assumed that this word was used in a different sense in an old dialect, it is not clear how and why it came to be used again to convey a totally different meaning.

It is improbable that Prof. Kremli had any evidence for the view that the word *adab* was derived from the Greek root *eduepers* meaning eloquent speech, other than a phonetic similarity. The introduction of a word or an idiom from one language into another requires certain conditions and prerequisites, paramount among which is the kind of linguistic relationship that exists between the two languages. Phonetic similarity or even a similarity in meaning alone cannot be considered evidence for the adoption of a word from one language by another. This point is worth noting because the word *adab* was widely used in Arabic at a time when the Arabs were not so familiar with the Greeks or their literary works that there could be linguistic interchanges between them.

The Arabs became acquainted with Greek books in the Abbasid period, and the word *adab* was widely used in the Amavid period. Also, as mentioned earlier, the Arabs were not thoroughly familiar with Greek literary works in any period, and no Greek book had been translated from Greek into Arabic. As a result, it would be incorrect to assume that the word Eduepes (?) entered the Arabic language abruptly and without any grounds, and was transformed into the word *adab*, thus acquiring a totally different meaning. To presume that the word was used in the past to denote eloquence of speech, and to take this meaning as evidence for such a view, cannot be supported because, the word *adab* was not used exclusively in the sense of eloquent speech.

[27] *Fil Adab-al-Jahili*, p. 20.

**Is the Root of *Adab*     In an article on *adab* and *adeeb*, the scholar
Originally Iranian?**     Moheet Tabataba'i has raised the question
whether the root of the word *adab* is
Iranian. He has reviewed the various views on the roots of this word.
According to him, it is probable that *adab* and *adeeb* were derived
from the Persian root of *dab* and *deep*, meaning to write.[28] In brief,
the reasons that he has offered for his position are as follows:

1. The word *deep* had an ancient usage in Iranian languages, and in
   the Tablet of Daryoosh, the word *deepi* is used to denote a written
   text; and in the Sassanid period, the writer was known as *dipeer*
   and the script as *dipeerieh*, as the place for writers was the *divan*,
   and where children were taught to be *dabirs* was called *dabeerestan*
   and *dabestan*.

2. As the Arabs, after they conquered Iran, adopted the codes of
   government from the Iranians, they also adopted the terms of
   the *divan*, the system of *dabestan* and *dabeerestan*, translated their
   titles verbatim into Arabic as *maktab* and *kottab* (based on the
   root to write in Arabic), and called the profession of teaching of
   knowledge and culture as *adeeb* and *mo'addeb*, and education as
   *ta'deeb*.

3. In the same manner that the Arabs adopted *maktab* and *kottab*
   from *dabestan* and *dabeerestan*, and maintained the words *divan*
   and *daftar* in their original form, would it not be possible that
   from the Persian roots of *dab* and *deep* they derived *adab* and
   *adeeb*?

The author has presented a number of possibilities of the extraction
of this word, but he has not iterated any of them because of lack
of conclusive evidence. Among these possibilities is that *aadab* was
derived from the root *da'ab*, as *aaram* is from the root *ra'am* and *aasa*
is from the root *sa*. Another is that the alphabet A as in *Vijeh* and
*Avijeh* was added to the words *dab* and *deep*, thus they became *adab*
and *adeeb*. Yet another possibility is that the alphabet A, which in
some branches of Pahlavi has been used instead of the letter B as in

---

[28] Refer to this article in the periodical *Amouzesh va Parvaresh*, vol. IX,
no. 1.

*bekhrad* and *benam* meaning one who has wisdom and one who has made a name, *adeeb* means that one who writes.

Without going into the details of this paper and the different possibilities presented therein, it can be said that the basis of the proposition presented by the author is closer to reality and worthy of interest, because the word *adab* initially devoted an Iranian sense, and its contents were mostly drawn from Pahlavi literature, and it is likely that its expression like its sense and context found its way into Arabic from the Pahlavi language. This issue is worthy of study, particularly the transformation of the word and its meaning before its usage became common in Arabic, and the similarity in its meaning in the Sassanid and Islamic periods.

# ELEVEN

# Persian Writing Code and Arabic Technical Prose

At a time when Islamic society was witnessing one of the biggest transformations in its history and Arab life was changing politically, culturally and socially, the Arabic prose of the *divan* also acquired a form which was unprecedented and unique.

From the late Amavid period Arabic writing or *kitabah* evolved into a new art, and with the emergence of competent *dabirs* who strengthened the foundations of Arabic prose, the grounds for its transformation were laid and the scope for taste and talent widened greatly. Thus, Arabic prose acquired a form vastly different from its humble origins in terms of style, structure, accuracy of meaning and beauty of expression, this was the first phase in the process of development of Arabic technical prose.

**Arabic Prose in the Jahili Period and the Dawn of Islam** In the Jahili period, a number of Arab tribes like the Jobba'an of Yemen in the south and Munzeris and Ghassanids in the north of the Arab Peninsula, who had trade or political relations with the neighbouring nations, were familiar with script and writing and used it in a limited way. Arabs in general did not have access to it, as there were few literates among them and the skill of writing was not appreciated by people at large. It is said that at the time of the emergence of Islam, no more than seventeen men and a few women of Quraish could write.[1] This was despite the fact that the Quraish was considered the most important and renowned among Arab tribes, which enjoyed more interactions with other na-

---

[1] Ibni Qutaybah, *Al-Ma'aref*, p. 153.

tions and cultures of that period. Unlike in the neighbouring countries of Iran and Rome, the art of writing was not popular among Arabs and they did not use it in their personal and social affairs.

A number of eminent researchers have alleged that although the Arabs in the Jahili period were familiar with composing poetry, they were not acquainted with technical prose and hence they did not use it. This is because the emergence of poetry which was oral preceded prose which was written. Also, poetry is the language of imagination and prose is the language of intellect, and there is no doubt that the growth and development of imagination among peoples and individuals has preceded the development of the intellect.[2] Several other researchers have asserted, merely on the basis of comparison with other nations, that the Arabs of the Jahili period were familiar with technical prose, as it is impossible that the Iranians, Indians, Egyptians and Greeks had technical prose five centuries before Christ, while the Arabs were still not familiar with it five centuries after Christ.[3]

Anis Maghdesi, a contemporary Arab scholar, has discussed this issue in his valuable book *Tatawwor Al Asaleeb al Nathriya*, and on the basis of reliable sources such as the narratives of ancient authors of literature and the Koran, he has provided valuable information in this regard.

1. In the Jahili period close to the rise of Islam there was a type of prose with a rhyme that was more common among clerics and in religious circles, and therefore it was known as *Saj' Kahenan*. This prose was close in style and structure to a number of *Surahs* of the Koran, particularly the first *Surahs*. Because of this similarity, some Arabs referred to the prophet as Kahin. This rhyming prose formed a link between poetry and simple prose, but it never reached the level of full-fledged prose.

2. On the basis of logical deduction it can be said that there was a kind of simple prose free of all kinds of complexity which was used by Arabs in social and commercial affairs, such as the prose

---

[2] '*Shawghi va Hafez*', pp. 62-8. Also see Nicholson, *Literary History of the Arabs*.

[3] Introduction to *Al-Nathr-al-Fanni*.

that was in use at the dawn of Islam. Whatever the form and style of Arab prose in that period, it did not progress and develop significantly and had limited influence on Arab life.

Arabic prose did not lose its simplicity in the first century of the Hijra. In this period, writers conveyed their messages using the simplest and shortest expressions and the most common words and they did not make any effort to beautify their expressions or ensure accurate structuring of their meanings. In fact, Arab prose had a natural flow and no rules had been developed for it.[4]

### The Period of Abdul Hamid and Ibni Mughaffa'

At the beginning of the second century of the Hijra, there was a transformation in Arabic prose, and the art of writing entered a new phase and acquired characteristics that were unknown to the Arabs. This transformation which had a significant impact was seen during the time of Abdul Hamid and Ibni Mughaffa'; Arab writers and historians have argued that these two scholars, particularly Abdul Hamid was the force behind this transformation. This period is therefore called the period of Abdul Hamid and Ibni Mughaffa'.

Abdul Hamid, who was given the title of *Kateb*, was one of the ingenious Iranian *dabirs* who served during the Caliphate of Marwan bin Mohammad, the last Amavid Caliph. He acquired a distinguished position in the art of writing because of his refined and new style. He founded a new style known as the *Hamidi* style, which was well known throughout the history of Arabic literature.

Abdul Hamid was an Iranian from Anbar. He went to Damascus and began to write under Salim, the *dabir* of Hisham bin Abdul Malek, who was an Iranian himself. When Marwan bin Mohammad was appointed *Wali* of Armenia, he accompanied him to Armenia, and when Marwan became the Caliph, Abdul Hamid continued to serve him and was the *dabir* in the *divan* of the Caliphate. However, he lost his life because of his loyalty to Marwan.[5]

---

[4] *Tatawor-al-Asalib-al-Nathriah*, pp. 1-10.

[5] For further reading on Abdul Hamid, see Estakhri, *Masalek-ul-Mamalek*, p. 145; *Wafiyat-al-A'yan*, vol. I, pp. 435-6; *Tabari*, part two, p. 839; *Al-Fehrest*, p. 118; *Morooj-al-Zahab*, vol. VI, p. 81.

Islamic authors who have written about Abdul Hamid have praised him for his eloquence and articulation in the art of writing, and have referred to the new style that he introduced in Arabic prose. This style was so extraordinary and innovative that some scholars have described this period as the beginning of the art of Arabic writing, and it was said, *'Bada'at al Kitabah bi Abdul Hamid'* (prose began with Abdul Hamid). Ibni Abde Rabbih[6] and Ibni Nadeem[7] have also lauded his work.

The reason for Abdul Hamid's fame as reflected in the writings of Arabic authors was that for the first time he brought Arabic prose out of its simple framework and adorned it with the beauty of form and meaning, and developed special codes for correspondence. In brief, he transformed Arabic writing into an art and strengthened the foundations of Arabic technical prose. He received the plaudits of his contemporaries for this innovative style which was imitated by the *dabirs* who succeeded him, and its significance and popularity continued throughout the history of Arabic literature.

Research on the factors that led to this transformation will clarify numerous issues in the cultural history of Iran and Islam. It is evident that the emergence of Arabic technical prose is the outcome of different factors both within the internal transformation of the Arabic language, and outside the context of that language and the Arab environment. It is not possible to determine the roots and causes of this transformation only through a study of Arab history or the characteristics of prose in the Jahili period and at the dawn of Islam, it is important to refer to the history of Iranian culture and civilization as well.

According to Abu Helal Askari, style introduced by Abdul Hamid in Arabic prose which led to this great transformation was an adaptation of the style of Persian prose. He has added, 'One who knows the use of each expression in its proper place in one language, when moving to another language, he will have the proper tools for expression in that language as well'. To demonstrate this issue, he has cited Abdul Hamid as an example, 'Do you not see that the models

---

[6]  *Eghd-ul-Farid*, vol. II, p. 206.
[7]  *Al-Fehrest*, p. 117.

that Abdul Hamid has left for the future, he had extracted from the Persian language and transferred to the Arabic language'.[8]

To determine the extent to which Arabic technical prose was influenced by the Persian style, it is important to review the characteristics of writing in Iran during the Sassanid period and determine its specifics to the extent possible.

**Writing Code in the Sassanid Period**　In chapter 3 there was a reference to the *dabirs* in the Sassanid court and their responsibilities. The most important advantage of the class of *dabirs* over other classes, which placed them at the helm of government affairs, even as *Bozorgfarmadar* or *Wazir A'azam*, was their wide base of knowledge, and particularly their writing skills, considered a great art in those days.

In the Sassanid period, the profession of *dabir* and service in the *divan* was a privilege of the aristocracy and nobility, but noble descent in itself was not sufficient for holding such a position, and proper type of knowledge and proficiency in writing skills were equally important. Therefore, those who aspired to the post of *dabir*, had to acquire the required knowledge in specialized institutions and master soundness of expression and beauty of script.

Among the reforms that Khosrow Anooshirvan introduced after resolving the problem of Mazdak, was his decree that the sons of the nobility whose fathers had been killed or who had lost their guardians be sent to an institute to acquire knowledge and culture for appointment to the *divan*.[9] Ferdowsi writes that Ardeshir Babakan had decreed that the best *dabirs*, as far as knowledge and writing skills were concerned, should be sent to work with other officials in the provinces, which demonstrates that *dabirs* were divided into levels on the basis of their knowledge and skills.[10] According to Ghalaghshandi,

As the shahs of Iran considered the profession and position of *dabirs* with distinction, they required that those who wished to enter into the service

---

[8] *Al-Sina'atain*, p. 51.

[9] *Tarikh Ibn-i-Batrigh*, p. 130. Manuscript in Beirut.

[10] Refer to the verses in the *Shahnameh*, Khavar edn, vol. IV, pp. 128-9.

of the *divan* be first tested by the chiefs of the *divan*, and if they were found worthy of the task, they would first be appointed with officials of the state in the provinces, and given a position relative to their knowledge and potentials. Then, gradually they would be promoted from one position to the next until they would occupy an elevated and distinguished position within the state organization.[11]

In addition to the specific technical knowledge that was required for their functions, the *dabirs* of the *divan* had to acquire a wide range of general information relevant to their era. Christensen has provided valuable information on the general context of civilization and culture in Iran in the Sassanid period.[12] It can be deduced from various references in Arabic writings that were borrowed from Pahlavi that the same wide range of knowledge that was expected of the *Kuttab* at the court of the Caliphate, which covered almost the same content as the field of *adab*, also applied to the *dabirs* of the Sassanid court, and the level of knowledge and proficiency that was expected from them.[13]

**Artistic Talent** Writers in the Sassanid period, particularly *dabirs* of the *divan*, attached great importance to the beauty of their writings, and they not only ensured that they used delicate paper, good ink and beautiful calligraphy, but also tried to convey their meanings in tasteful contexts, and present their expressions in an attractive form. This artistic taste attracted the attention of Arabs in the Islamic period, and there is a reference to it in the writings of that period. In his book *Al-Hayawan*, Jahiz quotes from Ibrahim Sindy on the importance that the Manavids attached to clean and smooth paper, black and bright ink, good calligraphy and their encouragement of calligraphers, 'I have not yet seen an equal to the paper and the script of their books'.[14]

---

[11] *Sobhi-al-A'asha*, vol. I, pp. 44-5.

[12] Refer to *L'Iran Sous les Sassanides*, p. 410.

[13] *Oyoon-al-Akhbar*, vol. I, p. 44; also the Foreword of *Adab-al-Kateb*; see *Al-Boldan* of *Ebne Faghih*.

[14] *Al-Hayawan*, vol. I, p. 28.

In Islamic sources pertaining to the Sassanid period, one often finds phrases like, this or that maxim or phrase was written in gold. It is known that Khosrow Anooshiravan decreed that the maxims of Bouzarjomehr be written in gold. On the order of Khosrow Parviz, all financial reports of the state that were presented to him had to be treated with rose water and saffron, because the odour of ordinary paper did not appeal to him.[15] The advance in the art of painting in this period is the best manifestation of this artistic bent, and also one of its outcomes.

This artistic bent was seen in some of the writings that reached the Arabs from the Sassanid period. Reference had been made to a book on the history of the Sassanids containing paintings of all the shahs of this dynasty. Hamzah Isfahani writes, that these paintings were coloured with great precision and detail. In his description of the arrest of Afsheen (one of the renowned commanders of Islam), Tabari has mentioned an Iranian book that was found in his house which contained blasphemous material and was decorated with gold and precious stones. Mani's book of *Arjang* was famous for its paintings which were considered masterpieces of that period.[16]

In addition to beauty in calligraphy and appearance, the Sassanids also paid great attention to the composition of phrases, and harmony in meaning; to ensure that their writings were the eloquent and beautiful, they strictly adhered to the rules and codes of eloquence. In historic sources of the Islamic period, the letters and statements of the Sassanid period are praised because of their high quality of eloquence.[17] One of the *Pand Namehs* attributed to Kasra was known as the *Ain ul Balaghah*. The tendency to use the adjective *balaghah* (eloquence) to praise Iranian writings indicates that this qualification was marked in those writings. A Pahlavi letter mentions the art of eloquence among the topics that were normally learnt in the Sassanid period.[18] Ferdowsi has referred to *balaghah* and good

[15] Balazori, *Fotooh-al-Boldan*, p. 464. the quote is from Ibni Moghaffa'.

[16] A few pages of this book were found in the excavations at Tourfan.

[17] Refer to *Tarikh Tabari*, pp. 820, 826, 846, 866; *Oyoon-al-Akhbar*, vol. I, p. 96.

[18] The Pahlavi paper '*Khosrow* and his *Gholam*'.

calligraphy as two of the characteristics of *dabirs*. Jahiz has compared Arab and Iranian eloquence and gave precedence to Arab eloquence because it was spontaneous, while Iranian eloquence had reached that level as a result of thought, contemplation, writing, learning and teaching.[19] The 'Code of Correspondence' includes a letter from Pahlavi writings; Jahiz has also mentioned an Iranian book entitled *Karvand* on this topic.[20]

Arabic writings occasionally included certain pieces on codes of expression that were borrowed from Pahlavi books and letters. Ibni Qutaybah has given a detailed account from the *Taj Nameh* on the functions of *dabirs*, which included several rules on the art and style of writing.[21] Certain books of literature while discussing the art of expression also refer to the opinions expressed by Iranians that have undoubtedly been borrowed from Pahlavi texts.[22]

It can be deduced from all these references that the art of writing and expression in the Sassanid period had its own codes that were recorded in books and letters which writers were expected to follow. Further, among the writings that reached the Arabs from the Sassanid period, were such letters, which were either independent pieces or part of books like the *Taj Nameh*, and through certain expressions found their way into Arabic writings.

**The Profession of Writing in the Secretariat of the Sassanid Court** It is clear that in the Sassanid period, a simple prose was used in ordinary conversation and writing, and an artistic prose was used in literary writings, official letters and *farmans*. Speeches by the Sassanid shahs on their coronation which have been recorded in history books, as well as the *Andarz Namehs* and the *Pand Namehs* that have been attributed to them or to others, were also written in this style. This artistic style was so conspicuous in some of these writings that even after they

[19] *Al-Bayaan wal Tabyeen*, vol. III, p. 20.
[20] Ibid., p. 10.
[21] *Oyoon-al-Akhbar*, vol. I, p. 46. Also copied in the *Nehayat al Erab*, vol. VII, p. 11.
[22] *Al-Sinaatain*, pp. 423-5.

were translated into Arabic, it was reflected to some extent in Arabic phrases.[23]

In the Sassanid *divan*, there were special *dabirs* for writing such technical letters. Usually when a *farman* or a letter from the *divan* had to be issued, one of the *dabirs*, the Iran *Dabir Bod*, briefly noted the topic in the presence of the shah, and after registration in the *Daftar Towghi'at*, the holder of the imperial seal who was called *Sahib Al Zimam* in Arabic stamped it with the special seal and another *dabir* rewrote it in the required literary style and format, thus, the contents of the stamped letter became an official correspondence that conformed to all the necessary intricacies of expression.

So much attention was focused on the prevailing style that a special kind of calligraphy had been developed for each kind of letter, from which no deviation was permitted. Ibni Mughaffa' has referred to seven forms of calligraphy in Persian, among which one was for the writing of *farmans* and *ahkam*, another for writing ordinary letters, and yet another for confidential letters, etc.[24]

**The Theory of Christensen**   On the basis of his scholarly work, Christensen has reached several conclusions on the technical prose and style of writing of letters in the Sassanid period. Reproduced here is a translation of what he has written:

Iranians have given from old times much attention to appearance. Official decrees and personal letters always had to be written in an artistic and appropriate style. In this period, wise sayings, ethical and religious sermons, poems, and pleasant charades (???) joined hands and produced a delicate and beautiful collection. In the style of writing and also in the writing of the titles of letters, so much care was taken that the social positions of both the sender and receiver were clearly obvious. In the letters that were exchanged between Sassanid shahs and one of their envoys, or a neighbouring monarch, the same concern for beauty of expression and pronunciation that existed in Pahlavi literary books or coronation statements is evident even more distinctly.[25]

Christensen has quoted from Nezami Arouzi on the responsibilities and functions of the *dabirs* and their qualifications. As Christensen

[23] Refer to Noeldke's Introduction to *Tarikh Tabari*.
[24] *Al-Fehrest*, pp. 13-14.
[25] Christensen, pp. 127-8.

has viewed the structure of the Islamic government and the administrative positions in that government such as that of the *wazir*, to be an exact copy of the administrative organization of Iran, he has also considered what Nezami has written as fully applicable to the Sassanid period.[26]

**Arabic Technical Prose**   In the second century of the Hijra there was a great transformation in Arabic prose, following which the foundation of technical prose and the grounds for its future progress were laid. As mentioned earlier, Abdul Hamid Katib was instrumental in this transformation.

The first century of Islam was not conducive to the progress of Arabic prose and the art of writing because the Arabs did not appreciate the profession of writing and Moslem puritans as well as conservatives did not consider writing and recording to be religiously desirable.[27] Although this period saw the emergence of some of the disciplines that later developed into distinct sciences such as *Qhira'ah, Tafseer, Fiqh* and *Hadith* which were debated in religious circles, topics like *riwayah* and poetry of the Jahili era were orally transmitted from generation to generation as the practice of writing or recording them had not yet been developed.

At that time the only institution where the art of writing was practised was the *divan* of the Caliphate, which had developed because of the expansion of the administrative organization of the state and had become a centre for skilled writers. Those who were instrumental in the development and progress of Arabic prose were the *dabirs* of the *divan*, who continuously added to the wealth of the Arabic language and its power and prepared it for even greater heights in later periods.

**The Styles of Abdul Hamid**   One can easily distinguish papers
**and Ibni Mughaffa'**   written by Abdul Hamid or Ibni Mughaffa' from those by early Arab writers. Among the characteristics of the writings of Abdul Hamid and Ibni Mughaffa', are the beauty of expression and style, precision

---

[26] This phrase can be found in Nezami Arouzi, *Chahar Maghaleh.*
[27] This has been covered in chapters 3 and 4 of this book.

of structure, harmony of meaning, depth of content, broadness of vision, focus of thought and many other intricacies that have colluded and distinguished these writings from earlier Arab writings.

One of the factors that distinguished the works of Ibni Mughaffa' and Abdul Hamid was that these two authors used the Arabic language for artful writing in new subjects and thus introduced new meanings and thoughts in the Arabic language. Not only were the letters that they wrote in the *divan* on political and administrative issues a novelty in the Arabic language, but even what they wrote on literary and ethical topics was, in the view of their contemporaries, innovative and unprecedented. Even today their writings appear far superior to those of their contemporaries as they are the product of broad vision, more mighty and productive minds.

This difference was not only due to the fact that Ibni Mughaffa' and Abdul Hamid were far more knowledgeable than their contemporaries, but also they dealt with a culture that was broader and represented a richer source. It is clear that the thoughts and meanings expressed by Abdul Hamid, Ibni Mughaffa' and their peers among the *dabirs* of the *divan* in their writings were borrowed from Iranian sources and expressed in the Arabic language, and it was in fact a group of *dabirs* who had translated the original Iranian works into Arabic.

The Iranian ancestry and culture of Ibni Mughaffa' is not in question. Abdul Hamid was also an Iranian of Anbar, and the quotations about him from Abu Helal Askari demonstrate his proficiency in Persian and Iranian literature. Moreover, the writings of these two authors that have survived are themselves proof of this, because in terms of subject and content they are similar to the ones in Pahlavi literature.

During the time of Jahiz, there was a heated debate and argument between the *Sho'oubyah*, i.e. those Iranians who did not accept the superiority of Arabs in the Islamic world, and Arabs who considered themselves superior to non-Arab Moslems, and each side presented its own arguments in support of its position. One of the issues that the *Sho'oubyah* bragged about was the heritage of Iranian civilization and culture that had been translated and was widely popular in Islamic society. In the defence of the Arabs Jahiz says:

What if these papers from the Iranians that are widely at the disposal of the people are not authentic, but fake? When people like Ibni Mughaffa' and Sahl bin Haroon and Abu Abdullah and Abdul Hamid and such, can write like that, what if those writings are not replicated from old writings, but have been recently written?[28]

Several points can be deduced from this quotation. First, at that time translations of many Iranian works were widely used by scholars and *dabirs*. Second, these translations in terms of content and style were similar to the writings of Iranian *dabirs* like Sahl bin Haroon, Abdullah Mohammad bin Yazdad bin Suwayd, Abdul Hamid and Ibni Mughaffa'. In other words, what these *dabirs* produced approximated to the Pahlavi works that had been translated into Arabic.

The coverage of the *Aadab* of Ibni Mughaffa' it was noted that after the translation of Pahlavi works into Arabic, the first books that were written in Arabic in replicating those translations were so close to them in terms of content and structure, that even a number of the books of Ibni Mughaffa' have been considered by some to be translations, and by others to be his own writings. In any case, from what we find in the books of literature, and from the study of past literary works, it is clear that the papers of Ibni Mughaffa', whether they were his own writings or translations, were unprecedented in Arabic in terms of content and meaning. Commenting on the *Al Yateemah*, Abu Fazl Ahmad bin abi Taher has described it as eloquent and well written, 'The consensus is that no one has reached the level of Ibni Mughaffa', and no one has said before him what he has said.'[29] Ibni Nadeem has listed *Al-Yateemah* both among the translations and original writings of Ibni Mughaffa'. According to Baghelani, Ibni Mughaffa' adapted its contents from a book on *Pand* and *Hekmat*, which was attributed to Bouzarjomehr.

Thus, there is no doubt that the reason for the fame of Ibni Mughaffa's papers was that they dealt with topics and meanings that were novel in the Arabic environment, and were new for the Arabs.

---

[28] *Al-Bayaan wal Tabyeen*, vol. III, p. 20.

[29] *Rasa'el-al-Bolagha'*, p. 115; reference to the manuscript of *Al-Manthur wal Manzour, Dar-ol-Kotob*, Egypt.

In writing his papers, Ibni Mughaffa' opened a new chapter in Arabic literature, and used Arabic prose for new and varied subjects.

Despite being renowned in the history of Arabic prose, not many of the papers of Abdul Hamid have survived today. Two papers have survived: one is a letter that he wrote on behalf of Marwan, the last Amavid Caliph to his successor (designate?) Abdullah, and the other is a paper in which he addressed the *dabirs* of his era, explaining to them their responsibilities. In order to understand the source of Abdul Hamid's innovative capabilities and the new ideas that he introduced into Arabic prose, one has to rely on these two papers.

The first letter was written in an Arabic environment and was in conformity with it, nevertheless, in terms of subject and content, it is similar to the letters seen in Pahlavi literature, and their Arabic translations were widely in use by scholars, *dabirs* and writers. This letter deals with the rules of sound government and through it Abdul Hamid introduced for the first time new areas in Arabic literature and Arabic writing. The letter covers topics such as discipline and politics, government, education, particularly the upbringing of the nobility and royalty, the arts of war, understanding people, the treatment of subordinates, the needy and the like,[30] that were all unprecedented in Arabic prose in the *divan*.

While discussing Pahlavi writings on applied wisdom and ethics that were translated into Arabic, it was explained that one type of such books were in the form of *Andarz Nameh* from a Sassanid shah to his successor on various subjects such as the rules of government, the reign of shahs, and ethical teachings, and the translation of such writings were known in Arabic as *O'hood* and *Wasaya*. Reference had been made to a number of such pieces like the *Ahde Ardeshir*, and *Ahde Anooshiravan*, and *Ahde Qobad*, and *Ahde Shapoor*, of which traces have survived in Arabic books.

This type of books became popular in the Islamic community as well, and Islamic writers continued to produce these books for several centuries. This category of books includes the *Pand Nameh*,

---

[30] For more information on this paper, refer to *Omara'-al-Bayan*, vol. I, p. 51.

the *Saboktakin*, the *Qaboos Nameh*, the *Syasat Nameh* and the like in Islamic Persian literature.

It must be borne in mind that although this type of writing in Arabic was the product of the Arabic and Islamic environment, it was in essence an imitation of similar Iranian writings. Since the letter of Abdul Hamid was the first of such letters, it aroused unprecedented interest and became a model for other writers, because in those days, the *dabirs* of the *divan* and also the Caliphs attached great importance to such issues. Included in this category was an elaborate letter from Taher bin Husayn to his son Abdullah, which has been transcribed by Ibni Khaldoon. Records reveal that when Ma'moon read this letter he was so impressed by it that he ordered that it be circulated to all the envoys of the state in the provinces and they should follow its recommendations.[31]

The second letter by Abdul Hamid was addressed to the class of *dabirs* on the rules and protocols of their profession and position. This letter, according to Ghalqashandi, became the basis of all the procedures and practices that the *dabirs* of the *divan* had to follow.[32] After what we have covered about the administrative institutions of the Caliphate and the interest of the *dabirs* of the *divan* to imitate the Sassanid Court, there is no need to mention the extent to which the likes of this letter were influenced by Iranian models. As we have seen, not only the profession of *dabirs* in the Caliphate was an imitation of the Sassanid Empire, but the *dabirs* themselves made an effort to copy Iranian practices, and also enforced them at the Court of the Caliphs.

It is clear from the excerpts borrowed from Pahlavi books such as the *Taj Nameh* by Moslem authors on the responsibilities and practices of *dabirs*, that such pieces of Pahlavi literature were translated into Arabic. Although not many such excerpts are available today, but it can be concluded that this category of writing produced in the first centuries of Islam, like the letter of Abdul Hamid, was in terms of content similar to works translated from Pahlavi.

---

[31] Refer to this letter in the Foreword of Ibni Khaldoon, pp. 303-11.
[32] *Sobhi-al-A'asha*, vol. I, p. 48.

There are other indications of the similarity between Abdul Hamid's letter and Iranian writings, and these are related to the resemblance between parts of this letter and parts of translated Pahlavi books. In his description of *dabirs*, Ibni Qutaybah has quoted from the *Moobadan Moobad* in the *Oyoon-al-Akhbar*. Undoubtedly, this quote originally appeared in a Pahlavi work, because all material drawn from Pahlavi books are generally attributed to one of the shahs or the Moobadan or the savants. What is noteworthy in this quote is its closeness to a part of Abdul Hamid's letter, and the personal style of the two authors is not taken into account which is different as they belong to different eras, the similarity is so prominent that the two cannot be regarded as unrelated and one appears to be based on the other.

While comparing the excerpt quoted by Ibni Qutaybah[33] and a part of the letter of Abdul Hamid[34] it is easy to see the extent to which Abdul Hamid and his peers among the *dabirs* of the Caliphate relied on Iranian sources in the selection of topics, meanings and ideas.

**The Transformation of Arabic Prose in Terms of Form and Style**   In addition to the developments that took place in Arabic prose in terms of meaning and thought, during the time of Abdul Hamid and Ibni Mughaffa', Arabic prose also underwent transformation in form and style which is worthy of study and scrutiny. For this, it is important to review the styles of Ibni Mughaffa' and Abdul Hamid, the two writers who are perceived as the fathers of the art of writing in Arabic.

Ibni Mughaffa' is known for his free style in which he tied the words and phrases completely to the meaning, and returned it to its simple and natural form. This style is known in Arabic as the *Mursal* style. It was not invented by Ibni Mughaffa', as being close to the nature of the language it existed in Arabic before him. The way he has used this style in his books was unprecedented in Arabic literature, because he was the first person who wrote numerous books on *adab*, in this style.

---

[33] *Oyoon-al-Akhbar*, vol. I, p. 47.
[34] Refer to this paper in the *Sobhi-al-A'asha*, vol. I, pp. 85-9.

To clarify this point, it is worthwhile to examine the literary books of the second and third centuries of the Hijra and review their styles. During this period, writers mainly focused on collection and selection; in other words, they collected various tales and narratives from different sources and transcribed them using the same phrases that they had heard, they did not alter their contents and sufficed by adding words at the beginning of each tale, such as so and so said, or so and so informed, to indicate that they were quoting others. For example, in the *Oyoon-al-Akhbar*, various tales have been narrated one after the other without any thought given to the relevance and harmony of the subjects. Therefore, these books were collections of diverse information, rather than coherent writings that reflected the thought, personality and the style of the writer. The works of Ibni Mughaffa' are different. Regardless of whether he has borrowed material from earlier or contemporary sources or Pahlavi books, his writings reflect his own astute insight and unique style. Although the topics of his books are wisdom and advice, which are in themselves unharmonious, he has used his unique skill to present a harmonious account on these topics, thus avoiding the scatterization of coverage that is seen in similar Arabic books.

This new style of writing which is evident in the works of Ibni Mughaffa', is not an imitation of that of his contemporaries, as there were no books or letters written in a similar style in those days and the art of writing in the Arabic language had not reached such heights. Therefore, there is no doubt that this style was a product of Ibni Mughaffa's wider cultural base and his familiarity with Pahlavi books. Their close similarity reveals the extent to which the development of the art of writing in Islam depended upon the literary works of Iran.

Abdul Hamid, according to literary historians, developed a new style which he had adopted from the Persian language. Anis Maqdesi, conducted a valuable study on this and discussed the extent to which Abdul Hamid was influenced by the Iranian style: The reason why historians of literature have considered Abdul Hamid and not Ibni Mughaffa' as the 'innovator of the Iranian style', despite the fact that Ibni Mughaffa' was better known for his affection for Iran, the translation of Pahlavi works, and dependence on Iranian sources, was that the Arabs found Abdul Hamid's style innovative as Ibni Mughaffa's style was not unprecedented in Arabic. The most important characteristics of Abdul Hamid's writing, for which he was famous, are his use of phrases and elaborate coverage of issues, and harmony of sentences, which in Arabic is known as *tawazon*. There is some doubt that Abdul Hamid adopted his style of *tawazon* from the Persian style of prose, and to clarify this doubt it is important to establish two points: first, to determine that in the days of Abdul Hamid or earlier, the common style of Persian writing was the style of *tawazon*, and second, to determine that this style was unprecedented in old Arabic prose; neither of these two points have been established yet.

According to Maqdesi, Abdul Hamid did not adopt the *tawazon* style from Iran, because this style was prevalent in Arabic, Abdul Hamid adopted it in his writings and thus transformed it into a distinct style. Maqdesi has added that Abdul Hamid borrowed from the Iranian style of writing the lengthy, elaborate and descriptive coverage of a subject which was unprecedented among the Arabs, since they had a simple and nomadic life, they had a simple style of writing, free of any artistic complexity, the Iranians, on the other hand, had a sophisticated civilization, and beauty of expression was important in their writings and was considered a sign of eloquence.

**A General View**   Before returning to the discussion of the unique style of Abdul Hamid and whether or not the *tawazon* style existed in Persian or Pahlavi, it may be appropriate to view Arabic prose in general and some of its acquired characteristics.

When one says that Arabic technical prose emerged as a result of the taste and insight of Iranian *dabirs*, and developed because of their familiarity with Iranian culture and ways, it does not mean that all the various styles that developed in Arabic and all the verbal tools of expression and meaning used in this language, were adopted from Iran. Every language has its own structure and character that definitely impacts its character, and for this reason some specific writing techniques may be pleasant in one language and unpleasant in another. Further, after the advent of Islam, because of the fact that Arabic became the language of religion and spread among various nations, and many scholars expressed a desire to expand and develop this language, and competent writers and authors arose, and numerous other factors, the Arabic language had ample opportunities for evolution, which were not available to Pahlavi or Persian. In the later centuries, because of the momentum of the development of the tools of expression in Arabic, this language was based on solid scientific foundations, which did not exist earlier in Iran or in any of the Iranian languages.

On the basis of this discussion it may be concluded that one element in this area that found its way from Iran to the Arabs and paved the way for subsequent development in Arabic prose was artistic taste. Before the emergence of Islam and prior to the Iranian influence on the Caliphate, the art of writing, like all other aspects of Arab social and personal life, was simple. The Arabs did not have elaborate rules of behaviour, their expression was devoid of all etiquette except their natural instinct, and no frameworks and structures had been developed for their art of writing. On the contrary, in Sassanid Iran, writing was considered an art, and the writer put in great effort to ensure the beauty of his expressions and strictly adhered to established norms and practices. In the Islamic era, when the task of Arabic writing was entrusted to the *dabirs* of the *divan*, this artistic taste gradually found its way into Arabic writing and soon norms were developed that were appropriate to the Arabic and Islamic environment.

Artistic taste was first seen in the appearance of the letters that were written, whether in the quality of paper used or the beauty of the script, etc., which was of interest to several Amavid Caliphs. Since this was new to the Arabs, Arabic writings mention that Walid bin Abdul Malek was the first Caliph who evinced an interest in the art of writing and demanded that fine paper be used, he appointed *dabirs* who had a beautiful handwriting, and refined the correspondence of the *divan*. However, these instructions were not followed after Walid, as artistic taste was not yet finally established in Arabic society. During the times of Omar bin Abdul Aziz and Yazid bin Walid, old practices were revived. From the end of the Amavid period and the beginning of the Abbasid period, when the centre of the Caliphate shifted to Baghdad, the environment was conducive to artistic taste and insight.

In the Sassanid period, much attention was focused on beautiful preambles to orations, letters, etc. Such preambles that were generally in praise of God and expressed gratitude for his bliss, can be seen in the orations and letters of the Sassanid shahs narrated in Ferdowsi's *Shah Nameh* and a number of Arabic literary and historical sources. A tale narrated by Bihaghi, makes clear that more attention was paid to these preambles than to the main text. According to him, after his victory over Bahram Choobin, Khosrow Parviz instructed the *dabirs* to record the events that led to his victory. When they presented their writings to Khosrow, the preamble did not appeal to him, and a junior *dabir* wrote an eloquent preamble which greatly pleased him and he ordered that the *dabir* be promoted.[35]

Such a practice did not exist among the Arabs either in the Jahili period or at the dawn of Islam, and prior to Abdul Hamid's time letters in Arabic were written without an introduction and a conclusion. They began with the main subject and ended with it. Since the days of Abdul Hamid, preambles gradually became common and similar phrases were introduced into the text and between paragraphs, and this area became a main concern for the *dabirs* and there was competition among them to demonstrate their artistic skills. Of course, the preambles to Arabic letters in the Islamic era were different from those written by the Sassanid *dabirs;* but despite the differences, it can be said that the Arab *dabirs* adopted this practice from the Iranian *dabirs* and their letters.

While discussing the style of correspondence in the Sassanid period, a reference had made to Christensen who had elaborated on the careful thought given in the correspondence to the social positions of the sender and the receiver and the relationship between them. This is because at the time, particular titles and phrases were used for each position and level, and therefore a letter was written keeping in view who was the sender and the receiver; it was perhaps similar to the way that Persian correspondence was drafted until recently. This style of correspondence was unprecedented in Arabic writing. Arab society was not divided into different classes, and there was no hint of class distinctions in Arab letters; similar phrases and

---

[35] *Al-Mahasen wal Masawe'*, p. 48.

expressions were used and this continued for quite some time after the advent of Islam. From the second century onwards, Arab *dabirs* began to focus on the classification of words and phrases on the one hand, and the social positions of the addressees on the other; and over time, choosing the appropriate words and phrases keeping in view the situation at hand as well as the position of the receiver became a prerequisite for eloquence, so that in the later centuries, the *dabirs* of the *divan* knew no bounds in the excessive use of titles.

Jahiz provides a phrase that clarifies the first phase of the evolution of this style in Arabic prose.[36] A study of Ibni Modabber's paper 'The Virgin Letter' clearly demonstrates the extent to which this issue was of concern to writers, and the speed at which it covered its initial phases of evolution.[37]

The use of lengthy and elaborate phrases was a general characteristic of Persian prose which found its way into Arabic. As mentioned earlier, artistic phraseology and playing with words and expressions were a result of the lifestyle and opulence of the Iranians, and as the Arabs had not adopted such a lifestyle, they were not aware of this type of writing.

**The Rhymed Style in the Translations of Iranian Works** Since adequate information is not available about the old Pahlavi texts, one cannot say with certainty about the origin of the rhymed style that was the basic characteristic of the writings of Abdul Hamid. However, it may be appropriate to draw attention to the following point.

While referring to Noeldke's views on the sophisticated phraseology of some of the Pahlavi works, it was said that in the Arabic translation of those works into Arabic, some of those artistic characteristics were diluted, but others were reflected in a number of Arabic books such as the *Tarikh Tabari*. If one accepts this view that the artistic characteristics seen in a number of Arabic translations of Iranian works are a reflection of their original Pahlavi texts, then one can say that the balance of the paragraphs and the harmony of the

---

[36] *Al-Bayaan wal Tabyeen*, vol. I, p. 129.

[37] This paper was published in Egypt in 1931.

sentences are the basis of the rhymed style, which were considered among the favoured expressional qualifications of the art of writing in Iran as well.

A scrutiny of the Arabic translations of Pahlavi writings that have survived in a number of Arabic books reveals that they fall into one or two categories: either they are from books of sciences or the arts that were written for educational purposes, or they are a part of literary pieces like coronation orations or official correspondence or the *Andarz Namehs*. The first type was necessarily void of artistic sophistication and was therefore written in a simple language and free style. The second type was generally written in a literary and artistic style, and reputed balanced paragraphs, harmonious expressions, and an abundance of elaborate sentences and synonyms.

However, the question remains whether the artistic characteristics evident in Arabic texts translated from Pahlavi are a reflection of the characteristics of their original Pahlavi texts, or whether they are due to the artistic inputs of their translators. The first probability appears to be closer to reality, although there is no conclusive evidence for this view.

# Bibliography

*Adab and Akhlagh in Iran Before Islam and its Impact on the Islamic Period*, Tehran, 1352 Hijrah (solar).

*Adab-al-Kateb*, Abdullah bin Muslim Ibni Qutaybah, Leiden, 1901.

*Adab-al-Kuttaab*, Abu Bakr Muhammad Souli, Cairo, 1341 Hijrah (lunar).

*Ahde Ardeshir*, Abbas Ehsan, Beirut, 1966.

*Ahsan ul Taqaseem*, Abu Abdallah Shamseddin al Maghdesi, Leiden, 1906.

*Akhbar al Ulamaa' be Akhbar al Hukamaa'*, Jamaluddin Ghafti, Leipzig, 1904.

*Al-Aghani*, Abul Faraj Isfahani, Dar al Kutub, Cairo.

*Al-Akhbar al Baghyah*, Abu Reyhan Birooni, Leipzig, 1872.

*Al-Akhbar-al-Tewal*, Abu Hanifah Dinevari, Leiden, 1888.

*Al-A'lagh al Nafisah*, Abu Ali Ahmad bin Rastah, Leiden, 1892.

Al-Awraagh (manuscript), Abu Bakr Muhammad Souli, Dar al Kutub, Cairo.

*Al-Bayaan wal Tabyeen*, Amru bin Bahr Jahiz, Cairo, 1932.

*Al-Eshteghagh*, Abu Bakr Muhammad Ibni Doraid, with corrections by Wustenfeld, 1853.

*Al Fakhri fil Aadaab al Sultaniyah*, Fakhreddin bin Yahya Balazori, Ehlurt, 1860.

*Al-Fehrest*, Muhammad bin Ishaq Ibni Nadeem, Leipzig, 1872.

*Al-Hayawan*, Amru bin Bahr Jahiz, Cairo, 1323-5 Hijrah (lunar).

*Al-Buldan*, Ahmad bin Abu Ya'ghoob Ya'ghoobi, Leiden, 1861.

*Al Dorrat-ul Yatimah*, Abdullah Ibni Mughaffa', *Al-Mughtabas*, vol. 3, Damascus.

*Al Ighd al Fareed*, Ibn Abd Rabbeh, Cairo, 1302 Hijrah (lunar).

*Al Kamel fil Tareekh*, Ezzeddin Ibnil Athir, Leiden, 1876.

*Al-Ma'aref*, Abdullah bin Moslem Ibni Qutaybah, Leipzig, 1860.

*Al-Mahasen wal Addad*, Amru bin Bahr Jahiz, Leiden, 1898.

*Al-Mahasen wal Masawe'*, Ebrahim bin Muhammad Bihaghi, Gissen, 1902.

*Al Motarjemoon wal Naghalah anil Faresiyah fil Ghoroon al Islamiyah al Oulah*, Mohammad Mohammadi-Malayeri, Beirut, 1966.

*Al Mukhtasar fi Akhbaar al Bashar*, Esma'eel bin Ali Abul Fidaa', Cairo, 1325 Hijrah (lunar).

*Al-Nathr-al-Fanni*, Zaki Mubarak, Cairo, 1934.

*Al Resalah al Azhraa'*, Ibni Mudabber, Leiden, 1931.

*Al-Sina'atain*, Abu Hilal Askari, Cairo, 1319 Hijrah (lunar).

*Al-Taj fi Akhlagh al Molook*, Amru bin Bahr Jahiz, Cairo, 1914.

*Al Tafdhil bayna Balaghatai al Arab wal Ajam*, Al Askari, quoted from Al Tuhfah Al Bahiyah, 1302 Hijrah (lunar).

*Al-Tanbih wal Eshraf*, Abul Hasan Ali Al Mas'oodi, Leiden, 1893-4.

*Al Tarjamah wal Naghl a'nil Faresiah fil ghoroon al Islamiyah al Ulah* (Translation and Transcription from Persian in the First Centuries of Islam), Mohammad Mohammadi-Malayeri, Beirut, 1964.

*Al Wozara' wal Kottab*, Muhammad bin Abdoos Jahshiari, Vienna, 1926.

An Important Source for the Study of Iranian Literature in the Sassanid Period, Mohammad Mohammadi-Malayeri, an article in *Iranshenasi*, Tehran, 1346 Hijrah (solar).

*The Bible*, Arabic edition, Beirut, 1875.

*Chahar Maghaleh*, Nezami Arouzi, Berlin, 1927.

*Duha-al-Islam*, Ahmad Amin, Cairo, 1936.

*Fajr-al-Islam*, Ahmad Amin, Cairo, 1933.

*Fil Adab-al-Jahili*, Taha Hussain, Cairo, 1933.

*Fotooh-al-Boldan*, Ahmad bin Yahya al Balazori, Grifzwald, 1868.

*Gaah Shomari dar Iran Ghadeem*, Seyed Hasan Taghi Zadeh, Tehran, 1316 Hijrah (solar).

*Gaatha* (Persian translation and introduction), Ebrahim Pourdavood, Bombay, 1927.

*Gojasteh Abalish*, ed. Sadegh Hedayat, Tehran. (This paper was translated, edited and published earlier by Bartholomi in Paris in 1887.)

*Ibni Mughaffa'*, Khalil Mardum Beik, Damascus, 1930.

*The Introduction of Ibni Khaldoon*, Abdul Rahman bin Muhammad, Beirut, 1900.

*Javdan Kherad*, Ahmad bin Muhammad Moskouyeh, Beirut, Saint Joseph University, manuscript at Al Maktabah al Sharghiyah (the Eastern Library).

*Kashf-ul-Zonoon*, Mustafa bin Abdallah Haaj Khalifah, Leipzig-Leiden, 1835, 1858.

*Mafatih-al-Oloom*, Muhammad bin Ahmad Kharazmi, Cairo, 1342 Hijrah (lunar).

*Masalek-ul-Mamalek*, Ebrahim bin Muhammad al Mas'oodi, Leiden, 1889.

*Mo'jam-ul-Buldan*, Abu Abdallah Shahabeddin Yaghoot, Leipzig, 1866-73.

*Mojam al-Udabaa'*, Abu Abdallah Shahabeddin Yaghoot, Leiden, 1909-16.
*Morooj al-Zahab*, Abul Hassan Ali al Mas'oodi, Paris, 1861-71.
*Morooj al-Zahab, Al Mas'oodi*, ed. Charles Pella, Beirut, 1966.
*Mukhtasar Ketab al Buldan*, Abu Bakr Ahmad Ibni Faghih, Leiden, 1855.
*Nameh (letter of) Tansar*, ed. Mojtaba Minavi, Tehran, 1311 Hijrah (solar).
*Nehayat al Erab*, Shahabeddin Ahmad Nowairi, Cairo, 1923.
*Neyrangestan*, Sadegh Hedayat, Tehran.
*Nozam al Jawhar*, Ibni Batrigh, Beirut (manuscript at Al Maktabah al Sharghiyah, the Eastern Library).
*Nuzhat al Mushtagh*, Shareef Edrisi, Leiden, 1968.
*Oyoon-al-Akhbar*, Abdullah bin Muslim Ibni Qutaybah, Dar al Kutub, Cairo.
*Qamoos al Lughah*, Muhammad bin Ya'ghoob Firooz Abadi, Tehran, 1277 Hijrah (lunar).
*Rasa'el Ibni Mughaffa'*, Yusuf Abu Halghah, Beirut, 1960.
*Rasa'el-al-Baghaa'*, Muhammad Kurd Ali, Al Zhaher Press, 1326 Hijrah (lunar).
Search for Persian Words in the Arabic Language, Mohammad Mohammadi-Malayeri, Article in *Al Derasat Al Adabiyah*, Lebanese University, Beirut, 1964.
*The Shahnameh of Ferdowsi*, Khavar Press, Tehran, 1310-12 Hijrah (solar).
*Sharh Nahj al Balaghah*, Ibn Abil Hadid, Tehran, 1271 Hijrah (lunar).
*Shawghi wa Hafez*, Taha Hussain, Cairo, 1933.
*Sina Molouk al Ardh wal Anbiaa'*, Hamzah Esfahani, Calcutta, 1866.
*Sirat al Rasool*, Muhammad Ibni Ishagh, Gottingen, 1858-60.
*Sourat al Ardh*, Muhammad bin Ali Ibni Hawghal, Leiden, 1938-9.
*Sourat Bilad Araagh al Ajam min Ketaab al Masalek wal Mamalek*, Muhammad bin Ali Ibni Hawghal, Leiden, 1822.
The Story of Hormozan and the Familiarization of Arab Moslems with the Diwan System in Iran, Mohammad Mohammadi-Malayeri, Article in *Maghalaat va Barresiha*, Tehran University, 1351 Hijrah (solar).
*Sobhi-al-A'asha*, Ahmad bin Ali Ghalghashandi, Cairo, 1337 Hijrah (lunar).
*Tabaqat-al-Omam*, Qhadhi Sa'ed bin Ahmad al Andalusi, Cairo, Alsa'adah Press.
*Tarikh al Adab al Arabi*, Brookelman (History of Arab Literature, Arabic translation by Prof. Abdul Haleem al Najjar), Cairo, 1968.
*Tatawor-al-Asalib-al-Nathriah*, Anis al Maghdesi, Beirut, 1935.
*Tarikh al Tamaddun al Islami* (History of Islamic Civilization), Georgi Zaidan, Cairo, 1922.
*Tarikh e Gozideh*, Hamdullah Mostowfi Ghazvini, London, 1910.

*Tarikh Mukhtasar al Duwal,* Ibnul Ibri, Beirut, 1890.

*Tazkareh Dowlatshah Samarqandi,* Brill, 1900.

*Teraz al Majales, Shahab al Din Ahmad Khafaji,* Cairo, 1284 Hijrah (lunar).

*Thalaath Rasa'el HI Jahiz,* Amru bin Bahr Jahiz, Cairo, 1344 Hijrah (lunar).

*Umara' al Bayan,* Muhammad Kurd Ali, Cairo, 1937.

*Wafiyat-al-A'yan,* Shamseddin Ahmad Ibni Khallakan, Cairo, 1275 Hijrah (lunar).

*Zahr-al-Aadaab,* Abu Ishagh Ebrahim Al Husri, Cairo, 1327 Hijrah (lunar).

What has been quoted in this book from the Russian orientalist Inostranzev is from a number of articles that the Parsi scholar Nariman translated into English and published in a book titled *Iranian Influence on Moslem Literature,* published in Bombay in 1918.

# Index